CW00469118

Toxicity review 26

Xylenes

G M Bell
R O Shillaker
M D J Padgham
P Standring

CONTENTS

Summary *1*

Identity *2*

Disposition and metabolism *2*
Studies in animals *2*
Studies in humans *7*

Toxicity to animals *10*
Acute toxicity *10*
Skin and eye irritancy and sensitisation *13*
Sub-acute toxicity *14*
Genotoxicity *18*
Carcinogenicity and chronic toxicity *19*
Effects on fertility and reproduction *20*

Toxicity to humans *24*
Acute toxicity *24*
Irritancy and sensitisation *26*
Effects of repeated exposure *26*
Genotoxicity *28*
Carcinogenicity *28*
Effects on reproduction *28*

Tables

1   Acute toxicity of xylenes to animals *29*
1.1   Inhalation studies
1.2   Oral studies
1.3   Dermal studies
1.4   Parenteral studies
1.5   *In vitro* studies

2   Sub-acute toxicity of xylenes to animals *71*
2.1   Inhalation studies
2.2   Oral studies
2.3   Dermal studies
2.4   Parenteral studies

3   Genotoxicity of xylenes *115*

4   Carcinogenicity studies of xylenes in animals *128*

5   Reproductive toxicity studies of xylenes in animals *130*

Appendix: Summary of metabolism and toxicity of ethylbenzene *151*

References *152*

Any enquiries regarding this publication should be
addressed to the Health and Safety Executive at any
area office or to one of the following Information Centres:

Health and Safety Executive
Library and Information Services
Broad Lane
SHEFFIELD S3 7HQ
Tel: (0742) 752539
Telex: 54556

Health and Safety Executive
Library and Information Services
Baynards House
1 Chepstow Place
Westbourne Grove
LONDON W2 4TF
Tel: (071) 221 0870
Telex: 25683

This publication represents a continuation of the HSE
Toxicity Review series, setting out the available scientific
evidence on the biological impact of substances
suspected of being hazardous to man. It has been
prepared primarily for the WATCH (Working Group on
the Assessment of Toxic Substances) panel of the
Health and Safety Commission's Advisory Committee on
Toxic Substances, in order to assist its members in
analysing the risks involved in working with the
substance(s) and in determining what controls of
exposure may be appropriate.

These Toxicity Reviews are critical summaries of the
literature and, as far as can be ascertained, are accurate
at the time of preparation.

The Health and Safety Executive is publishing these
papers in order to contribute information to scientific and
public debate on the level of risk involved in exposure to
such substances, on the acceptability of such risk and
on the the control measures that need to be adopted.

Titles already published:

TR1	Styrene
TR2	Formaldehyde
TR3	Carbon disulphide
TR4	Benzene
TR5	Pentachlorophenol
TR6	Trichloroethylene
TR7	Cadmium and its compounds
TR8	Trimellitic anhydride-(TMA)
	4,4' Methylenebis (2-chloroaniline)-(MBOCA)
	N-Nitrosodiethanolamine-(NDELA)
TR9	1,1,1, Trichloroethane
TR10	Glycol ethers
TR11	1,3-Butadiene and related compounds
TR12	Dichloromethane (methylene chloride)
TR13	Vinylidene chloride
TR14	Review of the toxicity of the esters of o-phthalic acid (phthalate esters)
TR15	Carcinogenic hazard of wood dusts
	Carcinogenicity of crystalline silica
TR16	Inorganic arsenic compounds
TR17	Tetrachloroethylene
TR18	N-Hexane
TR19	Toxicity of nickel and its organic compounds
TR20	Toluene
TR21	Chromium
TR22	Bis(chloromethyl)ether

ISBN 0 11 885697 9

SUMMARY

Identity and metabolism

Xylenes are colourless, volatile liquids that exist either as the individual o-, m- and p-isomers, or as commercial grade xylene containing varying proportions of the isomers. Vapours of xylenes are rapidly absorbed via the respiratory tract. Xylenes are well-absorbed orally in animals and liquid m-xylene has been shown to be well-absorbed through human skin. Xylenes are highly soluble in blood and fat, and are widely distributed in the body. Only a small proportion of absorbed m-xylene has been detected in human subcutaneous fat. Although accumulation of xylenes in human blood and in animal body fat and brain tissue has been demonstrated during exposure for 1 to 2 weeks, concentrations in animal fat fell on prolonged exposure (possibly due to xylenes inducing their own metabolism). Low levels of xylenes and their metabolites have been detected in the fetuses of exposed rodents. Xylenes are extensively metabolised in humans, with about 90% of the absorbed dose being excreted in urine as the glycine conjugate of methylbenzoic acid following inhalation of up to 200 ppm vapour or dermal exposure to the liquid. There is evidence that excretion of methylbenzoic acid conjugates can be reduced by exposure to certain other chemicals. No significant differences in the disposition and metabolism of the three xylene isomers have been demonstrated in humans, although some quantitative differences have been identified in animals.

Toxicity to animals

Xylenes have a low acute toxicity. Inhalation LC_{50} values in excess of 4000 ppm and oral LD_{50} values in excess of 3500 mg/kg have been reported. Death is caused by respiratory failure due to CNS depression. At high vapour concentrations there is a major effect on the CNS and a biphasic response with initial excitation followed by depression, particularly for p-xylene, has been observed. Elevated serum hepatic enzyme levels and decreased lung cytochrome P450 levels have been noted. Vapours of xylenes are respiratory tract irritants.

Single application of liquid xylenes can cause overt skin irritation. Eschar formation and blistering have been reported after repeated exposure. A single instillation of liquid xylenes into the eye caused predominantly slight conjunctival irritation. No skin sensitisation data are available.

Hearing loss, mainly at high frequencies, was the major finding with sub-acute exposure. It was observed following repeated exposure to 800 ppm and above for 6 weeks or to 1450 ppm for 3 days. A no-effect level was not determined and reversibility was not assessed.

Apart from this single study of hearing loss, xylenes have been shown to have low toxicity following repeated inhalation exposure and oral administration. The most commonly reported finding was a functional hypertrophy of the liver observed at exposure levels of 50 ppm and above.

There is no evidence from numerous studies with different end-points that xylenes are genotoxic. There is no evidence of carcinogenicity due to xylenes, following chronic oral administration, in the rat or mouse; the data for the male rat are, however, limited.

In reproductive toxicology studies there is no evidence of teratogenicity following inhalation exposure but delayed development has been observed. Following oral administration teratogenicity was observed at 683 mg/kg (o- and p-xylene) and 870 mg/kg (m-xylene). These dose levels were at or above those causing increased resorptions.

Toxicity to humans

Following single inhalation exposure or oral ingestion, the signs of toxicity predominantly involve the CNS. Headache, nausea and vomiting, dizziness and vertigo have all been reported at an inhalation exposure level estimated to be 700 ppm. In controlled exposure studies, a slight impairment of vestibular and visual functions and reaction time was observed at exposure levels of 200 ppm m-xylene and above; no effects were noted at exposure levels of up to 160 ppm. Death, attributed to respiratory depression following loss of consciousness, has been observed, with an exposure level required for loss of consciousness being estimated as 10,000 ppm. Apparent complete recovery was observed in survivors. There was evidence of an interaction between m-xylene and ethanol (resulting in further impairment of visual functions and reaction times) at low m-xylene levels (145-150 ppm) with a functional tolerance developing at higher exposure levels (275-290 ppm).

Exposure to vapours of xylenes at concentrations of 200 ppm and above has caused eye, nose and throat irritation. Corneal lesions have been documented following occupational exposure to xylene vapour. Liquid xylenes are irritant to human skin and eyes. Xylenes did not result in sensitisation in a skin sensitisation study and there is no evidence, despite widespread use, that xylenes cause sensitisation by skin contact.

In controlled, repeated-exposure studies there was no evidence of accumulative effects but there was some evidence of tolerance or adaption. Following repeated exposure of workers to xylenes, or solvents containing significant amounts of xylenes, episodes of depression, extreme fatigue, anxiety and sleep disorders were frequently reported. There was a gradual reduction in the severity of most symptoms after cessation of exposure. Insufficient data are available for any conclusions to be made on the effects of xylenes on neurophysiological or psychological functions, liver or kidney function or haematology parameters. Much of the data comes from studies on occupational groups such as painters and printers who have a mixed pattern of solvent exposure.

Similarly, insufficient data are available for any conclusions to be made on the genotoxic or carcinogenic potential of xylenes or on the potential effects on reproduction.

IDENTITY

Xylenes are colourless, volatile liquids with an empirical formula of C_8H_{10} and a molecular weight of 106.17. There are three structural isomers:

| | ortho(o)-xylene (1,2-dimethyl benzene) | meta(m)-xylene 1,3-dimethylbenzene | para(p)-xylene 1,4-dimethylbenzene |

The IUPAC and CAS preferred names are 1,2-, 1,3- and 1,4-dimethylbenzene although IUPAC still permits the trivial name xylene and the three isomers are usually called *ortho-*, *meta-* and *para-* xylene. Synonyms include xylol and xylen. Commercial grade xylene is predominantly a mixture of the three isomers, in widely varying proportions, and up to 40% ethylbenzene (Eb). Minor constituents include aliphatic hydrocarbons, C_9 aromatic hydrocarbons and toluene.

The physico-chemical properties of the individual isomers are tabulated below[1-5].

	ortho	meta	para
CAS Registry Number	95-47-6	108-38-3	106-42-3
Melting Point, °C	-25.2	-47.9	13.3
Boiling Point, °C (760 mm Hg)	144.4	139.1	138.3
Relative Density (20/4)	0.880	0.864	0.861
Vapour Pressure mm Hg (20 °C)	5	6	6.5
Vapour Density (air = 1)	3.7	3.7	3.7
Solubility in water, mg/l (25 °C)	171	147	156
n-Octanol-water partition coefficient (log P)	3.12	3.20	3.15
Flash Point, °C (closed cup)	32	25	27

An odour recognition threshold (for 50% of subjects) of approximately 1 ppm has been determined for a xylene mixture[6]. *o*-Xylene is reported to have a characteristic, sweet odour.

The main uses of xylene mixtures are for blending into petrol and as a solvent or thinner. Of the individual isomers, *p*-xylene is commercially the most important, being used predominantly in the production of polyester.

Throughout this review the following convention applies to the material used.

o-, *m*-, *p*-xylene: individual isomers.

Xylene:	defined isomer mixtures (composition details always stated) and material of undefined composition.
Xylenes:	a general term covering individual isomers and material of defined and undefined composition.

A volume of 1 ml of liquid xylenes has been taken to be equivalent to a weight of 870 mg and a concentration of 1 ppm xylenes in air to be equivalent to 4.35 mg/m^3.

Since ethylbenzene is an important component of commercial grade xylene, a brief summary of the metabolism and toxicity of ethylbenzene is provided as an Appendix (see p151).

DISPOSITION AND METABOLISM

Studies in animals

In vivo studies

Absorption

Rapid xylene absorption was recorded following whole-body exposure of mice to radiolabelled (ring ^{14}C-) *m*-xylene vapour for 10 minutes[7,8]. The autoradiograms suggested that absorption was primarily via the respiratory tract.

The levels of urinary metabolites indicate that all xylene isomers are well-absorbed orally by rats[9,10]. Peak xylene blood levels were noted in rats 4 hours after an oral dose of 0.5-4 g *m*-xylene/kg or 1.1 g *p*-xylene/kg[9,11].

In a briefly reported study with mice, a percutaneous absorption rate of 0.3 µg/cm^2/minute was calculated for liquid *m*-xylene applied dermally[12].

Distribution

Rat

The distribution of xylene equivalents (xylene plus its metabolites) has been studied in male rats exposed to about 50 ppm radiolabelled (methyl ^{14}C-) *p*-xylene vapour for up to 8 hours[13]. The highest concentrations were present in the kidneys (20 to 40 times the concentration in arterial blood during exposure) and subcutaneous fat. Concentrations in excess of those in blood were also present in the ischiadic nerve. Cerebrum, cerebellum, muscle and spleen concentrations were clearly below those in blood. Elimination half-lives for xylene equivalents from subcutaneous fat of 2 to 7 hours were estimated and some activity was still present in the kidneys 6 hours post exposure. A separate experiment with rats exposed to 257 ppm radiolabelled p-xylene indicated that both xylene and its metabolites were present in all tissues examined (blood, subcutaneous fat, cerebrum, muscles and liver), with about 75% of xylene equivalents in subcutaneous fat being xylene itself.

o-Xylene can cross the placenta of pregnant rats, but the concentrations measured in fetal blood and amniotic fluid immediately post exposure were less than in maternal blood[14]. Maternal blood concentration of o-xylene were seen to rise with increasing exposure concentrations following inhalation of up to 700 ppm vapour for 2 hours. Male rats exposed to up to 300-460 ppm m-xylene for 6 hours or more showed an increase in blood concentrations of m-xylene, at the end of exposure, which were in excess of the proportional increase in the atmospheric concentration[11,15]. Elimination from blood has been reported to be biphasic, with only trace levels of m-xylene remaining 16 hours after exposure to 690 ppm for 8 hours[11]. No accumulation of m-xylene in blood was noted on exposure to up to 460 ppm, 6 hours/day for 9 days or to 230 ppm, 6 hours/day, 6 days/week for 32 days.

The concentration of m-xylene in perirenal fat and brain (cerebrum) showed a positive correlation with exposure concentration when rats were exposed to 50 to 750 ppm m-xylene vapour 6 hours/day, 5 days/week for 1 or 2 weeks[16,17]. The concentration in fat was markedly greater than in brain, and in both tissues accumulation occurred from weeks 1 to 2. No xylene was detected in either tissue after a 2-week exposure-free period.

Accumulation of xylene in perirenal fat has also been noted in rats exposed to 300 ppm xylene (80% m-, 12% p-) vapour, 6 hours/day, 5 days/week for 1 or 2 weeks[18]. However, in a similar study with 300 ppm m-xylene, no accumulation in perirenal fat or brain tissue was recorded[16]. Xylene levels in the perirenal fat of rats exposed to 300 ppm xylene (19.2% o-, 43.0% m-, 19.5% p-, 18.3% Eb) vapour, 6 hours/day, 5 days/week for 18 weeks showed a progressive increase over the first 2 weeks and then declined[19]. The decline was attributed to xylene inducing its own metabolism. A result consistent with this effect was also obtained in a similar study with rats exposed to 300 ppm xylene (85% m-, 15% o- plus p-)[20].

Mouse

Two studies of the tissue distribution of ^{14}C-labelled xylenes and their metabolites have been conducted using low-temperature, whole body autoradiography[7,8,21]. The distribution of total radioactivity, 'volatile' radioactivity (considered to be unmetabolised xylenes), 'non-volatile' radioactivity (xylene metabolites) and tightly bound radioactivity (metabolites presumed to be covalently bound to cell macromolecules) was compared.

Whole-body autoradiography of male mice exposed to about 330 ppm radiolabelled (ring [14]C-) m-xylene vapour for 10 minutes revealed very high levels of radioactivity immediately post exposure in body fat, bone-marrow, brain (white matter), spinal cord, spinal nerves, liver and kidney[7,8]. Radioactivity in the nervous system and fatty tissues appeared to be due to xylene alone and was present for up to 1 and 8 hours, respectively. High levels of xylene metabolites were recorded in blood, lung, liver and kidney. Metabolites were recorded in the kidney for up to 8 hours post exposure (indicating rapid excretion of metabolites), and in the intestinal contents, bronchi and nasal mucosa up to 24 hours. No radioactivity was present in the body at 48 hours. In a separate experiment with the same exposure regime, it was shown that 8 hours post exposure the concentration of radioactivity (measured by liquid scintillation counting) in liver, kidney and body fat was greater than in blood.

Low-temperature autoradiographic and liquid scintillation techniques have also been used to study the distribution of radioactivity following exposure of pregnant mice to about 2000 ppm ^{14}C-labelled p-xylene vapour for 10 minutes[21]. High concentrations of xylene were recorded immediately post exposure in the adult brain (including cerebellum) and lung, with lesser amounts in kidney and liver. Xylene metabolites were also present in these tissues immediately post exposure, with particularly high concentrations in the kidney. Elimination of xylene and metabolites from these tissues was rapid, with low concentrations being recorded at 1 and 4 hours, respectively. Radioactivity in fat was investigated from 30 minutes post exposure, when the concentration of xylene was much higher than in other tissues; elevated concentrations were still present at 4 hours. Pronounced retention of xylene metabolites was noted in the nasal mucosa and olfactory bulb of the maternal brain at 4 and 24 hours.

p-Xylene appeared to pass immediately from dam to embryo/fetus at all stages of gestation studied (days 11, 14, 17). However, the concentration of xylene in the fetus was low (2% of that in maternal brain immediately post exposure) and was rapidly cleared. Fetal concentrations of metabolites were also low compared to

3

concentrations in the mother. Xylene was evenly distributed in the fetus following exposure on day 11 but was located primarily in the liver following exposure on day 17. Uptake of radioactivity by uterine fluid was noted.

In neither of these two mouse studies was any radioactivity found to be firmly bound to tissues, which suggests the absence of reactive metabolites[7,8,21].

A tissue distribution study with pregnant mice dosed orally with radiolabelled *m*-xylene, at 870 mg/kg, has been reported briefly as an abstract[22]. Radioactivity was detected in fetuses following dosing on days 12 or 15 of gestation but had virtually disappeared 24 hours post dose. At least 95% of radioactivity found in the fetus was attributed to xylene metabolites.

Rabbit

In an early study with rabbits exposed to xylene (27% *o*-, 52% *m*-,21% *p*-) vapour over several months, the concentration of xylene in the adrenals, bone-marrow and spleen was reported to be in excess of that in blood[23]. However, the limited nature of the investigation makes it impossible to draw any firm conclusions.

Metabolism and elimination

The metabolism and elimination of xylenes have chiefly been studied in the rat.

Rat

All xylene isomers appear to be excreted predominantly as metabolites in urine[10,24,25]. Exhalation of unchanged *m*-xylene has been documented in one study[24]. Exhalation was greatest 4 hours after intraperitoneal injection, with 13% of the dose being exhaled unchanged within 10 hours.

The principal metabolic pathway involved side-chain oxidation to form methylbenzoic acid, apparently via methylbenzyl alcohol and methylbenzyl aldehyde (Figure 1). Methylbenzoic acid is then conjugated with glycine (to form methylhippuric acid) or glucuronic acid and excreted in urine[25-27]. Studies indicate that conjugation with glycine predominates for *m*- and *p*-xylene[10,24-26,28]. For example, following an intraperitoneal *m*-xylene dose of 87-348 mg/kg, 53-75% was excreted as *m*-methylhippuric acid in urine collected up to 24 hours[28]. In the case of *o*-xylene, glucuronide formation has been reported to predominate over glycine conjugation[10,27].

The existence of a separate minor pathway resulting in the urinary excretion of thioethers (believed to be

mercapturic acids) has been investigated[29,30]. The pathway appears to be more important for *o*-xylene than for the other isomers: following an intraperitoneal dose of 319 mg/kg the proportion excreted as mercapturic acids was calculated to be 10% for *o*-xylene as compared to 0.6-1.3% for *m*- and *p*-xylene. In the case of *o*-xylene the main thiometabolite is believed to be *o*-methylbenzyl mercapturic acid and to be formed by *o*-methylbenzyl alcohol undergoing sequential sulphation and glutathione conjugation.

There is evidence that a small amount of *m*-methylbenzyl alcohol is excreted in rat urine following conjugation with sulphates or glucuronic acid[26].

Hydroxylation of the aromatic ring with the formation and urinary excretion of dimethylphenols (apparently as conjugates) has been reported to be another minor metabolic pathway in rats[26,31].

Mouse

Male mice which retained a calculated dose of 108.5 mg/kg, following exposure to about 330 ppm radiolabelled *m*-xylene vapour for 10 minutes, eliminated 66.2% of the dose in urine and 3.4% as radiolabelled *m*-xylene in exhaled breath over the following 8 hours[7,8]. Significant biliary excretion of xylene metabolites was also noted.

In the brief abstract for another study with radiolabelled *m*-xylene, ^{14}C excretion by pregnant mice was reported to be principally in urine and expired air following oral administration[22]. Approximately 99% of ^{14}C excretion in urine was in the form of metabolites.

No information is available on the identity of metabolites of xylenes in the mouse.

Other Species

Methylbenzoic acid and dimethylphenols have been reported in the hydrolysed urine of guinea pigs and rabbits exposed to each of the xylene isomers[23]. In an early study, it was concluded that, following oral dosing of 1-2 g xylenes to rabbits, all isomers were metabolised chiefly to methylbenzoic acid[33]. Methylbenzoic acid was considered to be mostly as the glycine conjugate (methylhippuric acid), while for *o*-xylene conjugation with glucuronic acid or excretion as unconjugated methylbenzoic acid predominated.

Excretion of *m*-xylene in the bile of dogs has been reported, but this was only a very small amount (less than 0.05% of an intravenous dose within 2 hours of dosing)[34].

Figure 1 Proposed metabolic pathways of *m*-xylene in rats and man

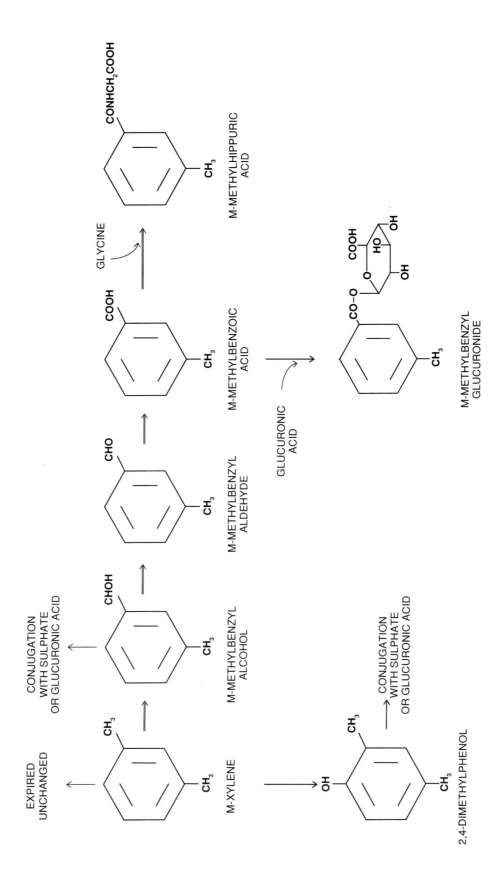

Summary of in vivo studies in animals

Xylenes are well-absorbed orally. Rapid absorption via the respiratory tract has been demonstrated for *m*-xylene. Appreciable dermal absorption of liquid *m*-xylene was noted in one limited report. Xylenes and/or their metabolites were distributed widely in rodents following inhalation of *m*-or *p*-xylene, the highest tissue concentrations being in body fat. High concentrations have also been recorded in kidneys, nervous tissue, liver and bone-marrow. Accumulation of xylenes in body fat and brain tissue has been demonstrated in some but not all studies during exposure for up to 2 weeks; a subsequent decline in the concentration of xylenes has been noted on prolonged exposure. Only low levels of xylenes and metabolites were detected in fetuses of exposed dams. All xylenes appear to be excreted by rodents predominantly as metabolites in urine, with exhalation of unchanged xylenes and biliary excretion of metabolites being of lesser importance. Xylenes are metabolised in rats, principally by side chain oxidation to form methylbenzoic acid, which is excreted in urine following conjugation with glycine or glucuronic acid. Minor urinary metabolites include conjugated dimethylphenols and conjugated thioethers. Quantitative differences in metabolism between *o*-xylene and the other two isomers have been identified.

In vitro animal studies

Absorption and distribution

The rate of absorption of liquid *o*-xylene across excised rat skin was calculated to be 0.103 μg/cm^2/minute at steady state, following an initial lag phase of 2.20 hours[35]. Similar values were obtained for ethylbenzene. The rate of absorption was less than for toluene, styrene or benzene, but greater than for the five aliphatic hydrocarbons tested.

Partition coefficients have been determined *in vitro* for *m*-xylene vapour using tissue homogenates and blood[36,37]. The following blood/air values have been reported: 20 (pig blood), 21 (rabbit plasma) and 37 (rabbit blood). Tissue/blood values for rabbits were 1.6-2.1 (muscle, kidney, heart and lung), 3.0-3.3 (liver and brain), 42 (bone-marrow) and 146 (retroperitoneal fat). The relatively low value for brain tissue has been attributed to the significant content of phospholipids in which xylenes are much less soluble than in neutral fat[38].

Metabolism

A metabolic and kinetic study of *p*-xylene has been conducted using isolated, perfused rabbit livers and lungs[39]. In this study, plasma clearance (per whole

organ) of *p*-xylene by lung, including elimination of unchanged *p*-xylene vapour, was about 50% of that by liver. However, on a weight-for-weight basis, the lung cleared *p*-xylene more rapidly from the circulation than did the liver and the rate of metabolism of *p*-xylene per unit weight was also higher. In a separate briefly reported investigation, it was calculated that, on the basis of *in vitro* measurements, the rate of metabolism per organ for a range of organic solvents, including *m*-xylene, would be markedly greater in rabbit liver than lung, although activity per unit of cytochrome P450 would be greater in the lung[40].

The organ perfusion study also identified differences between the metabolic pathways in rabbit liver and lung[39]. In the liver *p*-methylhippuric acid was the major metabolite detected but in the lung this side chain oxidation pathway progressed primarily to *p*-methylbenzyl alcohol, with smaller amounts of *p*-methylbenzoic acid and no *p*-methylhippuric acid being detected. Another difference was the formation of 2,5-dimethylphenol by the lungs, in small amounts, but not by the liver.

Some information on the metabolism of xylenes by rat subcellular fractions is available. In contrast to rabbits, it has been reported that rat lung enzymes have only negligible activity towards organic solvents in comparison with rat liver enzymes[40]. Metabolism of *m*-and *p*-xylene to *m*-and *p*-methylbenzyl alcohol has been found to be greater for hepatic than pulmonary microsomes[41,42]. Further metabolism of *p*-methylbenzyl alcohol to *p*-methylbenzoic acid occurred in the presence of a hepatic but not pulmonary cytosolic fraction. The formation of methylbenzyl alcohol and dimethylphenol by hepatic and pulmonary microsomes is dependent on cytochrome P450. Evidence that xylenes can induce metabolism has been obtained from studies in which the activities of liver microsomal enzymes and concentrations of cytochrome P450 were increased following daily exposure to xylenes[16,43]. Metabolism of *m*-xylene by a microsome/cytosol preparation of cerebral tissue was reported to be very slow[16].

Summary of in vitro animal studies

Absorption of liquid *o*-xylene across rat skin *in vitro* was comparable to that measured for xylenes *in vivo*. The body fat/blood and bone-marrow/blood partition coefficients for *m*-xylene were consistent with the high concentration of *m*-xylene in these tissues *in vivo*. The hypothesis based on *in vivo* observations that xylenes can induce their own metabolism is supported by *in vitro* data. There is evidence from *in vitro* experiments that clearance and metabolism of xylenes (expressed per whole organ) is greater for rabbit liver than lung. Metabolism of *m*-xylene by a subcellular cerebral fraction of rats was very slow.

Effects of other chemicals on the metabolism of xylenes by animals

The effects of exposure to toluene, ethanol or phenobarbital on the metabolism of xylenes have been investigated in several studies. There is evidence that exposure to toluene or ethanol can either enhance or inhibit the metabolism of xylenes, the response appearing to be related particularly to the timing of this exposure[18-20,43-47]. Pre-treatment with phenobarbital increases the metabolism of xylenes; *in vitro* data suggest that this is a feature of the liver and not the lung[9,24,49-51]. Limited data are available on the effects of some other chemicals[45,50,52,53].

Studies in humans

Absorption

Absorption of xylenes has been investigated following inhalation and dermal exposure to the vapour and dermal application of the liquid. No studies of oral absorption have been reported.

Inhalation

Pulmonary retention of *m*-xylene, as determined by measurement of atmospheric and exhaled concentrations, became relatively constant (at about 60%) after the first 5 to 10 minutes' exposure to 100 ppm[54]. In another study, pulmonary retention of 62-64% was reported for each xylene isomer on exposure to 45-90 ppm for 1 to 7 hours[55]. Retention was also relatively constant, averaging 59%, in individuals exposed to stable or periodically varying *m*-xylene concentrations (70-220 ppm) while at rest or undergoing intermittent physical exercise (100 W for 10 minutes, four times per day)[56]. A slight reduction in retention (from 63 to 51%) was noted when resting individuals subsequently underwent moderately heavy physical exercise (150 W for 30 minutes) during exposure to 100 ppm xylene (8.8% *o*-, 49.4% *m*-, 1.4% *p*-, 40.4% Eb)[57]. However, increased pulmonary ventilation during exercise was calculated to be associated with a clear increase in total uptake of xylenes[56,57].

Further evidence that xylenes are well-absorbed by the lungs comes from measurements of xylene levels in alveolar air[57,58]. In resting individuals exposed to 100 and 200 ppm xylene (8.8% *o*-, 49.4% *m*-, 1.4% *p*-, 40.4% Eb), the alveolar air level was about 15% of that in inspired air[57]. A value of 36% was, however, recorded for individuals undergoing heavy exercise (150 W for 30 minutes) during exposure to 100 ppm.

The ethylbenzene to *m*-plus *p*-xylene ratio for xylene in inspired air has been found to be similar to that in alveolar air (*o*-xylene was not measured), thus indicating similar rates of pulmonary absorption for ethylbenzene and xylenes[59].

Xylenes are rapidly absorbed into blood following inhalation exposure. Resting individuals exposed to 100-200 ppm xylene (8.8% *o*-, 49.4% *m*-, 1.4% *p*-, 40.4% Eb) had levels of xylene in alveolar air and blood approaching apparent plateau levels within about 15 minutes, higher levels being attained at 200 ppm[57]. Light physical exercise during exposure to 100 ppm greatly increased the blood levels of xylene, with a plateau level being reached after about 2 hours. Studies by another group of investigators using exposure to 100-290 ppm *m*-xylene revealed a rapid rise in xylene blood levels during the first hour of exposure and then a much more gradual increase for the remainder of the exposure period (the next 2-3 hours)[54,60]. On repeated exposure to 100 ppm (6 hours/day for 4.5 days), blood levels indicated that some accumulation of *m*-xylene had occurred.

In vitro human blood/air partition coefficients of 26-38, calculated for each of the xylene isomers, demonstrate that xylenes are highly soluble in blood[61]. Similar values (30-40) were obtained for the ratio of xylene concentrations in arterial blood/alveolar air in individuals undergoing physical exercise during exposure to 100-200 ppm xylene (defined above)[57]. A low value (about 15) was obtained for resting individuals. Values of 12-15 have also been recorded for the venous blood/end exhaled air ratio in apparently resting individuals exposed to 20-70 ppm *p*-xylene[62]. The lower values for resting individuals could be due to incomplete equilibrium. In blood, *m*-xylene is mainly associated with serum proteins[54].

Dermal

Dermal absorption of xylenes has been investigated following exposure to the liquid or vapour. In early studies, liquid xylenes (about 0.2 ml of the individual isomers or an undefined mixture) were applied under a watch glass to the forearm[63,64]. Dermal uptake, ie transfer across skin (absorption) plus retention within the skin, was calculated by measuring how much of the applied material remained on the skin surface after 5-15 minutes.

Uptake values of 50-160 µg/cm^2/minute were reported for the three isomers and for the undefined xylene mixture (these values are considered to be markedly in excess of true dermal absorption).

More recently, dermal absorption has been investigated following hand immersion in liquid *m*-xylene for 15-20 minutes, with precautions being taken to prevent inhalation exposure[65,66]. In one study, absorption, estimated from the urinary level of the metabolite *m*-methylhippuric acid, was calculated to be about 2 μg/cm^2/minute in eight volunteers[65]. Another subject, who had a history of atopic dermatitis but had "healthy skin" prior to exposure, exhibited three times greater absorption. The amount (about 35 mg) an individual in the main group absorbed through both hands was estimated to be similar to that absorbed following inhalation exposure to 100 ppm for the same period. Peak *m*-xylene concentrations appeared in the draining venous blood 4-6 minutes after exposure.

A similar mean value for dermal absorption, 2.45 μg/cm^2/minute, was obtained by another group of investigators from measurements of urinary levels of *m*-methylhippuric acid and the amount of *m*-xylene in exhaled breath[66]. Variation in absorption of up to 6.2 times between individuals, as compared with up to two times within the same individual, was reported. Two types of barrier cream were tested but neither was shown to be effective in preventing dermal absorption. *m*-Xylene was usually detectable in breath 10 minutes after exposure commenced, with peak levels 10 minutes post exposure.

Dermal absorption of *m*-xylene vapour has been investigated in volunteers exposed to 300 ppm (two men) or 600 ppm (three men) for 3.5 hours while breathing air through a full facepiece respirator to avoid inhalation exposure[67]. The subjects wore pyjamas and periodically performed sufficient exercise to cause a rise in skin temperature and perspiration. Dermal absorption (calculated in a manner similar to that used in the hand immersion studies) appeared to be directly dependent on vapour concentration and at 600 ppm was of the order of 0.01 μg/cm^2/minute. This figure is only approximate because of variability in the measurements for the limited number of subjects investigated. Absorption was said to be more than three times greater in an individual with skin abrasions associated with atopic dermatitis. In a further experiment within the same study, three subjects were exposed to 20 ppm, but in this case they remained sedentary and had no respiratory protection, ie both dermal and pulmonary absorption could occur. The amount of *m*-xylene absorbed in this experiment was calculated to be nearly equivalent to that following dermal-only exposure to 600 ppm. (Thus further illustrating the limited importance of dermal absorption of *m*-xylene vapour.) Blood levels of *m*-xylene were similar and in both experiments had almost reached a plateau by the end of the exposure period.

Distribution

Little information on the distribution of xylenes in humans is available. A high peritoneal fat/air partition coefficient (3605) has been determined for *m*-xylene vapour *in vitro*[37]. The times required for equilibrium levels of *m*-xylene to be reached in tissues have been calculated from physiological parameters to be a matter of minutes for well-perfused parenchymal organs, a few hours for muscle and several days for adipose tissue[38].

Post-mortem tissue analysis on a woman found to have a quantity of xylene mixture in her stomach revealed xylene to be present in all tissues investigated (xylene would appear to have been swallowed 4 days prior to death)[68]. The ratios of the three isomers were roughly similar in the stomach contents (3*o*-: 5*m*-: 2*p*-), blood (3:6:1) and adipose tissue (4:4:2). However, in the brain, liver, spleen, kidney and myocardium *o*-xylene accounted for approximately 80% of the xylene isomers. Only limited significance can be attached to the findings of this study because they are based on a single individual.

In an experiment with volunteers exposed to 100 to 200 ppm xylene (8.8% *o*-, 49.4% *m*-, 1.4% *p*-, 40.4% Eb) for 2 hours, the ethylbenzene to *m*-plus *p*-xylene ratio (*o*-xylene not measured) in subcutaneous adipose tissue up to 22 hours post exposure was similar to that in inspired air[59]. A negative correlation between the concentration of xylene in adipose tissue and the degree of obesity was reported. Total xylene uptake by an individual, however, showed a strong positive correlation with the amount of body fat. About 5% of xylene uptake remained in the adipose tissue 22 hours post exposure.

In another volunteer study, individuals were exposed to approximately 90-200 ppm, constant or time weighted average (TWA) concentration, *m*-xylene intermittently for about a week[69]. The proportion of absorbed *m*-xylene distributed to subcutaneous fat was calculated to be low, being about 4% in resting individuals and 8% in those undergoing exercise. Elimination from this fatty tissue was slow, a median elimination half-life of 58 hours having been calculated. (Thus, some accumulation of *m*-xylene in fatty tissue may be possible on repeated exposure.) The limited data suggest that elimination was monophasic. For two of the three exposure/activity regimes, a positive correlation was found between elimination half-life and relative fat mass.

Analysis of gas chromatographic-mass spectrometric profiles of low molecular weight organic compounds obtained from fetal cord blood and maternal blood at birth has shown that xylene (undefined) can cross the human placenta[70]. In this study of 11 births, no evidence for fetal accumulation of xylene was obtained.

Metabolite formation

Metabolism of xylenes by humans is similar to that described for rats in that it consists primarily of side-chain oxidation to form methylbenzoic acid (see Figure 1)[54-56]. In humans, methylbenzoic acid (all isomers) is then conjugated principally with glycine and excreted in urine as methylhippuric acid[55]. It has been estimated that glycine conjugation would be saturated in a man exposed to about 270 ppm xylene while undertaking moderately heavy physical work or to about 780 ppm while resting[71]. A small amount of the glucuronide ester of methylbenzoic acid, and trace levels of methylbenzyl alcohol, have also been detected in human urine following exposure to certain xylenes[27,72,73].

Hydroxylation of the aromatic ring with the formation, and urinary excretion, of dimethylphenols (apparently as conjugates) is a minor metabolic pathway in humans, as it is in rats[73]. In humans the following dimethylphenol isomers have been identified: 2,3- and 3,4- (with *o*-xylene), 2,4- (with *m*-xylene) and 2,5- (with *p*-xylene)[55].

Elimination

Absorbed xylenes are excreted predominantly as metabolites in urine, with small amounts excreted unchanged in exhaled air. Excretion in faeces has not been investigated but would appear to be unimportant. The apparent rate of clearance of *p*-xylene from blood has been calculated to be 2.6 l/kg/hour at 20 ppm and 1.6 l/kg/hour at 70 ppm[62].

Urinary excretion

Urinary excretion of total conjugates of *m*-methylbenzoic acid and 2,4- dimethylphenol conjugates has been measured following exposure of volunteers to a constant or TWA concentration of about 90-200 ppm *m*-xylene over a 5 day period[54,56]. At least 97% of the xylene absorbed was calculated to be excreted as *m*-methylbenzoic acid conjugates. 2,4-Dimethylphenol conjugates accounted for 1-2% of the metabolites measured. The same results were obtained for individuals at rest and undergoing intermittent physical exercise (100 W for 10 minutes).

Similarly, when volunteers were exposed to about 45 ppm of *o*-, *m*-, or *p*-xylene for 8 hours, it was estimated that 95-99% of the absorbed dose was excreted as methylhippuric acid in urine[55]. Dimethylphenol excretion (determined following acid hydrolysis of urine) accounted for 0.1-2% of the amount of each isomer absorbed. Only trace amounts of xylenes were detected in urine. Values of about 90% for the percentage of the absorbed dose of *m*-xylene excreted as methylhippuric acid have also been calculated following exposure to 100 ppm vapour for 4 hours and in a hand immersion experiment with liquid *m*-xylene[66,72]. Another group of investigators, however, estimated that 46% of absorbed *o*-xylene was excreted in urine as methylhippuric acid following exposure to 138 ppm vapour for 3 hours; only trace amounts of the glucuronide conjugate of *o*-methylbenzoic acid were detected[27].

Mean half-lives for urinary excretion of methylhippuric acids (*m*-plus *p*-isomers) of 3.6 and 30.1 hours were calculated for painters following exposure to xylene (undefined isomer mixture) at work[74]. There is some evidence for a positive association between the degree of obesity and the length of half-life. In a controlled-exposure study with resting subjects exposed to *m*-xylene vapour, urinary excretion of conjugates of *m*-methylbenzoic acid was described, from limited sampling points, as triphasic with approximate half-lives of 1-2, 10, and 20 hours[54]. Other investigators have reported that the time course of urinary excretion is similar for *o*-, *m*- and *p*-methylhippuric acid[55].

Following oral administration of *o*-xylene at 39 mg/kg, maximum urinary levels of glycine and glucuronide conjugates of *o*-methylbenzoic acid were recorded after 3 to 6 hours[27,75]. Excretion of the two conjugates was reported to be equivalent to 33.1% and 1.0%, respectively, of the dose administered; similar percentages were recorded after an oral dose of 78 mg/kg. In an equivalent experiment with *m*-xylene, only the glycine conjugate was measured. Peak excretion of this conjugate occurred 1 to 3 hours after the oral dose; total excretion was calculated to be equivalent to 53.1% of the dose administered.

Exhalation

It has been calculated for xylenes that following exposure to up to 200 ppm vapour about 4-5% of the amount estimated to be absorbed by the lungs is subsequently exhaled unchanged[54-57].

Elimination of *m*-xylene in exhaled breath has been reported to show a similar triphasic elimination profile to that for urinary excretion of total conjugates of *m*-methylbenzoic acid[54]. The initial half-life of about 1 hour agrees with the value obtained for *m*-xylene in breath (and blood) up to 3 hours post exposure by another group of investigators[72].

Effect of other chemicals on the metabolism of xylenes in man

Co-exposure to *m*-xylene and ethylbenzene vapour, on the consumption of ethanol or aspirin prior to inhalation exposure to *m*-xylene, has been shown to reduce urinary excretion of one or more xylene metabolites, including methylhippuric acid[60,72,73]. In the case of ethanol consumption, a clear increase in the *m*-xylene concentration in blood was also noted[60]. Other investigators have reported that co-exposure to toluene vapour decreased the ratio of the concentration of *p*-xylene in venous blood to that in end-exhaled air[62].

In a hand immersion experiment, dermal absorption of liquid *m*-xylene was inhibited by the presence of isobutanol[76].

Summary of the disposition and metabolism of xylenes in humans

Xylenes are rapidly absorbed via the respiratory tract. A pulmonary retention value of about 60% has been calculated on exposure to up to 100-200 ppm; this would appear to be the equilibrium value. Total respiratory uptake is clearly increased by physical exercise and is also positively correlated with the amount of body fat.

Liquid m-xylene is well-absorbed through the skin; values of about 2 μg/cm^2/minute have been obtained for normal skin. A higher value was obtained for an individual with a history of atopic dermatitis. Dermal absorption of m-xylene vapour (up to 600 ppm) would appear to be much more limited.

Xylenes are highly soluble in blood and fat, and are distributed widely in the body. However, only a small proportion of absorbed m-xylene is distributed to subcutaneous fat. Some accumulation of m-xylene in blood has been noted in one study on repeated exposure over a 5-day period.

Xylenes undergo extensive metabolism, with typically about 90% of the absorbed dose being excreted in urine as methylhippuric acid, the glycine conjugate of methylbenzoic acid, following inhalation (up to 200 ppm) or dermal (liquid) exposure. Most of the remainder is exhaled as unchanged xylene or excreted in urine as dimethylphenol conjugates or the glucuronide conjugate of methylbenzoic acid. Excretion of methylbenzoic acid conjugates, as well as xylenes in exhaled breath, exhibits multiphasic kinetics. Excretion of methylbenzoic acid conjugates can be reduced by exposure to ethylbenzene, ethanol or aspirin.

No significant differences in the disposition and metabolism of the three xylene isomers have been demonstrated.

TOXICITY TO ANIMALS

Acute toxicity

Inhalation

Most studies have been carried out in rats and mice. Summaries of the available data are presented in Table 1.1. In general, xylenes would appear to have a low acute inhalation toxicity.

o-Xylene

LC_{50} values, for 6-hour exposures, of 4330 ppm in the rat and 4595 ppm in the mouse have been reported[77,78].

Signs of toxicity in rats and mice were hypotonia, somnolence, narcosis, ataxia, prostration, clonic spasms and unconsciousness leading to death due to respiratory failure[77,79-81]. In mice, some deaths occurred during exposure and some were delayed to between days 5 and 10 post exposure[78].

In a study of conditioned behaviour in mice, an increased response rate was seen after a 30-minute exposure to 1400-2000 ppm[79]. At higher concentrations there was a marked decrease in response rate with an EC_{50} of 5179 ppm. This biphasic response indicates that there was excitation of the central nervous system (CNS) at low concentrations and depression at higher concentrations. The depressant effect on the CNS was found to increase the threshold for the onset of pentylenetetrazol (PTZ)-induced convulsions in mice, with an EC_{50} of 1339 ppm[82]. However, in a study of prenarcotic motor behaviour in rats, no significant effects were observed up to the narcotic threshold of 2180 ppm for a 4-hour exposure[80].

Irritation of the respiratory tract has been reported in the mouse, with an RD_{50} (dose causing a 50% decrease in respiratory rate) of 1467 ppm for an exposure of approximately 5 minutes[83,84]. The onset of the effect was generally rapid and the maximum decrease in respiratory rate was attained within a few minutes.

m-Xylene

In the rat and the mouse, LC_{50} values of 5984 ppm and 5267 ppm respectively have been reported following 6-hour exposures[77,78]. Deaths in the mouse study occurred within the 6-hour exposure period[78]. In an early study with mice exposed to 2010 ppm for 24 hours, deaths were reported 4 days after exposure[85].

As with o-xylene, signs of toxicity consisted of hypotonia, somnolence, narcosis, ataxia, prostration, clonic spasms and unconsciousness leading to death due to respiratory failure[77,79-81,86].

The biphasic CNS response of excitation at low concentrations and depression at higher concentrations observed in a conditioned behavioural study in mice occurred at similar exposure levels to those seen for o-xylene[79]. CNS depression was again found to increase the threshold for the onset of pentylenetetrazol (PTZ)-induced convulsions in mice with an EC_{50} of 2093 ppm[82]. The narcotic threshold of approximately 2100 ppm (4-hour exposure) determined in prenarcotic motor behaviour studies in rats was also similar to that observed for o-xylene[80,86].

Following exposure of rats to 75, 150, or 300 ppm for 24

hours, there were concentration-dependent decreases in pulmonary cytochrome P450 levels and mixed function oxygenase (MFO) enzyme activity, which were significant at all concentrations[15]. However, ultra-structural examination of the lungs of two animals from the high dose revealed no abnormalities.

p-Xylene

LC$_{50}$ values of 4740 ppm for a 4-hour exposure and 4591 ppm for a 6-hour exposure have been reported in the rat and 3907 ppm for a 6-hour exposure in the mouse[41, 77,78,87]. Some deaths occurred during exposure and others were delayed[77].

The signs of toxicity were similar to those reported for the other isomers.These were hypotonia, somnolence, muscular spasms, hyper-reactivity to noise, dyspnoea, ataxia, prostration and unconsciousness leading to death due to respiratory failure[77,79-81,88].

A study of conditioned behaviour in mice showed that *p*-xylene elicited a biphasic CNS response with excitation and depression at exposure levels similar to those seen for the *o*- and *m*-isomers[79]. In contrast to *o*- and *m*-xylene, marked activation together with incoordination and tremors were observed at concentrations between 400 and 1500 ppm in a study of prenarcotic motor behaviour in rats[80]. However, the narcotic threshold was similar to that for *o*- and *m*-xylene at 1940 ppm (4-hour exposure).

Concentration-dependent increases in serum activities of marker enzymes for hepatocellular and hepatobiliary damage in the rat occurred following a 4-hour exposure to 1000, 1500 or 2000 ppm *p*-xylene[89]. However, in other studies at higher exposure levels (sufficient to cause some mortality) no treatment-related macroscopic or microscopic hepatic lesions have been noted in the rat or mouse[77,85,88].

Following a 4-hour exposure to 1000 ppm, there was a marked decrease in pulmonary cytochrome P450 in rabbits and a significant decrease in NADPH cytochrome c reductase and MFO enzyme activity in rats[90,91].

Xylene

Rat 4-hour exposure studies to xylene of defined and undefined composition have led to reporting of LC$_{50}$ values of 6350, 6700 and 10 950 ppm[6,92,93]. In these studies, deaths occurred during the exposure period[6,92]. No LC$_{50}$ values for the mouse are available but experiments have been carried out at up to 7000 ppm for 30 minutes[79]. Signs of toxicity in rats and mice were narcosis, ataxia, prostration, clonic or tonic spasms and unconsciousness leading to death due to respiratory failure[6,79,94].

No signs of toxicity were reported following a 4-hour exposure to 580 and 530 ppm (7.63% *o*-, 65.01% *m*-, 7.84% *p*-, 19.27% Eb) in the rat and dog respectively[6].

In a conditioned behavioural study (xylene composition not defined) in the mouse, a biphasic CNS response was observed, with excitation and depression at similar exposure levels to those seen for the three individual isomers[79]. In the same type of study conducted in rats exposed to 113 ppm and above of xylene of undefined composition, there was a transient decrease in behavioural performance and, at higher concentrations, rapid development of tolerance[95-97].

Rats exposed to 1450 ppm xylene for 8 hours (10% *o*-, 80% *m*-, 10% *p*-) showed a slight increase (approximately 5 dB) in the auditory response threshold at 20 kHz[98].

A reversible decrease in respiratory rate, indicative of respiratory tract irritation, was reported in mice exposed to 1300 ppm and above (xylene composition defined previously) for 1 minute[6]. There was no observed effect of respiratory rate during exposure to 460 ppm.

In contrast to *p*-xylene, serum activities of marker enzymes for hepatoxicity in the rat showed no changes following a 4-hour exposure to 340-5480 ppm xylene of undefined composition[93,99]. At 5480 ppm there were raised liver triglyceride levels. Histological examination of the liver revealed no treatment-related abnormalities. In another study, no histological abnormalities were observed in the livers of cats following exposure to approximately 9500 ppm (xylene composition defined previously) for up to 2 hours[6].

Summary of acute inhalation toxicity

The acute toxicity of xylenes has been studied mainly in the rat and mouse. Xylenes are all of low acute toxicity by inhalation, with reported LC$_{50}$ values for 6-hour exposures in excess of 4000 ppm. Death is caused by respiratory failure due to CNS depression and there is some evidence of delayed deaths.

Effects on the CNS are the predominant finding, with excitation at lower concentrations and depression at higher concentrations. In the mouse, excitation occurred at 1400-2000 ppm and the EC$_{50}$ for depression was 5179 ppm following exposure to *o*-xylene. There was little difference between each individual isomer and xylene of undefined composition.

In the rat, the biphasic response was only noted with *p*-xylene in the concentration range approximately 400-1500 ppm. However, the concentration for the onset of narcosis was similar for all three isomers (1940-2180 ppm).

11

A slight increase in auditory response thresholds has been observed at 1450 ppm xylene (defined composition) in rats.

Irritation of the respiratory tract, manifest as a decrease in respiratory rate, has been observed; exposure to 1467 ppm o-xylene for 5 minutes reduced the rate by 50%.

In the rat, elevated serum enzyme activities indicative of hepatocellular damage have been observed at and above 1000 ppm in one study with p-xylene. However, no effects were seen in rats at exposure levels up to 5480 ppm xylene (undefined composition) and no histopathological lesions have been observed at higher exposure levels with p-xylene or xylene (defined or undefined composition).

Decreased pulmonary cytochrome P450 levels and/or MFO enzyme activity have been observed in rats at 75 ppm m-xylene and above and 1000 ppm p-xylene.

Oral

Most studies have been performed in the rat. Summaries of the available data are presented in Table 1.2. Xylenes have a low acute oral toxicity.

o-, m-, p-Xylene

LD_{50} values of 3608 mg/kg (o-xylene), 5011 and 6660 mg/kg (m-xylene), and 4029 mg/kg (p-xylene) have been reported in the rat[100,101].

Xylene

Following studies conducted in the rat, LD_{50} values of between 3523 and 8700 mg/kg have been reported for various mixtures of defined composition and a xylene of undefined composition[92,100,102,103]. In the mouse, values of 5627 and 5251 mg/kg for males and females respectively have been reported[102]. The xylene tested was 9.1% o-, 60.2% m-, 14.6% p- and 17.0% Eb. Most deaths occurred within 72 hours of dosing in rat studies[92,104]. Lethal doses of xylene of undefined composition were above 5100 mg/kg, 5950 mg/kg causing 67% mortality within 7 days[104]. Signs of toxicity at the lethal doses were CNS depression and, on histological examination, the only findings reported were "congestion of cells" in liver, kidney and spleen.

Dermal

All studies have been performed in the rabbit. Summaries of the available data are presented in Table 1.3. Xylenes are all of low acute dermal toxicity. o-Xylene had an LD_{50} value of above 20 000 mg/kg for a 24-hour exposure "under a sleeve"[105]. Signs of toxicity

included narcosis, which diminished at 24 hours, and marked skin irritation. An LD_{50} value of 12 180 mg/kg has been reported for a 24-hour exposure to m-xylene "under a sleeve"[101]. No data are available for p-xylene. In an acute toxicity study, no deaths were seen following a 4-hour exposure to xylene (composition undefined) at 1700 mg/kg[92].

Parenteral

Most studies have been conducted in the rat or mouse. The available data are summarised in Table 1.4. The reported studies used predominantly the intraperitoneal (i.p.) route but also included intravenous (i.v.), subcutaneous (s.c.) and intramuscular (i.m.) administration. Xylenes are all of low acute toxicity following parenteral administration.

Reported LD_{50} values were 2236 mg/kg (m-xylene), 3280 mg/kg (p-xylene) and 2459 mg/kg (xylene, undefined composition) in the rat by the i.p. route[41,87,106-108]. In the mouse LD_{50} values of 1364 mg/kg (o-xylene), 1731 mg/kg (m-xylene), 2109 mg/kg (p-xylene) and 1610 mg/kg (xylene, undefined composition), all i.p., have been reported[94,109].

In a number of studies, all three isomers were found to interfere with the modulation of the vestibular-oculomotor pathways in the rat[110].

The blood threshold levels for this effect were 170-200 µg/ml for each isomer administered by the i.v. route. Similar results have also been reported for m-xylene in the rabbit[111-117]. The vestibular-oculomotor effects occurred at lower blood levels in the rabbit (30 µg/ml) and some deaths due to respiratory distress were recorded at 100 µg/ml.

Although serum enzyme studies have shown some evidence of apparent hepatic toxicity in rat and guinea pig at xylene (undefined composition) dose levels of 652 mg/kg and 1000 or 2000 mg/kg respectively (i.p. administration), only minor histopathological changes have been reported[107,108,118]. A marked increase in serum aspartate aminotransferase (AST) activity and a slight increase in alanine aminotransferase (ALT) activity was seen following i.v. administration of 50 mg/kg m-xylene to the dog[34].

A dose-dependent depletion of hepatic glutathione has been demonstrated in the rat, with o-xylene exerting an effect at 50 mg/kg or above, in contrast to m-xylene at 425 mg/kg or above, and p-xylene (which had a potency similar to that of m-xylene), following i.p. administration[29]. The effects observed following administration of o-xylene were no longer present at 24 hours.

A decrease in rat pulmonary cytochrome P450 levels has been seen with all isomers administered i.p. at 531 mg/kg[119].

In vitro studies

The *in vitro* effects of xylenes have been investigated using a variety of tissues including liver, lung and erythrocytes. Summaries of the available data are presented in Table 1.5. A weakly inhibitory action on the activities of rat liver aryl hydrocarbon hydroxylase and 7-ethoxycoumarin O-deethylase has been demonstrated in microsomal preparations[120]. All three isomers caused comparable inhibition.

In a briefly reported study, treatment of perfused rabbit lung with approximately 11 mg *p*-xylene resulted in destruction of cytochrome P450 to a similar extent to that seen after treatment with the metabolite *p*-methylbenzyl aldehyde[121].

Xylenes have been reported to inhibit the hypotonic haemolysis of erythrocytes at low concentrations, with EC_{50} values of 29, 39 and 44 μg/ml respectively for the *o*-, *m*-, and *p*-isomers[122]. Erythrocyte stromatolysis has been reported with *o*-xylene at a concentration of approximately 44 μg/ml[123].

Overall summary of acute toxicity

All xylenes show essentially comparable acute toxic effects in rats and mice.

Xylenes have a low acute toxicity following inhalation exposure (LC_{50} values for 4- or 6-hour exposures to rats or mice being excess of 4000 ppm), dermal application and oral (LD_{50} values for rats and mice in excess of 3500 mg/kg) or parenteral administration. Death is caused by respiratory failure due to CNS depression.

The CNS appears to be the predominant target in all species examined, regardless of the route of administration. The main effects observed following inhalation exposure were excitation at lower concentrations (above 400 ppm for 4 hours with *p*-xylene) and depression at higher concentrations 1940-2180 ppm for 4 hours being the narcotic threshold values for all isomers).

Irritation of the respiratory tract has been observed, with a 5-minute exposure to 1467 ppm *o*-xylene reducing the respiratory rate by 50%.

Skin and eye irritancy and sensitisation

Skin irritation

Several studies indicate that xylenes are irritant. Erythema and oedema were induced following single application of unstated amounts of xylene (undefined composition) to rabbit or guinea pig skin[124-126]. Rapid onset of effects was observed and epithelial desquamation, with some histological evidence of epithelial necrosis, occurred after several days[124]. In the rabbit, irritation (graded as moderate by the authors) has been reported following 24-hour exposure to 0.5 ml xylene (undefined mixture of the individual isomers and Eb) under semi-occlusive conditions[92].

In an acute dermal study involving 24-hour occlusive application to rabbit skin, low volumes of *o*-xylene resulted in erythema and oedema while application of higher volumes resulted in fissuring[105].

Application of 0.5 ml *p*-xylene, under a Teflon chamber, to rabbit skin for 4 hours has been reported to produce a response which would be classified as irritant using EEC criteria[127,128].

Following repeated daily application of 0.5 ml xylene (composition as above) to rabbit skin, gradually increasing irritation was reported, with eschar being noted in at least half of the test animals within 10 days[92]. It is unclear whether a dressing was applied during treatment. In another study, following 10 to 20 applications of xylene (undefined composition) to open or semi-occluded rabbit skin over a 2-to-4 week period, moderate to marked irritation was reported, along with moderate "superficial" necrosis[103]. Blistering of the skin was also reported, particularly under the semi-occlusive dressing.

Eye irritation

Application of approximately 0.05 to 0.5 ml liquid xylenes (individual isomers or undefined composition) to the rabbit eye was reported to cause immediate discomfort and blepharospasm followed by slight conjunctival irritation and very slight, transient corneal necrosis[92,101,103,129].

A study conducted to a recent protocol reported that 0.1 ml liquid xylene (undefined composition) was mildly irritant to the rabbit eye[130]. No description of the eye lesions was given.

The exposure of cats to xylene (undefined composition) vapour concentrations causing overt irritation of the eyes and nose has been reported to give rise to corneal epithelial vacuoles[131]. This lesion was described as reversible, disappearing within 24 hours in all animals. In another study, a slight conjunctival response, but no corneal epithelial vacuoles, was reported following exposure of rabbits to "high concentrations" of xylene (undefined composition) vapour[132].

Skin sensitisation

No data are available.

Summary

Single application of liquid xylenes to skin produced skin irritation, with larger volumes causing fissuring particularly when occlusive conditions were employed. Following repeat application, eschar formation and blistering have been reported.

Instillation of liquid xylenes into the eye caused some discomfort, slight conjunctival irritation and very slight, transient corneal damage. There was some evidence of corneal epithelial vacuole formation following exposure to unknown concentrations of vapours of xylenes.

No skin sensitisation data are available.

Sub-acute toxicity

Inhalation

Most studies have been carried out in rats and mice. Summaries of the available data are presented in Table 2.1. Xylenes have a low inhalation toxicity following repeated exposure.

o-Xylene

There are no reports of treatment-related mortality. Decreased body weight gain was observed in rats exposed to 3500 ppm, 8 hours/day for 1 to 6 weeks[133]. Following exposure to 780 ppm, 8 hours/day, 5 days/week for 6 weeks or 78 ppm continuously for 90 days, no treatment-related toxic effects were observed on body weight gain, or on limited haematological or histopathological end points in the rat, dog or monkey[134]. However, with the former exposure schedule, persistent tremors were observed in one of the two dogs exposed and there was a marked decrease in body weight gain in guinea pigs.

Catecholamine levels and turnover in various parts of the hypothalamus were significantly increased, and dopamine turnover was significantly decreased in various parts of the forebrain, following exposure of rats to 2000 ppm, 6 hours/ day for 3 days[135]. There was also some evidence of altered adenohypophyseal hormone secretion.

Relative liver weight, levels of cytochrome P450 and cytochrome b_5, and the activity of some associated MFO enzymes, were reported to be increased in the rat liver following exposure to 3500 ppm, 8 hours/day for 4 weeks[136]. Following exposure at the same level for 6 weeks no treatment-related macroscopic or microscopic abnormalities were noted on histopathological examination of the liver[133]. However, ultrastructural examination revealed hepatocellular hypertrophy. There was a significant increase in relative liver and kidney weights, cytochrome P450 levels and the activity of some associated MFO enzymes following exposure of rats to 2000 ppm, 6 hours/day for 3 days[137,138]. The pattern of enzyme induction in the liver was reported to be consistent with that produced by phenobarbital-type agents. In this study, o-xylene also produced a significant decrease in cytochrome P450 levels and some associated MFO enzyme activities in the lung.

m-Xylene

Treatment-related mortality has not been reported. Following exposure to 1600 ppm, 4 hours/day, 5 days/week for 7 weeks, mice showed increased motor activity[139].

As with o-xylene, there was a significant increase in catecholamine levels and turnover in the hypothalamus and some evidence of altered adenohypophyseal hormone secretion following exposure of rats to 2000 ppm, 6 hours/day for 3 days[135]. A significant decrease in clonidine binding to α-adrenergic receptors in the hypothalamus was observed in mice exposed to 1600 ppm, 4 hours/day, 5 days/week for 7 weeks. It is not known whether this alteration was due to a decrease in receptor density or a change in receptor affinity. Following exposure of rats to 300 ppm, 7 hours/day for 16 weeks, there was some evidence, from behavioural tests, of CNS impairment[140]. However, the toxicological significance of these findings is uncertain.

Significant increases in relative liver weight, hepatic cytochrome P450 levels and the activity of some associated MFO enzymes were observed in rats exposed to 2000 ppm, 6 hours/day for 3 days[137,138]. Enzyme induction was reported to be similar to that produced by o-xylene. The activity of some hepatic MFO enzymes was significantly increased at all concentrations following exposure of rats to 50, 300, 400 or 750 ppm, 6 hours/day, 5 days/week for 1 or 2 weeks[16,141]. Following exposure to 750 ppm, 6 hours/day, 5 days/week for 1 or 2 weeks, there was no effect on serum alanine aminotransferase activity in the rat and no treatment-related abnormalities were observed on histopathological examination of the liver[141]. Decreased levels of reduced glutathione were observed in the liver at 300 ppm and above.

14

In the rat kidney there were significant increases in cytochrome P450 levels and the activity of some MFO enzymes following exposure to 2000 ppm, 6 hours/day for 3 days[138]. Following exposure of rats to 50, 300, 400 or 750 ppm, 6 hours/day, 5 days/week for 1 or 2 weeks, a consistent, significant increase in renal cytochrome P450 levels was observed at 400 ppm and above[16,141]. Significant increases in the activity of renal MFO enzymes were observed at all exposure levels.

Pulmonary cytochrome P450 levels and the activity of some MFO enzymes were significantly decreased in rats exposed to 300 ppm, 7 hours/day, 4 days/week for 5 weeks[15].

p-Xylene

No treatment-related mortality has been reported.

As with the other isomers, significant increases in catecholamine levels and turnover occurred in various parts of the rat hypothalamus following exposure to 2000 ppm, 6 hours/day for 3 days[135]. Similarly, there was some evidence of altered adenohypophyseal hormone secretion.

Increases in relative liver weight, hepatic cytochrome P450 levels and the activity of some associated MFO enzymes were also reported to be significant following exposure to 2000 ppm, 6 hours day for 3 days[137,138]. The same pattern of enzyme induction occurred as that produced by the o- and m-isomers. In this study, there was a significant increase in the activity of some renal MFO enzymes.

There was a significant decrease in the pulmonary microsomal levels of cytochrome P450 in the rat following exposure to 2000 ppm, 6 hours/day for 3 days and in the rabbit following exposure to 1000 ppm, 4 hours/day for 2 days[91,138].

Xylene

Substantial mortality was observed in mice exposed to 2300 ppm, 7 hours/day for up to 6 days (composition undefined)[142]. All animals were reported to adopt an abnormal body position and to exhibit ataxia of the rear limbs, progressing to paralysis. Sub-pleural bleeding was noted in some decedents at necropsy. At 1725 and 1150 ppm there were no deaths. However, ataxia was reported in two animals at the lowest exposure concentration. Following exposure of rats to 620, 980 or 1600 ppm, 18-20 hours/day for up to 7 days (composition undefined), narcosis and deaths were reported at the highest exposure concentration[143,144]. In another study, there were no treatment-related deaths

or toxic effects on body weight gain, haematology, clinical chemistry or at histopathological examination, following exposure of rats or dogs to 180, 460 or 810 ppm, 6 hours/day, 5 days/ week for 13 weeks (7.63% o-, 65.01% m-, 7.84% p-, 19.27% Eb)[6].

An increase (approximately 20 dB) in the auditory response threshold at 12 and 20 kHz has been reported following behavioural studies (multisensory conditioned avoidance) in rats exposed to 1450 ppm, 8 hours/day for 3 days (10% o-, 80% m-, 10% p-)[98]. Following exposure of rats for 14 hours/day, 7 days/week for 6 weeks (10% o-, 80% m-, 10% p-) there was an increase (approximately 10-30 dB) in auditory response thresholds at 12 kHz and above (800 ppm), 8 kHz and above (1000 ppm) and 2 kHz and above (1200 ppm)[98]. In this study, following exposure to 1200 ppm, there was a significant increase in brainsteam auditory evoked response (BAER) thresholds at 4, 8 and 16 kHz tone frequencies. At 1000 and 800 ppm the BAER threshold was markedly elevated at 16 kHz and only slightly elevated at 8 kHz. Thus xylene was demonstrated to cause hearing loss in rats following repeated exposure. A no-effect level was not determined. The reversibility of the hearing loss was not assessed in this study.

As with the individual isomers, significant increases in catecholamine levels and turnover in various parts of the rat forebrain and hypothalamus have been reported following exposure to 2000 ppm, 6 hours/day for 3 days (2.0% o-, 64.5% m-, 10.0% p-, 23.0% Eb)[135]. There was also some evidence of altered adenohypophyseal hormone secretion. In another study, noradrenaline levels in the hypothalamus were significantly increased and acetylcholine levels in the striatum significantly decreased following exposure of rats to 800 ppm for 30 days (composition undefined)[145].

There were concentration-dependent increases in hepatic cytochrome P450 levels and the activity of MFO enzymes, significant at all concentrations, following exposure of rats to 75, 250, 500, 1000 or 2000 ppm, 6 hours/day for 3 days (2.0% o-, 64.5% m-, 10.0% p-, 23.0% Eb)[146]. The pattern of enzyme induction was similar to that noted for the individual isomers and consistent with that produced by phenobarbital-type agents. Various other studies (using various xylene mixtures and of undefined composition), mainly by the same group of authors, have reported findings consistent with liver enzyme induction over this concentration range[18,19,137,138,146-148]. Relative liver weights were significantly increased in rats following exposure to 630 ppm, 6 hours/day, 5 days/week for 4 weeks (2.0% o-, 64.5% m-, 10.0% p-, 23.0% Eb)[147]. A marked, dose- dependent increase in the surface area of smooth endoplasmic reticulum was noted on ultrastructural examination of the liver following exposure of rats to either 1000 or 2000 ppm, 6 hours/day, 5 days/week for up to 18 weeks (19.2% *o*-, 43.0% *m*-, 19.5% *p*-, 18.3% Eb)[19,146].

As reported for the individual isomers, there were significant increases in renal cytochrome P450 levels and the activity of MFO enzymes following exposure of rats to 2000 ppm, 6 hours/day for 3 days (2.0% *o*-, 64.5% *m*-, 10.0% *p*-, 23.0% Eb)[138]. Marked, concentration-dependent increases in the activity of renal MFO enzymes have also been observed in rats exposed to 50, 400 or 750 ppm, 6 hours/day, 5 days/week for 2 weeks (composition undefined)[149]. Renal cytochrome P450 levels were reported to be only "moderately changed".

A marked decrease in the activity of pulmonary MFO enzymes occurred following exposure of rats to 2000 ppm, 6 hours/day for 3 days (composition defined above)[138].

Summary of inhalation studies

Hearing loss has been observed in rats, predominantly at higher frequencies, with marked increases in auditory response thresholds and brainsteam auditory evoked response thresholds following repeated exposure to 800 ppm and above for 6 weeks or to 1450 ppm for 3 days (10% *o*-, 80% *m*-, 10% *o*-). A no-effect level for hearing loss has not been established and reversibility was not assessed in the study.

Apart from the single study of hearing loss, xylenes have all been shown to be of low toxicity by repeated inhalation exposure. No mortality or toxicologically important findings were reported in rats or mice following exposure to 3500 ppm (*o*-) or 1600 ppm (*m*-), 4-8 hours/day for up to 17 weeks. No effects were observed following exposure of rats or dogs to 810 ppm, 6 hours/day, 5 days/week for 13 weeks. (7.63% *o*-, 65.01% *m*-, 7.84% 19.27% Eb). However, mortality was observed in mice exposed to 2300 ppm xylene (composition undefined), 7 hours/day for up to 6 days (no deaths at 1725 ppm) and rats exposed to 160 ppm xylene (composition undefined), 18-20 hours/day for up to 7 days (no deaths at 980 ppm).

The most commonly reported observation is phenobarbital-type liver enzyme induction, as well as kidney enzyme induction, with increases in the activity of hepatic and renal MFO enzymes noted following repeated exposure to 50 ppm and above. These effects may be considered to reflect a functional hypertrophy and not to be toxicologically important findings.

Decreased pulmonary cytochrome P450 and/or the activity of MFO enzymes has been noted following repeated exposure to 300 ppm and above.

Oral

Most studies have been performed in the rat. Summaries of the available data are presented in Table 2.2. Xylenes have a low toxicity by repeated oral administration.

o-Xylene

There is no clear evidence of treatment-related toxicity in any of the studies reported. Decreased body weight, compared to controls, was reported in rats administered 2166 mg/kg for 4 days or 1062 mg/kg for 3 days[150,151].

Following administration of 2166 mg/kg for 4 days to rats, significant increases in liver weight, cytochrome P450 levels, NADPH cytochrome c reductase activity and the activity of MFO enzymes was reported[150,152]. On histopathological examination, hypertrophy of the centrilobular hepatocytes and a widening of the centrilobular zone were observed. The authors reported that this was consistent with phenobarbital-type liver induction. However, on ultrastructural examination, only minimal proliferation of the smooth endoplasmic reticulum (SER) was noted in the centrilobular hepatocytes. In rats, after administration of 1062 mg/kg for 3 days, there were significant increases in liver weight, cytochrome b_5 levels and the activity of MFO enzymes[151]. Ageing rats fed a diet containing 200 ppm *o*-xylene for 1, 2, 4 or 6 months showed formation of vacuolar structures in the hepatocytes on ultrastructural examination[153].

There were significant increases in renal cytochrome b_5 levels and the activity of MFO enzymes following administration of 1062 mg/kg for 3 days to rats[151].

m-Xylene

Substantial mortality was observed following administration of 2000 mg/kg, 5 days/week for up to 4 weeks to rats[154]. Decreased body weight, compared to controls, was observed in rats administered 1062 mg/kg for 3 days and reduced terminal body weights were observed in rats administered 500 mg/kg, 5 days/week for 4 weeks[151,154].

In rats administered 2166 mg/kg for 4 days, there were significant increases in liver weight, cytochrome P450 levels (males only), NADPH cytochrome c reductase activity and the activity of MFO enzymes[150,152]. On histopathological and ultrastructural examination, the findings were similar to those observed with the *o*-isomer. Following administration of 1062 mg/kg for 3 days, there were significant increases in liver weight, cytochrome P450 and cytochrome b_5 levels, as well as NADPH cytochrome c reductase and the activity of MFO enzymes[151].

There was no significant effect on kidney weight following administration of 500 or 2000 mg/kg, 5 days/week for 4 weeks to rats and on histopathological examination no treatment-related abnormalities were noted[154]. However, in another study, following administration of 1062 mg/kg for 3 days to rats, there were significant increases in kidney weight, cytochrome P450 and b_5 levels, as well as increased NADPH cytochrome c reductase and the activity of MFO enzymes[151].

p-Xylene

Decreased body weight, compared to controls, was reported in rats administered 2166 mg/kg for 4 days or 1062 mg/kg for 3 days[150-152].

Following administration of 2166 mg/kg for 4 days, rats showed increases in liver weight, cytochrome P450 levels, NADPH cytochrome c reductase and the activity of MFO enzymes[150,152]. On histopathological and ultrastructural examination the findings were similar to those observed with the o- and m-isomers. Following administration of 1062 mg/kg for 3 days, there were significant increases in rat hepatic cytochrome b_5 levels, NADPH cytochrome c reductase activity and the activity of MFO enzymes[151]. In the same study, there were significant increases in renal cytochrome P450 and cytochrome b_5 levels as well as the activity of MFO enzymes.

Xylene

Following administration of 125, 250, 500, 1000 or 2000 mg/kg for up to 14 days to rats (9.1% o-, 60.2% m-, 13.6% p-, 17,0% Eb), substantial mortality was observed at the highest dose[102]. Mean body weight gain was markedly reduced in males at 250 mg/kg and above, and in females at 125 mg/kg and 1000 mg/kg and above. Shallow, laboured breathing and prostration were reported immediately after dosing at 2000 mg/kg. There were no treatment-related abnormalities observed at gross necropsy. Administration of 62.5, 125, 250, 500 or 1000 mg/kg, 5 days/week for 13 weeks (9.1% o-, 60.2% m-, 13.6% p-, 17.0% Eb) to rats resulted in no deaths or clinical signs of toxicity[102]. Body weight gain was slightly reduced at 1000 mg/kg. There were no treatment-related abnormalities observed at gross necropsy or on histopathological examination.

Following administration of 250, 500, 1000, 2000 or 4000 mg/kg for up 14 days (9.1% o-, 60.2% m-, 13.6% p-, 17.0% Eb) to mice, all animals died on the second day of dosing at 4000 mg/kg[102]. Mean body weight gain was markedly reduced in males at all dose levels. However, no consistent effects were observed in females. Shallow breathing and prostration were

observed at 2000 mg/kg during the first week of the study. There were no treatment-related abnormalities observed at gross necropsy. Administration of 125, 250, 500, 1000 or 2000 mg/kg, 5 days/week for 13 weeks (9.1% o-, 60.2% m-, 13.6% p-, 17.0% Eb) to mice resulted in no clear treatment-related mortality[102]. Decreased mean body weight and transient clinical signs, including weakness, lethargy, short and shallow breathing, unsteadiness and paresis, were observed at 2000 mg/kg. There were no treatment-related abnormalities observed at gross necropsy or histopathological examination.

Summary of oral studies

Xylenes are all of low toxicity following repeated oral administration. Mortalities were observed following administration of 2000 mg/kg for up to 14 days (rats) and 4000 mg/kg (mice) but no important findings were observed following administration of 1000 mg/kg (rats) or 2000 mg/kg (mice) for 90 days (9.1% o-, 60.2% m-, 13.6% p-, 17.0% Eb).

Phenobarbital-type hypertrophy of the liver was considered to represent a functional change and not to be a toxicologically important finding. Significant increases in cytochrome b_5 levels and the activity of MFO enzymes have been observed in both liver and kidney with all isomers following administration of 1062 mg/kg.

Dermal

One briefly reported study is summarised in Table 2.3. No significant conclusions can be drawn from this study.

Parenteral

Only limited data are available on the toxicity of xylenes by repeated parenteral administration. These are summarised in Table 2.4.

Significant mortality was observed at 870 mg/kg, but not at 435 or 174 mg/kg xylene (composition undefined), following daily s.c. administration for up to 4 weeks to rats[155]. In a poorly reported study, there was substantial mortality following i.m. administration of 86 mg/kg p-xylene for more than 4 weeks to rabbits[156].

Liquid droplet formation or fatty infiltration in the liver was reported to occur in studies using the i.p. route at 73 mg/kg o-xylene, or 86 mg/kg p-xylene, for 3 days in the rat[41,153].

Repeated s.c. administration of 435 mg/kg (composition undefined) for 6 weeks to rats was found to result in a decreased learning rate[155].

Following i.p. administration of 2123 mg/kg xylene (30% o-, 55% m-, 15% p-) for 3 days to rats, there was a significant increase in liver weight, cytochrome P450 levels, NADPH cytochrome c reductase and the activity of MFO enzymes[43].

Summary of sub-acute toxicity

The major finding was hearing loss, predominantly at high frequencies. This was observed following repeated inhalation exposure of rats to 800 ppm and above for 6 weeks or to 1450 ppm for 3 days. A no-effect level was not determined and reversibility was not assessed.

Apart from the single study of hearing loss, xylenes have been shown to have a low toxicity following repeated inhalation exposure and oral administration. Mortalities were observed following oral administration at 2000 mg/kg (rats) and 4000 mg/kg (mice). No toxicologically important findings were observed following 13 weeks' inhalation exposure 6 hours/day, 5 days/week to 810 ppm (rats and dogs) or oral administration of 1000 mg/kg (rats) or 2000 mg/kg (mice) for 13 weeks.

A phenobarbital-like effect on the liver was considered to reflect a functional hypertrophy and not to be of toxicological importance. The activity of MFO enzymes was found to be significantly increased in both liver and kidney following repeated inhalation exposure to 50 ppm or repeated oral administration of 1062 mg/kg.

Decreased pulmonary cytochrome P450 levels have been noted following repeated inhalation exposure to 300 ppm.

Genotoxicity

Xylenes have been evaluated for genotoxicity in a number of studies with a variety of end-points. Summaries of the available data are presented in Table 3.

o-Xylene

Negative results have been obtained, both with and without metabolic activation, in a number of apparently well-conducted reverse mutation assays with the usual strains of *Salmonella typhimurium* (TA 98, TA 100, TA 1535, TA 1537, TA 1538)[157-162]. These tests were conducted using plate incorporation or preincubation protocols.

In a micronucleus test, i.p. administration of two doses of up to 440 mg/kg, 24 hours apart, had no effect on the incidence of micronucleated polychromatic erythrocytes in the bone-marrow of mice[109]. The dose level was chosen following a LD_{50} sighting study. No toxicity or

effect on the polychromatic (PCE) to normochromatic (NCE) ratio was observed in the micronucleus test.

In a sperm head abnormality assay, i.p. administration of two doses of 440 or 1320 mg/kg, 24 hours apart, had no effect on the incidence of abnormal sperm in rats[163].

m-Xylene

A number of apparently well-conducted reverse mutation assays with *Salmonella typhimurium* (same strains as for o-xylene) have been reported[159-162,164]. Plate incorporation or preincubation protocols were used in these tests. Negative results were obtained both with and without metabolic activation.

In a micronucleus assay, there was no effect on the incidence of micronucleated polychromatic erythrocytes in the bone-marrow of mice following i.p. administration of two doses of up to 648 mg/kg, 24 hours apart[109]. No toxicity or effect on the PCE to NCE ratio was observed at the top dose level, which was chosen following a sighting LD_{50} study.

p-Xylene

Using preincubation or plate incorporation protocols, a number of apparently well-conducted reverse mutation assays with *Salmonella typhimurium* (same strains as for o-xylene) were reported[159-162,164,165]. Negative results have been obtained both with and without metabolic activation. A negative result was also obtained, both with and without metabolic activation, in a preincubation reverse mutation assay with *Escherichia coli* [165].

In a micronucleus assay in the bone-marrow of mice, i.p. administration of two doses of up to 646 mg/kg, 24 hours apart, had no effect on the incidence of micronucleated polychromatic erythrocytes[165]. The top dose level, set following a sighting LD_{50} study, did not result in toxicity or an effect on the PCE to NCE ratio being observed.

Xylene

In vitro tests for point mutations

Three apparently well-conducted reverse mutation assays with *Salmonella typhimurium* (same strains as for o-xylene) have been reported[166-168]. These tests have used suspension, plate incorporation or preincubation protocols with xylene of varying compositions (undefined or 11.40% o-, 52.07% m-, 0.31% p-, 36.08% Eb). In all tests, negative results were obtained both with and without metabolic activation. A negative result has also been obtained in an adequately conducted forward gene mutation assay with mouse L5178Y TK +/- cells, both with and without metabolic activation (11.40% o-,

52.07% *m*-, 0.31% *p*-, 36.08% Eb)[167].

In vivo tests for chromosome damage

The ability of xylenes to cause chromosome aberrations in bone-marrow cells has been evaluated using a number of exposure routes. A negative result was reported in rats following i.p. administration of up to 384 mg/kg on 1 day or daily for 5 days (11.40% *o*-, 52.07% *m*-, 0.31% *p*-, 36.08% Eb)[167]. However, the value of this study is limited as no effect on the mitotic index was observed at the top dose levels. A negative result was noted following oral administration of 625 mg/kg, daily for 10 days, to mice[169]. However, this study is also of limited value, because effects on the mitotic index, if any, were not reported and no positive control data were presented. A negative result was also claimed in an abstract report of a study using inhalation exposure of rats to 300 ppm (undefined xylene mixture), 6 hours/day, 5 days/week for 9, 14 or 18 weeks[170].

The ability of xylenes to induce micronuclei in bone-marrow polychromatic erythrocytes has been investigated in mice. Oral administration of 440 mg/kg (composition undefined) to mice gave a negative result[171]. However, it seems likely that this was well below a maximum tolerated dose. Oral administration of two doses of up to 1000 mg/kg (composition undefined), 24 hours apart to mice, also gave a negative result[169]. However, this study was only reported in limited detail.

Dominant lethal assays

Dominant lethal assays have been reported in both rat and mouse. In male rats, single i.p. administration of 870 mg/kg (composition undefined), followed by mating of each male with two females/week for 10 weeks, resulted in no adverse effects on reproduction[172]. Similarly, a single s.c. administration of 870 mg/kg (composition undefined) to male mice, followed by mating of each male with three females/week for 8 weeks, resulted in no adverse effects of reproduction[172]. Although it is not clear whether maximum tolerated doses were achieved in these studies, the dose levels used are considered to be satisfactory.

In a *Drosophila* recessive lethal study, reported in abstract form only, the authors claimed a significant increase in the incidence of recessive lethals when technical grade xylene (containing 18.3% Eb) was used[170]. (A negative result was claimed with the *o*- and *m*-isomers.) Little significance can be attached to this finding in view of the limited reporting.

In vitro indicator tests for DNA damage

Negative results were reported in differential toxicity assays with DNA repair-proficient and repair-deficient strains of *Bacillus subtilis* and *Escherichia coli*, both with and without metabolic activation (xylene of undefined composition)[173,174]. Negative results were also noted in a mitotic recombination assay with *Saccharomyces cerevisiae* D4 (11.40% *o*-, 52.07% *m*-, 0.31% *p*-, 36.08% Eb)[167]. However, the reporting of this study is inadequate.

Summary of genotoxicity studies

The genotoxicity of xylenes has been investigated in a variety of assays with different end-points and negative results were consistently obtained. There was no evidence of genotoxic activity in well-conducted bacterial reverse mutation assays or in a forward mutation assay with mammalian cells. There is no adequate study of clastogenic activity *in vitro*. *In vivo* tests for chromosome damage (both bone-marrow cytogenetics and micronucleus), including studies where the top dose was chosen following a sighting LD_{50} study, were negative. Negative results were also obtained in dominant lethal assays in rats and mice following administration of adequate maximum doses and in bacterial differential toxicity assays. Thus, it can be concluded that there is no evidence that xylenes are genotoxic.

Carcinogenicity and chronic toxicity

The carcinogenic potential of xylenes has been investigated in three *in vivo* rodent bioassays following oral administration. These studies are summaried in Table 4. There are no data available for the individual isomers.

Carcinogenicity studies

In a recently reported NTP bioassay, rats and mice were administered xylene (9.1% *o*-, 60.2% *m*-, 13.6% *p*-, 17.0% Eb) in corn oil, by gavage, for 103 weeks[102]. A retrospective audit revealed no major problems with the conduct of the studies or with the collection and documentation of the experimental data. However, it should be noted that a high proportion of male rats were killed following dosing accidents.

In this bioassay 50 F344/N rats of each sex were administered xylene at 0, 250 or 500 mg/kg (5 days/week). Male rats dosed at 500 mg/kg showed a clear reduction in survival (excluding accidental deaths) and, from week 64, a lower mean body weight than controls. Although no effects on survival or body weight were seen in female rats, the top dose was considered to be sufficiently high for the evaluation of carcinogenic potential. There was no evidence of organ toxicity on histopathological examination or of any treatment-related increase in the incidence of neoplasia. However, too few males survived to termination (50% at 250 mg/kg,

40% at 500 mg/kg) for the potential carcinogenicity of xylene to be evaluated in the male rat.

Groups of 50 B6C3F$_1$ mice of each sex were administered 0, 500 or 1000 mg/kg. There were no significant effects on survival or mean body weights. However, at 1000 mg/kg transient hyperactivity was reported in all mice from week 4. There was no evidence of organ toxicity on histopathological examination or of any treatment-related increase in the incidence of neoplasia. The highest dose was considered to be of sufficient magnitude for evaluation of the carcinogenic potential of xylene in the mouse.

In a poorly reported bioassay, 40 Sprague-Dawley rats of each sex were administered xylene (composition undefined) in olive oil, by gavage, at 500 mg/kg, 4-5 days/ week for 104 weeks[175,176]. The animals were then observed for the remainder of their lifespan (up to 141 weeks). A group of 50 Sprague-Dawley rats of each sex served as vehicle controls. At 134 weeks carcinoma of the oral cavity (10% test animals, 0% controls) and "acanthoma and dysplasias" of the forestomach (10% of test animals, 0% controls) were noted. The authors also recorded an increase in the proportion of test rats with malignant neoplasms compared to controls, at 141 weeks. However, the reporting of this study was so limited that no satisfactory assessment of the data is possible and thus no carcinogenicity evaluation can be made.

Other studies

A number of studies have investigated whether exposure to xylenes alters the incidence of experimentally induced skin neoplasia in mice[177-180]. The conduct, reporting and information contained in these studies does not allow any useful conclusions to be drawn.

Summary

There is no evidence of carcinogenicity or systemic toxicity in an adequately reported bioassay in which xylene was administered orally to rats or mice. However, in the study with male rats, survival was too low for any firm conclusions to be drawn.

Effects on fertility and reproduction

The effect of xylenes on the reproductive system has been evaluated in the rat, mouse and rabbit following inhalation exposure, the rat and mouse following oral administration and the hamster following dermal application. Summaries of the available data are presented in Table 5.

o-Xylene

In one teratogenicity study, by inhalation, CFY rats were exposed to 0, 34, 345 or 690 ppm continuously from days 7 to 14 of gestation[14,181-183]. There was a concentration-related reduction in maternal food consumption and weight gain during the exposure period, but no significant differences on day 21. No treatment-related effects on post-implantation loss or mean litter size were observed. In the groups exposed to 345 or 690 ppm there was evidence of delayed development. There was no increase in the incidence of fetuses with minor variations or malformations. No significant findings were noted at 34 ppm. It can be concluded that there was evidence of delayed development at 345 and 690 ppm, exposure levels causing slight maternal toxicity.

A teratogenicity study where CFLP mice were exposed, by inhalation, to 0 or 115 ppm for 4 hours, three times a day, from days 6 to 15 of gestation has been reported in summary form only[181,184]. There was evidence of delayed development in the exposed group but no increase in the incidence of post implantation loss, minor variants or malformations. However, the significance of these findings is limited because maternal toxicity, if seen, was not reported.

A teratogenicity study in the rabbit using continuous inhalation exposure to 0 or 115 ppm from days 7 to 20 of gestation has been reported in summary form only[184]. The significance of the results of this study (no significant effects on post-implantation loss, the incidence of delayed development, minor variants or malformations) is limited because no maternal toxicity was observed at this exposure level. However, exposure to 230 ppm of another isomer or mixed xylenes caused some maternal mortality.

A teratogenicity study in the mouse, reported in abstract form only, has been conducted using oral administration[185]. In this study, CD-1 mice were administered 0, 261, 683 or 870 mg/kg from days 6 to 15 or 0 or 870 mg/kg from days 12 to 15 of gestation. Following administration from days 6 to 15, maternal toxicity (not further described in the abstract) was observed at 683 and 870 mg/kg. A significantly increased incidence of resorptions and an increased incidence of cleft palate were reported at these dose levels. Administration of 870 mg/kg from days 12 to 15 resulted in increased maternal mortality but no increase in the incidence of malformations. No significant findings were reported at 261 mg/kg using either administration schedule. Thus, in this study, there was an increased incidence of malformations at 683 and 870 mg/kg, dose levels which significantly increased the incidence of resorptions and produced some maternal toxicity. No effects were observed at 261 mg/kg.

m-Xylene

m-Xylene has been evaluated in a developmental

toxicity screen[186]. In this study, ICR mice were administered, orally, 0 or 2000 mg/kg from days 8 to 12 of gestation and the dams delivered their young. One treated dam died and there was no effect on weight gain in the remaining dams. *m*-Xylene administration had no effect on the number of litters born, on the mean number of neonates per litter or mean neonate weight. It was concluded that *m*-xylene had no effects in this screen at 2000 mg/kg, a dose level which might result in some maternal mortality.

In a teratogenicity study, by inhalation, CFY rats were exposed to 0, 34, 345 or 690 ppm continuously from days 7 to 14 of gestation[14,181,183,187]. During the exposure period four dams exposed to 690 ppm died and maternal body weight gain was reduced at all exposure levels. At day 21, only the group exposed to 690 ppm had a reduced mean body weight. There was evidence of delayed development and an increased incidence of a minor variant (extra ribs). There were no significant effects on the embryo or fetus in the groups exposed to 34 or 345 ppm. It can be concluded that there was no increase in the incidence of malformations at 690 ppm, an exposure level which resulted in some maternal mortality. No effects were observed at 34 or 345 ppm.

A teratogenicity study where CFLP mice were exposed, by inhalation, to 0 or 115 ppm for 4 hours, three times a day, from days 6 to 15 of gestation has been reported in summary form only[181,184]. There was evidence of delayed development in the exposed group but no increase in the incidence of post-implantation loss, minor variants or malformations. Maternal toxicity, if seen, was not reported.

In the rabbit, a teratogenicity study using continuous inhalation exposure to 0 or 115 ppm from days 7 to 20 of gestation has been reported in summary form only[184]. A slightly increased incidence of post-implantation loss was noted. There were no significant effects on the incidence of delayed development, minor variants or malformations. However, no maternal toxicity was observed at this exposure level. (In experiments with *p*-xylene and mixed xylenes, some maternal mortality was observed at 230 ppm.)

There is an abstract report of a teratogenicity study in the mouse, conducted using oral administration[185]. In this study, CD-1 mice were administered 0, 261, 683 or 870 mg/kg from days 6 to 15 or 0 or 870 mg/kg from days 12 to 15 of gestation. Following administration from days 6 to 15, maternal toxicity (not further described in the abstract) was observed at 870 mg/kg in one experiment, but not in a second. A statistically significant increase in the incidence of cleft palate was observed at this dose level in the second, but not first,

experiment. The significance of the increased incidence of cleft palate is uncertain. These malformations were only seen in one study at a dose level at which no maternal toxicity was reported. However, in the repeat study, maternal toxicity was observed at this dose level, but no malformations. No effects were observed at 261 or 683 mg/kg in either experiment. Following administration from days 12 to 15, there was a significant increase in maternal mortality and in the incidence of malformations (mostly cleft palate) in the first experiment. No effects were observed in a second experiment. No effects were observed at 261 or 683 mg/kg in either experiment. It can be concluded that there was an increased incidence of malformations (in one experiment) at 870 mg/kg, a dose level at which maternal mortality was observed. The overall conclusion from these experiments is that there was an increased incidence of malformations at 870 mg/kg, a dose level where maternal mortality (administration days 12-15) or toxicity (administration days 6-15) was observed. No effects were observed at 261 or 683 mg/kg.

p-Xylene

In one teratogenicity study, CFY rats were exposed to 0, 34, 345 or 690 ppm continuously from days 7 to 14 of gestation[14,181,182,188]. At 690 ppm there was a reduction in maternal food consumption and body weight gain during the exposure period. No differences from the controls were observed on day 21. At this exposure level there were increased incidences of total resorptions and post-implantation losses, and the mean litter size was significantly reduced. Evidence of delayed development was observed at 690 ppm (reduced mean fetal weight). Delayed skeletal ossification was observed at all exposure levels. An increased incidence of a minor variant (extra ribs) was seen at 690 ppm. There was no increase in the incidence of fetuses with malformations. It was concluded that delayed development and an increased incidence of a minor variant were seen at 690 ppm, an exposure level resulting in some maternal toxicity. Delayed development (an increased incidence of fetuses with delayed skeletal ossification) was also reported at 34 and 345 ppm, exposure levels where maternal toxicity was not observed. A no-effect level for delayed development was not determined. The incidence of malformations was not increased.

In another teratogenicity study, rats were exposed to 0 or 114 ppm continuously from days 1 to 20 of gestation[189]. Signs of maternal toxicity were not reported. A significant increase in the incidence of both pre- and post-implantation losses was reported in the treated group. The incidence of delayed development and minor variants was not affected by treatment and no malformed fetuses were observed. Maternal toxicity, if seen, was not reported.

A teratogenicity study where mice were exposed, by inhalation, to 0 or 115 ppm for 4 hours, three times a day, from days 6 to 15 of gestation has been reported in summary form only[181,184]. There was evidence of delayed development in the exposed group but no increase in the incidence of post-implantation loss, minor variants or malformations. Maternal toxicity, if seen, was not reported.

In the rabbit, a teratogenicity study using continuous inhalation exposure to 0, 115 or 230 ppm from days 7 to 20 of gestation has been reported in summary form only[181,184]. At 230 ppm one dam died, three aborted and total resorption or fetal death in utero was observed in the remaining four dams. At 115 ppm no maternal toxicity was observed and there were no significant effects on post-implantation loss or on the incidence of delayed development, minor variants or malformations. Thus, in this study, exposure to 230 ppm resulted in limited maternal mortality and no viable fetuses. No effects on the dam or fetus were observed at 115 ppm.

There is an abstract report of a teratogenicity study in the mouse, conducted using oral administration[185]. In this study, CD-1 mice were administered 0, 261, 683 or 870 mg/kg from days 6 to 15 of gestation or 0 or 870 mg/kg from days 12 to 15 gestation. Following administration from days 6 to 15, maternal toxicity (not further described) was observed at 683 and 870 mg/kg. A significantly increased incidence of resorptions and an increased incidence of cleft palate were reported at these dose levels. Administration of 870 mg/kg from days 12 to 15 resulted in significant maternal mortality and an increased incidence of malformations (mostly cleft palate). No significant findings were reported at 261 mg/kg with either administration schedule. Thus, in this study, an increased incidence of malformations was observed at 683 and 870 mg/kg (administration days 6 to 15), dose levels which caused maternal toxicity and increased the incidence of resorptions. An increased incidence of malformations was also observed at 870 mg/kg (administration days 12 to 15), a dose level which caused significant maternal toxicity. No effects were observed at 261 mg/kg.

A behavioural teratogenicity study has been conducted in the rat[190]. In this study, the animals were exposed, by inhalation, to 0, 800 or 1600 ppm, 6 hours a day from days 7 to 16 of gestation. Maternal weight gain was reduced in the group exposed to 1600 ppm. There were no significant effects on mean litter size or pup weight to post-natal day (PD)3 or on pup growth rate, locomotor activity or acoustic startle response to PD65 at either exposure level. In conclusion, exposure to p-xylene at 1600 ppm, an exposure level causing some maternal toxicity, had no significant effect on pup post-natal

viability, growth or indicators of CNS development.

Xylene

Single generation study

A single generation study with a teratology element has been conducted in Sprague-Dawley rats[191]. Animals were exposed to 0, 60, 250 or 500 ppm (20.4% o-, 44.2% m-, 20.3% p-, 12.8% Eb), 6 hours a day, during a 131-day pre-mating period. Exposures continued throughout the mating period (males) or until mating occurred (females). The mated females were further exposed from days 1 to 20 of gestation and days 5 to 20 of lactation. Additionally, at 500 ppm, exposed males were mated with unexposed females and vice versa. Approximately one third of the pregnant females exposed to 0 or 500 ppm were used in the teratogenicity study. The remaining animals delivered their young.

There were no mortalities in the treated groups during the study. Body weight gain was significantly higher during the mating period in females exposed to 60 or 250 ppm. There were no treatment-related effects on mating, fertility, pregnancy indices, the mean duration of gestation, mean litter size or mean day 1 pup weight. During the lactation period there were no toxicologically important effects on the pups, including gonad weights on day 21. On day 49, in the group where both parents had been exposed to 500 ppm, mean pup weight (both male and female) was significantly lower than controls but there was no effect on pup gonad weights.

In the teratology study, there were no toxicologically important effects on the number of implantation sites, live fetuses, live fetuses per implant or sex distribution. There was no increase in the incidence of fetuses with delayed development or malformations in the groups exposed to xylene.

Thus, at exposure levels of up to 500 ppm, xylene had no toxicologically important effects on male or female reproductive performance. There was no evidence of delayed development in the fetuses or of teratogenicity. A minor effect on body weight in early adult life in animals whose parents were exposed to 500 ppm was noted. However, as no toxicity was noted in the parental animals during pre-mating or mating or gestation (females only), a maximum tolerated dose may not have been achieved. Thus, the potential for xylene to affect male or female reproductive performance or to affect the developing fetus may not have been fully assessed in this study.

Teratogenicity studies

Continuous inhalation exposure studies

Three studies by the same group of workers have been

performed in CFY rats. In the first study, rats were exposed continuously to 0 or 230 ppm (10% o-, 50% m-, 20% p-, 20% Eb) from days 9 to 14 of gestation[192]. There were no effects on maternal body weight gain, or post-implantation loss and there was no evidence of delayed development in the fetuses from the exposed group. An increased incidence of minor variants (extra ribs and fused sternebrae) and three malformations (none in the control group) were observed in the exposed group. It was concluded that there was an increased incidence of minor variants at 230 ppm, an exposure level where no maternal toxicity was observed. The authors considered the three malformations to be an incidental finding and not evidence of teratogenicity.

In the second study, rats were exposed continuously to 0, 53, 437 or 772 ppm (10% o-, 50% m-, 20% p-, 20% Eb) from days 7 to 15 of gestation[181,184,193]. (Data in the original Hungarian language report[193] were apparently re-presented after reassessment in the other two reports.) At 772 ppm one dam died and body weight gain was reduced during the exposure period and group mean body weight was significantly below the control mean on day 21. Post-implantation loss was increased but there was no effect on mean litter size. Delayed development was observed at this exposure level (772 ppm) and there was an increased incidence of a minor variant (extra ribs). There was no effect on the incidence of malformations. At the lower exposure levels, there was no effect on maternal body weight gain. The only significant finding in the fetuses at these exposure levels was delayed development. It was concluded that at 772 ppm, an exposure level causing some maternal mortality, delayed development and an increased incidence of a minor variant were observed. At lower exposure levels, not causing maternal toxicity, delayed development was noted. There was no evidence of teratogenicity at any exposure level.

The third study was reported in summary form only[194]. In this study, rats were exposed to 0 or 138 ppm (composition undefined) from days 7 to 15 of gestation. Maternal body weight gain was reduced and relative liver weight increased. Increased incidences of delayed development and a minor variant (extra ribs) were reported. There was no effect on post-implantation loss or on the incidence of malformations. At a higher exposure level (828 ppm continuously from day 10 to 13 of gestation) it was reported that xylene increased the fetotoxic and teratogenic potential of co-administered acetylsalicylic acid (aspirin) by a mechanism which increased the plasma concentration of free salicylic acid.

A teratogenicity study in the rabbit using continuous inhalation exposure to 0, 115 or 230 ppm (10% o-, 50% m-, 20% p-, 20% Eb) from days 7 to 20 of gestation has been reported in summary form only[181,184]. At 230

ppm three dams died, six aborted and total resorption or fetal death in utero was observed in the remaining dam. At 115 ppm no maternal toxicity was observed and there were no significant effects on post-implantation loss or on the incidence of delayed development, minor variants or malformations. Thus, in this study, exposure to 230 ppm resulted in significant maternal mortality and no viable fetuses. No effects on the dam or fetus were observed at 115 ppm.

Discontinuous inhalation exposure studies

Two studies in the rat have been reported. In the first, Sprague-Dawley rats were exposed to 0, 100 or 400 ppm (11.4% o-, 52.1% m-, 0.3% p-, 36.1% Eb), 6 hours a day, from days 6 to 15 of gestation[195]. No maternal toxicity was observed. There were no treatment-related effects on the number of implantation sites or live or dead fetuses, litter size or mean fetal weight. There was no evidence of delayed development or teratogenicity. Thus, in this study, exposure to up to 400 ppm xylene had no toxicologically important effects. However, a maximum tolerated dose may not have been achieved and the teratogenic potential of xylene may not have been fully assessed in this study.

In the second study, Wistar rats were exposed to 0, 2, 11, or 114 ppm (composition undefined), 6 hours a day, 5 days a week from days 1 to 21 of gestation[196]. Some of the dams were killed on day 21 of gestation for the teratology study and the remainder delivered their young. The authors reported increased post-implantation loss, malformations and impaired post-natal development of the offspring of rats exposed to 11 or 114 ppm xylene. However, no conclusions can be drawn from this study because of poor reporting.

There are two studies reported using discontinuous exposure in the mouse. In the first, CFLP mice were exposed to 0, 115 or 230 ppm (10% o-, 50% m-, 20% p-, 20% Eb) for 4 hours, three times a day, from days 6 to 15 of gestation[181,184]. The data were presented in summary form only and maternal toxicity was not reported. No effects were observed at 115 ppm. At 230 ppm the significance of the observed delayed development (with no evidence of effects on post-implantation loss, minor variants or malformations) is unclear in the absence of reporting of maternal toxicity.

In the second study, ICR mice were exposed to 0, 500, 1000, 2000 or 4000 ppm (composition undefined), 6 hours a day, from days 6 to 12 of gestation[197]. The study was reported only as an abstract which did not include reporting of maternal toxicity. Two thirds of the dams were killed on day 17 of gestation for the teratology study and the remainder delivered their young. Fetal weight was significantly decreased at 2000 and 4000 ppm. There was a dose-related increase in the incidence of extra ribs and delayed ossification of the sternebrae. In the groups which delivered their young, delayed development of hair and teeth and decreased body weight gain were noted at 4000 ppm with no effects on the time of eye or ear opening or coordinated walking. As maternal toxicity, if observed, was not reported, it is not possible to determine whether these findings are due directly to xylene administration or secondary to effects of the dam.

Other routes of administration

A study using oral administration has been conducted in the mouse[198]. In this study, CD-1 mice were treated with 0, 520, 1030, 2060, 2580, 3100 or 4130 mg/kg (9.1% o-, 60.2% m-, 13.6% p-, 17.0% Eb) on days 6 to 15 of gestation. All animals administered 4130 mg/kg and 13 out of 38 animals administered 3100 mg/kg died. Maternal body weight gain was significantly reduced in the survivors at 3100 mg/kg and liver weight was increased at both 2060 and 2580 mg/kg. Mean fetal weight was significantly decreased at and above 2060 mg/kg. There was a dose-related increase in the incidence of resorptions. This was statistically significance at 3100 mg/kg. The incidence of both cleft palate (2060 mg/kg and above) and bilateral wavy ribs (2580 mg/kg and above) was increased. It was concluded that delayed development was observed from 2060 mg/kg and the increased incidence of cleft palate at 2060 and 2580 mg/kg was indicative of teratogenicity. At 2580 mg/kg the multiple bilateral wavy ribs were considered to be possibly indicative of teratogenicity.

No conclusions can be drawn from the teratogenicity study using dermal application to hamsters as insufficient data are available from the summary report[199].

Summary of effects on the reproductive system

In a single generation study in the rat using discontinuous exposure, a no-effect level for effects on the parental animals, the fetus, or the pups up to post-natal day 49, of 500 ppm (mixed xylenes) has been determined. No single generation studies using the individual isomers are available.

In teratogenicity studies using continuous inhalation exposure to rats, no teratogenicity has been observed at exposure levels of up 690 ppm (o-, m-, or p- isomers) or 772 ppm (mixed xylenes). These exposure levels are above that causing significant maternal and fetal mortality in the rabbit (230 ppm). No continuous inhalation exposure studies in the mouse are available. No-effect levels for delayed development in the rat vary because of the wide intervals between doses; they were

345 ppm (m-), 34 ppm (o-) and not determined for p- or mixed xylenes. In the rabbit, no teratogenicity or fetotoxicity was seen at 115 ppm for all isomers and mixed xylenes.

Using discontinuous exposures with mixed xylenes, no-effect levels for delayed development of 400 ppm (exposure for 6 hours a day) (rat) and 115 ppm (3 x 4 hour exposures per day) or 1000 ppm (exposures for 6 hours a day) (mouse) have been determined. No teratogenicity studies with the individual isomers in the rat or rabbit are available. In the mouse, delayed development was seen at 115 ppm with all isomers (3 x 4-hour exposures per day), the only exposure level tested. No teratogenicity was observed in any study.

Oral administration of high doses of mixed xylenes (2060 and 2580 mg/kg) to mice resulted in an increased incidence of malformations (primarily cleft palate) in the absence of clear evidence of maternal toxicity. An increased incidence of cleft palate was also reported in the same strain of mice following oral administration of all isomers at maternally toxic doses (683 or 870 mg/kg).

In studies where the dams delivered their offspring, there were no effects on pup body weight or attainment of development landmarks following discontinuous exposure of p-xylene at 1600 ppm to rats or xylene (undefined) at 2000 ppm to mice.

Thus, although delayed development has been observed following inhalation exposure to both rats and mice, the importance of these findings is uncertain. There is no evidence of an increased incidence of malformations except following oral administration at high doses to mice.

TOXICITY TO HUMANS

Acute toxicity

There are reports of death and acute poisoning following both over exposure to vapours and oral ingestion of solvents containing substantial amounts of xylenes[200-204]. No accurate estimates of exposure levels or amount of xylene ingested are available. Death has been attributed to respiratory depression following loss of consciousness[202]. The exposure level required for loss of consciousness has been estimated to be 10 000 ppm[200]. Pulmonary congestion and oedema were observed at autopsy following both inhalation exposure and oral ingestion[200,202]. Among survivors, coma, EEG changes, amnesia, mental confusion and ocular nystagmus have been reported[200,201,204]. There is also evidence of gastrointestinal and respiratory symptoms and impaired renal and hepatic function[200,201,203,204].

At concentrations high enough to cause gross loss of attention and stupor, xylenes can have a cardiotoxic effect and extrasystolic arrythmia with systolic murmur, problems in intravenricular conduction, a nodal rhythm and ischaemia of the heart muscle have been documented[205,206]. At lower concentrations (estimated to be up to 700 ppm for up to 1 hour), headache, nausea, eye/nose/throat irritation, dizziness, vertigo and vomiting have been reported[207].

Recovery appears to be complete in most non-fatal cases, but occasional attacks of dizziness and clouding of vision were observed 24 months after oral ingestion of an unknown quantity of xylene by one subject[201].

Major and minor seizures following the use of a xylene based modelling glue have been observed on several occasions in one subject[208]. Such seizures were not seen following the use of a similar glue containing a different solvent. A convulsive seizure possibly provoked by industrial exposure to xylenes has also been reported in a single subject on one occasion[209].

Studies using controlled exposure

A number of volunteer studies have been conducted, predominantly by a single group of investigators. These studies have investigated effects on the central nervous system (CNS) and the peripheral nervous system (PNS) functions following exposure to predominantly m-xylene, but also to p-xylene or mixed xylenes (defined in one study as 12.1% o-, 54.5% m-, 12.8% p-and 20.7% Eb)[210-226]. No significant effects on vestibular or visual function, reaction times, coordination, eye muscle tone or peripheral senses were observed during 4-hour exposures to a constant concentration of up to 160 ppm. Slight impairment of vestibular function (body balance and positional nystagmus), visual function and reaction times were observed at higher exposure levels (200 to 390 ppm). However, some enhancement in vestibular function compared to control values has also been observed at 200 ppm. No effects were observed in subjective signs or tests for coordination, eye muscle tone, peripheral senses and short term memory at these higher constant exposure levels. The effects reported above were also seen at similar exposure levels during studies using fluctuating concentrations of between 135 and 400 ppm during the 4-hour exposures (200 ppm TWA, 10-minute peak exposures). There was some evidence of an improvement in body balance and visual function following exercise (100 W for 10 minutes). This may indicate an arousal reaction, resulting from the exercise, which overcame the effects of the increased concentration of xylenes in the blood.

In other studies, dizziness was reported by four out of six volunteers exposed to 690 ppm of p-xylene for 15

minutes[6]. No important effect on the ECG was noted in groups of six subjects exposed to xylene (8.8% o-, 49.4% m-, 1.4% p-, 40.4% Eb) for 2 hours at either 200 ppm with 90 minutes' exercise (50 W) or 100 ppm with 90 minutes' exercise (50, 100 or 150 W)[57].

Co-exposure studies with other solvents

Controlled exposure studies using m-xylene in combination with either ethanol or 1,1,1-trichloroethane (TCE) and p-xylene in combination with toluene have been reported[60,211-220,225,227]. Vestibular function, as measured by body balance and positional nystagmus, was unaffected by exposure to 145-150 ppm m-xylene and minimally affected by ethanol (0.8 g/kg). The effects of combined exposure on vestibular function were additive. At higher xylene exposure levels (275-290 ppm) in combination with ethanol (0.8 g/kg) there was evidence of functional tolerance. At these concentrations xylene appeared to antagonise the effect of ethanol on vestibular function. Visual function and reaction times were impaired by exposure to either 275-290 ppm m-xylene or 0.8 g/kg ethanol. In experiments with combined exposures at this level, there was evidence that the effects on visual function and reaction times were not additive. Volunteers have experienced nausea and vomiting when exposed to xylene (275-290 ppm) and ethanol (0.8 g/kg) in combination but not individually.

Conspicuous dermal flushing has been observed in one volunteer following ingestion of ethanol (0.8 g/kg) and exposure to m-xylene (300 ppm). These effects were not observed in volunteers exposed to xylene or ethanol individually. In a study of co-exposure to m-xylene and TCE, exposure of volunteers to 200 ppm m-xylene alone resulted in minor effects on vestibular and visual functions and reaction times. Simultaneous exposure to 400 ppm TCE had no further effect[218,219]. In another study, exposure to p-xylene (approx 60 ppm) and toluene (approx 30 ppm) had no effect on reaction times, short-term memory or heart rate[225].

Summary

The signs of toxicity following acute exposure to xylenes predominantly involve the CNS. Death after acute exposure has been attributed to respiratory depression following loss of consciousness. The exposure level required for loss of consciousness has been estimated to be 10 000 ppm. Recovery in non-fatal cases appears to be complete, but impaired renal and hepatic function and gastrointestinal and respiratory symptoms have been reported during the recovery period. Headache, nausea and vomiting, eye/nose/throat irritation, dizziness and vertigo have been reported following exposure estimated to be at 700 ppm for up to 1 hour. Slight impairment of vestibular and visual functions and reaction times were observed at exposures of 200 ppm *m*-xylene and above. No effects were observed at exposure levels of up to 160 ppm. No effect on subjective signs or tests for coordination, eye muscle tone, peripheral senses or short term memory were observed in these studies at exposure levels of up to 390 ppm. There was evidence of an improvement in vestibular and visual function following exercise. Co-exposure studies with ethanol have shown that at low xylene exposures (145-150 ppm) the combined effects were additive. At higher xylene exposure levels (275-290 ppm) there was evidence that combined exposure results for visual function and reaction times were not additive and ethanol appeared to antagonise the effects of xylene on vestibular function. An increased incidence of nausea and vomiting was reported at these high xylene exposure levels and a case of dermal flushing was reported. Insufficient data are available to rank the relative effects of the individual xylene isomers.

Irritancy and sensitisation

Skin, eye and respiratory irritation are frequently reported as subjective symptoms following occupational exposure to vapours of undefined xylenes[131,132, 228,229]. However, few experimental studies on this aspect have been published.

The skin irritancy of liquid xylene isomers has been only briefly reported[64- 66,76]. In one study, 0.015 ml of each isomer was applied, under occlusion, to forearm skin for between 5 and 10 minutes[64]. *p*-Xylene was considered to have the most marked irritant effect, with erythema and an itchy response being observed 30 seconds after application. All reactions had disappeared between 4 and 5 hours after application. The reactions with *o*- and *m*-xylene were less marked and disappeared within 10-20 minutes of the end of the application period.

In the other studies, both hands of subjects were immersed in pure *m*-xylene[65, 66,76]. A burning sensation was noticed soon after commencing a 15-20 minute exposure. This sensation had subsided within 60 minutes of exposure termination. An erythematous reaction was observed in the exposed skin. This had disappeared within a few hours. In one study, a toxic eczema requiring local corticosteroid therapy was observed in one subject[65]. The affected skin only returned to a normal appearance after 4 days.

Four out of six subjects tested experienced eye irritation following exposure to 460 or 690 ppm xylene vapour (7.6% *o*-, 65.0% *m*-, 7.8% *p*-, 19.3% Eb) for 15 minutes[6]. One subject reported eye irritation at 230 ppm and no subjects reported irritation at 110 ppm. In another study, there was no significant effect on the

reporting of irritation to the eyes, nose and throat by volunteers following exposure to 98, 196 or 392 ppm mixed xylene vapour for 30 minutes[226]. In a third study, 200 ppm undefined xylene vapour caused irritation to the eyes, nose and throat during exposures of between 3 and 5 minutes[230]. Corneal lesions have been reported in furniture polishers exposed to solvent vapours in varnishes and thinners (including one containing virtually pure xylene)[131,132]. In seven out of eight polishers the corneal lesions disappeared completely 8 to 11 days after cessation of exposure[132]. Isolated corneal vacuoles could still be seen in one polisher 30 days after cessation of exposure. The eye irritancy of liquid xylenes has not been reported.

The skin sensitisation potential of undefined xylene has been investigated in one study using a non-adjuvant maximisation test[231]. None of the 24 test subjects showed evidence of sensitisation. There is also no evidence, despite widespread usage, of skin sensitisation to xylenes.

Summary

Exposure to vapours of xylenes causes eye, nose and throat irritation. These signs were observed at 200 ppm in one study and, in 1 of 6 subjects, at 230 ppm in another study. The skin irritancy of liquid xylenes has been poorly reported. Transient erythema, itchy and burning sensations have been documented. Of the three isomers, *p*-xylene caused the greatest response. Corneal lesions have been documented following occupational exposure to vapours of xylenes. No evidence of sensitisation has been observed in one study in volunteers nor, despite widespread usage and exposure, in practice.

Effects of repeated exposure

General health surveys

Subjective symptoms have been observed in both case reports and surveys of workers exposed to xylenes or solvent mixtures containing significant amounts of xylenes[209,228,232-236]. Exposure levels and duration of exposure were not always reported. Concentrations of xylenes of up to 350 ppm were reported in one case report where exposure was to solvent containing 75% xylenes for up to 0.5 hours a day, for 2 months[232]. Episodes of depression, extreme fatigue, headache, anxiety, giddiness, feeling of drunkenness and sleep disorders were the most frequently reported symptoms. When follow-up studies were conducted after cessation of exposure a gradual reduction in the severity of symptoms was observed.

Concentrations of 32 ppm at the work station and 14.3

ppm in the ambient air were reported in a study of eight female laboratory technicians exposed to xylene (5-15% o-, 50-70% m-, 10-25% p-) for approximately 4 hours a day, for a mean duration of 8 years (range 6 months to 16 years)[237]. A group of 11 laboratory technicians (sex not stated) of similar mean age, and range and education level, but who did not handle solvents, comprised the control group. Anxiety, disorders of sleep, memory and concentration and episodes of depression were more frequently reported by the group exposed to xylene. However, in this study percutaneous exposure to xylene, which was not quantified, also occurred (total exposure was assessed by urinary methylhippuric acid concentrations). Thus, it is not possible to relate directly the symptoms reported by the xylene exposed group in this study to the atmospheric xylene levels.

Effects on the central and peripheral nervous systems

Controlled exposure studies

Four studies of controlled exposure to m-xylene have been reported[218,238-240]. In three of the these studies, exposure was to 100 ppm, 6 hours a day, for 4 days and then 200 ppm for 3 hours on the fifth day. After the weekend, exposure continued for 1 day for 6 hours at 100 ppm in one study[239]. In the other two studies, the continued exposures were to fluctuating concentrations of 64-200 ppm (100 ppm TWA) for 6 hours a day, for 2 days and 128-400 ppm (200 ppm TWA) for 3 hours on the third day[238,240]. In the fourth study, exposures were to fluctuating concentrations of 64-200 ppm (100 ppm TWA) for 6 hours a day, for 4 days and again for 1 day after the weekend. For the fifth day of the first week the exposure was to 135-400 ppm (200 ppm TWA) for 3 hours[239]. Some impairment of vestibular function (body balance) was observed following each exposure at or above 200 ppm in all studies. There was also some evidence of an impairment of reaction time and coordination[238,239]. No effects were observed in subjective signs or tests for eye muscle tone or peripheral senses. Most of the observed effects were also seen following acute exposure to similar exposure levels. There was no evidence of cumulative effects but there was evidence (at about 200 ppm) of tolerance or adaption to m-xylene exposure.

Case reports and studies of occupational groups

A number of studies, primarily from Scandinavia, have claimed neurophysiological and psychological disorders (often described as pre-senile dementia) in workers (eg car spray painters) occupationally exposed to solvent mixtures including xylenes[241-250].

In none of these studies was exposure to xylenes alone nor were xylenes the main solvents in a mixture. It is not possible to separate the effects due to the individual solvents present in the mixtures. Hence, no conclusions can be drawn regarding the effects of xylenes on neurophysiological or psychological functions in occupational groups.

Studies investigating other sub-acute effects

Liver damage, as measured by raised activities of serum enzymes and/or raised albumin and bilirubin concentrations and histological changes in biopsy samples, has been documented during clinical examination of individuals and occupational groups (eg painters) chronically exposed to solvent vapours, including xylenes[251-256]. Other studies have not confirmed the presence of liver disease[229,257-259]. However, no study reports exposure to pure xylenes (and in many cases xylenes were only a small proportion of total exposure). Consequently, no definite conclusions can be drawn on the occurrence of liver damage in humans repeatedly exposed to xylenes.

Effects on the kidney have been examined in a study of eight subjects (age range 34-61 years) who had worked at degreasing metal surfaces with mixed xylenes for at least 9 years[260]. Exposure levels, determined at the time of the study, occasionally reached 100 ppm and it was assumed that this level had been exceeded in earlier years. Urinanalysis (parameters measured not specified) was reported to show no pathological findings, but no data were presented.

A number of case reports and case control studies have reported effects on kidney function in humans exposed to organic solvents[261-269]. In most of these studies, no information was given on the solvents used, exposure levels or duration of exposure. Thus, no conclusions can be drawn on the occurrence of kidney damage in humans repeatedly exposed to xylenes.

A study has reported data indicating a decreased peripheral blood platelet count in 12 of 27 men intermittently exposed to mixed xylenes at a level of up to 200 ppm over an unspecified period of time[270]. Use of xylenes was stopped due to a change in working practice and platelet counts rapidly returned to normal. As it was reported that there was no evidence of aplastic anaemia in any of these men, it was assumed that other peripheral blood cell series (including lymphocytes and leukocytes) were evaluated and found to be normal.

A recent haematology study of 35 male spray varnishers exposed to xylene (0.5-3.4 ppm o-, 3.2-11.7 ppm m-, 0.9-4.3 ppm p-, 1.4-7.5 ppm Eb and also toluene <1.5 ppm), n-butanol (<1.2 ppm), 1,1,1-trichloroethane (<35.5 ppm) and several C9-aromatics but not benzene has been reported[271]. The results of this study showed that mean peripheral erythrocyte numbers and haemoglobin levels were decreased in the exposed compared with the control group. The neutrophil: lymphocyte ratio was inverted due to increased lymphocyte and decreased segmented neutrophil numbers. Platelet counts were within the normal range. However, because of the exposure to other solvents these effects cannot be definitely attributed to exposure to xylenes.

There are some studies where investigators report effects on haematology, particularly peripheral white blood cell numbers and function[272-274]. However, exposure to benzene and other petroleum based products also occurred. It is therefore not possible to attribute these effects to exposure to xylenes.

Summary of effects of repeated exposure

In controlled exposure studies, some impairment of vestibular function (at exposure levels of 200 ppm and above), and also reaction times in tests for coordination, have been reported. In these studies there was no evidence of cumulative effects but some evidence of tolerance or adaption.

The effects of repeated exposure to xylenes has not been adequately investigated. Most occupational studies have reported on exposure to a wide range of solvents in particular industries (eg spray painting). The solvents used and the exposure levels were often poorly defined. Episodes of depression, extreme fatigue, headache, anxiety and sleep disorders were the most frequently reported subjective signs of repeated exposure to xylenes. After cessation of exposure there was usually a gradual reduction in the severity of most symptoms.

Claims of neurophysiological and psychological disorders in occupational groups exposed to solvents (including xylenes) have been made. However, no conclusions on the effects of xylenes can be made. No conclusions can be made regarding the effects of xylenes on liver or kidney function.

An effect on peripheral blood erythrocyte numbers, haemoglobin levels and white cell numbers and ratio was noted in one study and an effect on platelet numbers in another study. As these studies yielded different findings it is not possible to make any conclusions on the effects of xylenes on the haemopoietic system.

Genotoxicty

Only limited studies have been carried out on the potential genotoxicity of xylenes to man. Sister chromatid exchange (SCE) in peripheral lymphocyte cultures was investigated in one study[275]. No significant differences in SCE frequencies, compared to a control group of 34 subjects, were noted in two groups of 23 workers who had been exposed for between 4 months and 23 years (mean 9.43 and 9.88 years respectively) to xylene (mixed xylenes containing Eb). The groups were selected at random but age (mean and range) and smoking habits were very similar in the different groups. The exposure levels were determined weekly and the mean values for the two groups over the previous 12 months were 11 and 13 ppm respectively. However, this study is of limited value as only 20 metaphases were examined per subject.

Two other studies are available but these have investigated workers co-exposed to xylene (composition undefined) and other solvents including benzene[276,277]. Consequently it is not possible to attribute the increased incidence of chromosome aberrations, reported in the first study, to exposure to xylenes. The second study reported that there were effects on sister chromatid exchange frequencies.

No conclusions can be drawn from any of these studies because of their small size, co-exposure to other solvents, or the small number of metaphases examined.

Carcinogenicity

There are no epidemiological studies available which have specifically investigated carcinogenicity following exposure to xylenes. Consequently, no conclusions can be made on the carcinogenic potential of xylenes in humans.

Effects on reproduction

There is little available information on the possible effects of xylenes on reproduction. In one study, university laboratory employees exposed to xylene (composition undefined) in the first trimester of pregnancy were studied[278]. Exposure levels were not stated. The miscarriage rate from 194 pregnancies studied was not significantly different from the control group of university laboratory employees not engaged in laboratory work involving exposure to solvents during the first trimester of pregnancy.

Overall, no conclusions can be made on the effects of exposure to xylenes on reproduction in humans because of the inadequate information available. A similar conclusion has been made previously[344].

Table 1: ACUTE TOXICITY OF XYLENES TO ANIMALS
Table 1.1: Inhalation Studies

Species	Concentration/dose/ duration	Observations
o-Xylene		
Rat (77) Sprague-Dawley 12 males/group	4330 ppm for 6 h.	LC_{50} value. 95% confidence limits 4247-4432 ppm. Signs of intoxication reported were hypotonia and somnolence. Autopsy on animals surviving the 14 d observation period revealed no macroscopic lesions of lungs, liver or kidneys.
Rat (85) Probably Wistar 10 animals/group Sex not given	a) 1531, 3062, or 6125 ppm for 24 h. b) 12 250 ppm for 12 h.	a) No deaths at 1531 ppm, one death at 3062 ppm and 8 deaths at 6125 ppm. b) A total of 2 deaths, one after 2 h. Autopsy of animals which died revealed no macroscopic or microsopic organ lesions. However a limited range of tissues was examined.
Rat (80) CFY 8 males/group	Six concentrations (not stated), up to anaesthesia, in the range of approximately 150-2500 ppm. 1, 2, 3 or 4 h exposure.	Study of the effect on prenarcotic motor behaviour. No significant effects on group motor activity were observed. Narcosis occurred at higher concentrations, with a threshold of 2180 ppm for a 4 h exposure.
Mouse (78) OF-1 20-25 females/group	4595 ppm for 6 h.	LC_{50} value. 95% confidence limits 4468-4744 ppm. Deaths occurred during exposure and there were also delayed deaths between days 5 and 10 post exposure.
Mouse (85) 10 animals/group Strain and sex not given	a) 1531, 3062 or 6125 ppm for 24 h. b) 12 250 ppm for 12 h.	a) No deaths at 1531 ppm, 4 deaths at 3062 ppm, and 9 deaths at 6125 ppm (8 deaths within 22 h). b) 2 deaths (1 death after 9 h). Autopsy of animals which died revealed no macroscopic or microscopic organ lesions. However a limited range of tissues was examined.

Table 1: ACUTE TOXICITY OF XYLENES TO ANIMALS
Table 1.1 Inhalation Studies

Species	Concentration/dose/ duration	Observations
Mouse (81) Strain, sex and numbers not given	Concentration range not stated. 2 h exposure.	Study to determine the minimum 2 h vapour concentration to cause: i) the animal to fall on its side ii) loss of reflexes iii) death. The effects observed included increasing dullness, followed by general anaesthesia, resting on side and clonic spasms. Reflexes were retained almost to point of death. Death occurred due to respiratory paralysis, seen with continued heart beat. Severe effects on peripheral circulation observed, including widening of the visible vessels of eyes and reddening of ears, nose, paws and tail. Minimum vapour concentrations for falling on side and death were 3400-4600 and 6900 ppm respectively.
Mouse (83, 84) OF-1 6 males/group	At least four concentrations (not stated). Approximately 5 min exposure.	A study of irritation of the respiratory tract, using the reflex decrease in respiratory rate. RD_{50} (exposure level reducing respiratory rate by 50%) 1467 ppm. 95% confidence limits 1406-1530 ppm. The onset of response was generally rapid and the maximum decrease in respiratory rate was attained within a few minutes.

Table 1: ACUTE TOXICITY OF XYLENES TO ANIMALS
Table 1.1 Inhalation Studies

Species	Concentration/dose/ duration	Observations
Mouse (79) CD-1		Study of the effects on a) behavioural test for milk reinforcement (Inter Response Time, IRT>10sec) and on b) a motor coordination test (inverted screen).
a) 15 males	a) A range of concentrations from 500 to 7000 ppm. Animals exposed for 30 min to ascending concentrations, on Tuesday and Friday of each week, and to air (control) on Thursday.	a) The animals were trained and then tested (for 15 min) immediately after each exposure. There was an increase in response rate at intermediate concentrations (1400-2000 ppm) and a marked decrease at 7000 ppm, due to gross ataxia and prostration in the animals. There was a concentration-dependent decrease in reinforcement rate. The lowest concentration for significantly affecting behavioural performance was 1400 ppm. The EC_{50}, for decreasing the response rate was 5179 ppm (4446-6076 ppm). There was a moderate disruption of response patterning, with an increase in IRT less than 10 sec at 1400-4000 ppm, and a increase in IRT after 22 sec at 7000 ppm.
b) 2 x 6 males	b) At least 3 concentrations from 2000 to 7000 ppm. Exposure period not stated.	b) The animals were tested at 1, 5, 15, 30, 45 and up to 60 min after exposure. The minimally effective concentration for failure of test was 3000 ppm. The EC_{50} for failure of test was 3640 ppm (3389-3910 ppm). The animals required 5 to 15 minutes recovery for normal test performance. These studies indicate that o-xylene gave a biphasic response with exposure concentration, causing excitation at low concentrations and depression at higher concentrations. These effects were reversible.
Mouse (82) OF-1 10 males/group	Concentration range not stated. 4 h exposure.	Study to determine the concentration required to cause a 50% increase in the seizure threshold for pentylenetetrazol induced convulsions.
	Animals also received pentylenetetrazol by intravenous infusion.	ED_{50} 1339 ppm. 95% confidence limits 1270 - 1392 ppm.

Table 1: ACUTE TOXICITY OF XYLENES TO ANIMALS
Table 1.1 Inhalation Studies

Species	Concentration/dose/duration	Observations
Mouse (279) OF-1 10 males/group	0, 1010, 1101, 1207 or 1234 ppm for 4 h.	A study to observe effects in the 'behavioural despair' swimming test. Immediately after exposure the mice were placed in a vertical glass cylinder containing water. The total period of immobility in the first 3 min in the water was measured. No deaths reported. The duration of immobility was reduced in a concentration dependent manner. ID_{50} 1127 ppm. 95% confidence limits 1068 - 1182 ppm. The significance of these findings is unclear.
Mouse (280) ddY strain 3 males/group	5 drops (estimated at up to 28 000 ppm). One hour previously, the animals were injected i.p. with 0.4 ml of physiological saline or i) Inosine ii) NAD iii) Glucuronic acid lactone iv) Inosine & NAD v) Inosine & glucuronic acid lactone vi) Inosine & glucuronic acid lactone & NAD.	Study of the effect of inosine, NAD and glucuronic acid lactone on survival time with acute intoxication. All combinations were found to increase the mean survival time. Inosine and glucuronic acid lactone was the most effective combination and produced an approximate doubling in survival time (146 min cf 78 min for saline). It was suggested that this result was due to improved biotransformation of xylene.

_m_-Xylene

Species	Concentration/dose/duration	Observations
Rat (77) Spague-Dawley 12 males/group	5984 ppm for 6 h.	LC_{50} value. 95% confidence limits 5796-6181 ppm. Signs of intoxication reported were hypotonia and somnolence. Autopsy on animals surviving the 14 day observation period revealed no macroscopic lesions of lungs, liver or kidneys.
Rat (85) Probably Wistar 10 animals/group Sex not given	a) 1005 or 2010 ppm for 24 h. b) 8040 ppm for 12 h.	a) No deaths at 1005 and 2010 ppm. b) One death reported. Autopsy of the animal which died revealed no macroscopic or microscopic organ lesions. However a limited range of tissues was examined.

Table 1: ACUTE TOXICITY OF XYLENES TO ANIMALS
Table 1.1 Inhalation Studies

Species	Concentration/dose/duration	Observations
Rat (101) Carworth-Wistar 6 animals/group Males and females	Concentration range not stated. 4 h exposure.	An acute inhalation study. At 8000 ppm, 10 out of 12 animals died.
Rat (86) CFY 8 males/group	Six concentrations from 150 to 2080 ppm. 4 h exposure.	Study to determine the effect on motor activity. m-Xylene gave a slight activation of group motor activity at lower concentrations. At higher concentrations depression was observed, 2080 ppm rapidly leading to narcosis.
Rat (80) CFY 8 males/group	Six concentrations (not stated), up to anaesthesia, in the range of approximately 130-2500 ppm. 1, 2, 3 or 4 h exposure.	Study of the effect on prenarcotic motor behaviour. A biphasic effect on group motor activity was reported. Slight exposure-dependent, activation, with inco-ordination, was observed at the lower concentrations of 130-1500 ppm. Depression occurred at higher concentrations, with a threshold for narcosis of 2100 ppm, for a 4 h exposure.
Rat (281) 4 animals/group Strain and sex not given	560, 1000, 1780 and 3000 ppm for 2 h. Animals exposed to ascending then descending concentrations on Tuesday and Friday of each week, and to air (control) on Thursday.	Study of the effect on fixed interval 5 min (FI 5) liquid reinforcement, the animals being tested immediately after exposure. At 3000 ppm there was an initial decrease in response rate, followed by an increase across the behavioural session. At the lower concentrations there was an initial increase in response rates. Reported in abstract form only.
Rat (15) Wistar 6 males/group	0, 75, 150 or 300 ppm for 24 h.	Study of the effect on lung cytochrome P450 activities. There was a significant decrease in cytochrome P450 concentration at all concentrations, and a significant, dose-dependent decrease in 7-ethoxycoumarin O-deethylase activity. There were significant increases in epoxide hydrolase activity at 150 and 300 ppm

33

Table 1: ACUTE TOXICITY OF XYLENES TO ANIMALS
Table 1.1 Inhalation Studies

Species	Concentration/dose/ duration	Observations
		There was no consistent effect on the content of NADPH-cytochrome c reductase, cytochrome b_5 or non-protein thiol groups.
		Scanning electron microscopy revealed no lung abnormalities in 2 animals exposed to 300 ppm.
Mouse (78) OF-1 20-25 females/group	5267 ppm for 6 h.	LC_{50} value. 95% confidence limits 5025-5490 ppm.
Mouse (85) 10 animals/group Strain and sex not given	a) 1005 or 2010 ppm for 24 h.	a) No deaths at 1005 ppm. 5 deaths at 2010 ppm, occurring 4 d after exposure.
	b) 8040 ppm for 12 h.	b) 6 deaths, with 4 within 7 h.
		Autopsy of animals which died revealed no macroscopic or microscopic organ lesions. However a limited range of tissues was examined.
Mouse (81) Strain, sex and numbers not given	Concentration range not stated. 2 h exposure.	Study to determine the minimum 2 h vapour concentration to cause:
		i) the animal to fall on its side ii) loss of reflexes iii) death.
		The effects observed included increasing dullness, followed by general anaesthesia, resting on side and clonic cramps. Reflexes were retained almost to point of death. Death occurred due to respiratory paralysis, seen with continued heart beat.
		Severe effects on peripheral circulation observed, including widening of the visible vessels of eyes and reddening of ears, nose, paws and tail.
		Minimum vapour concentrations for falling on side, loss of reflexes and death were 2300-3400, approximately 3400, and 11 500 ppm respectively.
Mouse CD-1		Study of the effects on a) behavioural test for milk reinforcement (Inter Response Time, IRT>10sec) and on b) a motor coordination test (inverted screen).

Table 1: ACUTE TOXICITY OF XYLENES TO ANIMALS
Table 1.1 Inhalation Studies

Species	Concentration/dose/ duration	Observations
a) 15 males	a) A range of concentations from 500 to 7000 ppm. Animals exposed for 30 min to ascending concentrations, on Tuesday and Friday of each week, and to air (control) on Thursday.	a) The animals were trained and then tested (for 15 min) immediately after each exposure. There was an increase in response rate at intermediate concentrations (1400-2000 ppm) and a marked decrease at 7000 ppm, due to gross ataxia and prostration in the animals. There was a concentration-dependent decrease in reinforcement rate. The lowest concentration for significantly affecting behavioural performance was 1400 ppm. The EC_{50}, for decreasing the response rate, was 6176 ppm (5508-7780 ppm). There was a moderate disruption of response patterning, with an increase in IRT less than 10 sec at 1400-4000 ppm, and a increase in IRT after 22 sec at 7000 ppm.
b) 2 x 6 males	b) At least 3 concentrations from 2000 to 7000 ppm. Exposure period not stated.	b) The animals were tested at 1, 5, 15, 30, 45 and up to 60 min, after exposure. The minimally effective concentration for failure of test was 3000 ppm. The EC_{50} for failure of test was 3790 ppm (3450-4164 ppm). The animals required 5 to 15 min recovery for normal test performance. These studies indicate that m-xylene gave a biphasic response with exposure concentration, causing excitation at low concentrations and depression at higher concentrations. These effects were reversible.
Mouse (82) OF-1 10 males/group	Concentration range not stated. 4 h exposure. Animals also received pentylenetetrazol by intravenous infusion.	Study to determine the concentration required to cause a 50% increase in the seizure threshold for pentylenetetrazol induced convulsions. ED_{50} 2093 ppm. 95% confidence limits 2001-2176 ppm.
Dog (282) Breed, sex and numbers not given	A range of concentrations up to approximately 8000 ppm, for 1-3 min. The animals were anaesthetised throughout the study.	Study to determine the effect of organic solvents on systemic blood pressure. Above a threshold concentration, of approximately 4500 ppm, there was a concentration-related fall in blood pressure. Other structurally unrelated organic solvents gave similar results.

Table 1: ACUTE TOXICITY OF XYLENES TO ANIMALS
Table 1.1 Inhalation Studies

Species	Concentration/dose/ duration	Observations
p-**Xylene**		
Rat (77) Sprague-Dawley 12 males/group	4591 ppm for 6 h.	LC_{50} value. 95% confidence limits 4353-5049 ppm. Some delayed deaths were reported. Signs of intoxication reported were hypotonia and somnolence as well as stereotypy, trembling and muscular spasms. Autopsy on animals surviving the 14 d observation period revealed no macroscopic lesions of lungs, liver or kidneys.
Rat (41, 87) Sprague-Dawley Female Numbers not given	4740 ppm for 4 h. Animals were pretreated i.p. with i) 75 mg/kg phenobarbital or ii) 15 mg/kg chlorpromazine or iii) 20 mg/kg 3-methylcholanthrene for 3 days prior to exposure.	A study of the effect of inducers on acute xylene toxicity. LC_{50} value. 95% confidence limits 4520-4960 ppm. Pretreatment with inducers slightly increased the LC_{50} (20, 5 and 9% respectively).
Rat (85) Probably Wistar 10 animals/group Sex not given	a) 2451 ppm for 24 h. b) 4912 ppm for 24-28 h. c) 19 650 ppm for 12 h.	a) No deaths reported. b) No deaths reported. c) 8 deaths reported, 4 after 6 h. Autopsy of animals which died revealed no macroscopic or microscopic organ lesions. However a limited range of tissues was examined.
Rat (88) Long-Evans a) 2 males/group b) 2 males/group	a) 4000 ppm. Exposure period not stated. b) 20 000 ppm. Exposure period not stated.	Study to examine the neurotoxicity of some organic solvents. a) No clinical effects were observed. b) Signs reported include dyspnoea, ataxia, hyperreactivity to noise, rigid tails and carpopedal spasm. Signs consistent with tremors, eg generalised quivering leading to violent twitching,

Table 1: ACUTE TOXICITY OF XYLENES TO ANIMALS
Table 1.1 Inhalation Studies

Species	Concentration/dose/duration	Observations
		were also reported along with profuse salivation.
c) 12 males/group	c) 10 000 ppm. Exposure period not stated.	c) 5 animals died, with one exhibiting severe tonic/clonic spasms. Necropsy revealed no gross lesions, other than those due to some local irritation of the respiratory tract. There were no treatment related microscopic lesions to the CNS.
Rat (283) Long Evans All animals were surgically prepared. 16 males per group	0,800 or 1600 ppm for 4 h	Study of the effect of xylene on the functional integrity of the visual system using flash-evoked potentials. The animals were tested 16-120 min after exposure. Only FEP peak N3 was measured. The peak amplitude was reduced in the group exposed to 1600 ppm. There was evidence that this reduction was greatest immediately after exposure. Peak amplitude returned towards control levels with increasing length of time between exposure and measurement. No differences between control and exposed group peak values were observed 75 min after exposure. Thus in this study xylene altered the processing of visual information. The authors suggest that this may be secondary to changes in arousal or excitability.
Rat (284) Long Evans 8-16 males per group	0 or 1600 ppm. Animals exposed for 4 h and tested each day for 5 days.	Study of the effect on two learning tasks and motor activity. Animals were trained and then tested on the same day as each exposure. Signs of toxicity (including unsteadiness and fine tremor) largely disappeared 30 min post exposure. In the autoshaping test, when the force required to depress the lever was 0.IN, acquisition was faster in treated animals but this was not observed at 0.2N. p - Xylene suppressed response rates in a reversal learning paradigm without affecting reversal rate. Vertically - directed motor activity was unaffected by p - Xylene; horizontally - directed activity was increased (approx 30%). This hyperactivity returned to control levels at the end of each days test and declined across the 5 daily tests.

Table 1: ACUTE TOXICITY OF XYLENES TO ANIMALS
Table 1.1 Inhalation Studies

Species	Concentration/dose/ duration	Observations
		This study indicated an effect of p - xylene on motor control rather than on cognitive capacity.
Rat (285) Long Evans All animals were maintained on a water-restricted schedule		A study of flavour aversion induced by xylene.
a) 6-10 males per group	0, 50, 100, 200, 400, 800 or 1600 ppm for 4 h	Concentration: effect study. Animals were presented with saccharin in place of water immediately prior to xylene exposures. Aversion testing was performed 3 days later by offering a choice between saccharin and water.
		Xylene inhalation induced a significant concentration - related fall in relative saccharin intake (approx 25% fall at 50-200 ppm and 100% at 1600 ppm)
		There was no significant treatment-related effect on total fluid intake.
b) 7 males per group	0 or 400 ppm for 0.5, 1, 2, 4 or 8 h	Duration: effect study. Animals were presented with saccharin and aversion-tested as for a). Relative saccharin intake declined from 0.4 at 0.5 h to approximately 0.1 at 2-8 h (control intake remained at approximately 0.55 throughout).
		There was no significant treatment-related effect on total fluid intake.
		Comparing the effects at constant concentration and constant duration indicated that xylene concentration was the primary determinant of the response.
c) 10 males per group	0, 200 or 400 ppm for 4 h	In this study animals were presented with saccharin in place of water 24 h before exposure to xylene. Aversion testing was as for a).
		In this study xylene had no effect on relative saccharin intake. There was no significant effect on total fluid intake.
		Thus in these studies xylene exposure immediately after saccharin presentation induced a flavour aversion to saccharin. This aversion was not seen if the period between saccharin presentation and xylene exposure was 24 hours.

Table 1: ACUTE TOXICITY OF XYLENES TO ANIMALS
Table 1.1 Inhalation Studies

Species	Concentration/dose/ duration	Observations
Rat (80) CFY 8 males/group	Eight concentrations (not stated) up to anaesthesia in the range of approximately 150-2500 ppm. 1, 2, 3 or 4 h exposure.	Study of the effect on prenarcotic motor behaviour. A biphasic effect on group motor activity was reported. Marked, exposure-dependent activation, with inco-ordination and tremors was observed at the lower concentrations of 400-1500 ppm. Depression occurred at higher concentrations, with a threshold for narcosis of 1940 ppm, for a 4 h exposure.
Rat (89) Sprague-Dawley 16 females/group	0, 1000, 1500 or 2000 ppm for 4 h.	Study of the effect on serum enzyme activities determined at 4 h and 24 h after the beginning of exposure. Aspartate aminotransferase (AST) was unchanged at 4 h but at 24 h showed a significant, concentration-related increase. Alanine aminotransferase (ALT) was significantly increased at 4 h in the 1500 and 2000 ppm groups. This activity was increased at 24 h, being significant at all 3 exposure levels. Glucose-6-phosphate dehydrogenase (G-6-PDH) was significantly increased at 4 and 24 h in the 1500 and 2000 ppm exposure groups. The increase was concentration-dependent. Isocitric dehydrogenase (ICD) was significantly increased at 4 h for the highest exposure group. At 24 h there was a significant increase at 1500 and 2000 ppm. Glutathione reductase (GSS-Rase) was increased in a significant, concentration-dependent manner, at 4 h and 24 h for the 1500 and 2000 ppm groups. Lactic dehydrogenase (LDH) was increased at 4 and 24 h at 1000 ppm. At 1500 ppm it was significantly lower than controls at 4 h but significantly increased at 24 h. At 2000 ppm it was significantly increased at both 4 and 24 h.

Table 1: ACUTE TOXICITY OF XYLENES TO ANIMALS
Table 1.1 Inhalation Studies

Species	Concentration/dose/ duration	Observations
		5'-Nucleotidase was significantly decreased at 4 h and increased at 24 h at 1000 ppm. At 1500 ppm and 2000 ppm, activity was unchanged at 4 h, but significantly increased at 24 h in a concentration-dependent manner. Acetylcholinesterase activity was significantly increased, in a concentration-dependent manner, at 4 h. These activities reverted to levels below control values at 24 h. The increased activity of AST, ALT, ICD and LDH are indicative of hepatocellular damage and increased 5'-nucleotidase is indicative of hepatobiliary damage.
Rat (91) Sprague-Dawley 4 females/group	0 or 1000 ppm for 4 h.	Study of the effect on lung microsomal activity. There was a significant inhibition of NADPH - cytochrome c reductase activity immediately and at 20 h (48 and 55% of controls) whereas there was a small, but significant, inhibition in NADH-cytochrome c reductase at 20 h (95%). There was a significant decrease in benzphetamine N-demethylase activity at 20 h (33%).
Mouse (78) OF-1 20-25 females/group	3907 ppm for 6 h.	LC_{50} value. 95% confidence limits 3747-4015 ppm.

Table 1: ACUTE TOXICITY OF XYLENES TO ANIMALS
Table 1.1 Inhalation Studies

Species	Concentration/dose/duration	Observations
Mouse (85) 10 animals/group Strain and sex not given	a) 2451 ppm for 24 h. b) 4912 ppm for 24-28 h. c) 19 650 ppm for 12 h.	a) No deaths reported. b) No deaths reported. c) 9 deaths, with 6 deaths within 6 h. Autopsy of animals which died revealed no macroscopic or microscopic organ lesions. However a limited range of tissues was examined.
Mouse (81) Strain, sex and numbers not given.	Concentration range not stated. 2 h exposure.	Study to determine the minimum 2 h vapour concentration to cause: i) the animal to fall on its side ii) loss of reflexes iii) death. The effects observed included continuous shivering of the entire body with a rigid tail. The shivering became progressively weaker and strong individual spasms of the body occurred. Breathing became gradually slower and towards the end of the exposure the animal was usually resting almost quietly. Reflexes continued until one minute before death, which occurred due to respiratory paralysis. Minimum vapour concentrations for falling on side and death were 2300 and 3400-8000 ppm.

Table 1: ACUTE TOXICITY OF XYLENES TO ANIMALS
Table 1.1 Inhalation Studies

Species	Concentration/dose/ duration	Observations
Mouse (79) CD-1		Study of the effects on a) behavioural test for milk reinforcement (Inter Response Time, IRT>10sec) and on b) a motor co-ordination test (inverted screen).
a) 15 males	a) A range of concentrations from 500 to 7000 ppm. Animals exposed for 30 min to ascending concentrations, on Tuesday and Friday of each week, and to air (control) on Thursday.	a) The animals were trained and then tested (for 15 min) immediately after each exposure. There was an increase in response rate at intermediate concentrations (1400-2000 ppm) and a marked decrease at 7000 ppm, due to gross ataxia and prostration in the animals.
		There was a concentration-dependent decrease in reinforcement rate. The lowest concentration for significantly affecting behavioural performance was 1400 ppm.
		The EC_{50}, for decreasing the response rate, was 5611 ppm (5105-6427 ppm). There was a moderate disruption of response patterning, with an increase in IRT less than 10 sec at 1400-4000 ppm, and a increase in IRT after 22 sec at 7000 ppm.
b) 2 x 6 males	b) At least 3 concentrations from 2000 to 7000 ppm. Exposure period not stated.	b) The animals were tested at 1, 5, 15, 30, 45 and up to 60 min, after exposure. The minimally effective concentration for failure of test was 3000 ppm.
		The EC_{50} for failure of test was 2676 ppm (2063-3470 ppm). The animals required 5 to 15 min recovery for normal test performance. These studies indicate that p-xylene gave a biphasic response causing excitation at low concentrations and depression at higher concentrations. These effects were reversible.
Rabbit (90)	0 or 1000 ppm for 4 h	Study of the effect on lung microsomal activity.
		There was a marked decrease in the pulmonary cytochrome P-450 concentration (55% of controls).
		Study presented in abstract form only.

Table 1: ACUTE TOXICITY OF XYLENES TO ANIMALS
Table 1.1 Inhalation Studies

Species	Concentration/dose/ duration	Observations
Xylene		
Rat (92) Long-Evans 10 males/group	6350 ppm for 4 h. Xylene undefined.	LC_{50} value. 95% confidence limits 4670-8640 ppm. Survivors were comatose but recovered shortly after removal from chamber.
Rat (6) Harlan-Wistar a) 10 males/group	a) 6700 ppm for 4 h.	a) LC_{50} value. 95% confidence limits 5100-8500 ppm. There were no deaths up to 2800 ppm, but 6000 ppm killed four animals and 9900 ppm killed all animals. There was a concentration-dependent, reversible narcosis manifest as poor coordination and prostration. In the highest exposure group 2 animals exhibited atelectasis, haemorrhage and interlobular oedema of the lungs. No signs of distress were seen at 580 ppm.
b) 5 males/group	b) <u>ca</u> 11 000 ppm.	b) Study to determine the time period lethal to 50% of the animals (Lt_{50}). Lt_{50} 92 min. There was immediate eye irritation, irritation of extremities at 5 min, prostration at 20 min and tremors at 45 min.
c) 5 males/group	c) 0 or <u>ca</u> 15 000 ppm for 45 min. Xylene used was; 7.63% o-xylene 65.01% m-xylene 7.84% p-xylene 19.27% ethylbenzene.	c) Exposure had no effect on erythrocyte osmotic fragility.
Rat (93) Sprague-Dawley Female Numbers not given		An acute study, using serum sorbitol dehydrogenase (SDH) and aspartate aminotransferase (AST) activities, and liver triglyceride levels as markers for liver damage.
	a) 10 950 ppm for 4 h.	a) LC_{50} value (24 h). 95% confidence limits 10 060 - 11 920 ppm.

Table 1: ACUTE TOXICITY OF XYLENES TO ANIMALS
Table 1.1 Inhalation Studies

Species	Concentration/dose/ duration	Observations
	b) 0, 340, 680, 1370, 2740 or 5480 ppm for 4 h. Xylene undefined.	b) There was no effect on enzyme activities. However there were raised hepatic triglyceride levels at the highest concentration. Liver histology revealed no abnormalities. Full data were not presented.
Rat (99) Sprague-Dawley Females		A study to determine LD_{50} values and the relative hepatotoxicity of some organic solvents using sorbitol dehydrogenase activity as a marker enzyme.
a) 10 per group	a) 10 950 ppm for 4 h.	a) LC_{50} value. 95% confidence limits 10 050-11 950 ppm.
b) 6 per group	b) 1370 ppm for 4 h. A group was then sacrified at 3 h intervals from 12 to 36 h after the beginning of exposure.	b) There was no effect on serum activity of sorbitol dehydrogerase (SDH) at any time.
c) 6 per group	c) 0, 340, 680, 1370, 2470 or 5480 ppm for 4 h. Xylene undefined.	c) There was no effect on serum SDH activity at 20 h. There were no histological changes observed in the livers of animals exposed to 5480 ppm.
Rat (94) 9 females/group Strain not given	Initial concentration of 15 000 ppm. Approximately 1 h exposure Xylene undefined.	Study of the time course of anaesthesia due to xylene. The animals displayed abnormal behaviour including flight attempts, salivation, biting, restless breathing and unusual positions. Subsequently animals fell over and paralytic symptoms were seen in the hind paws. As narcosis developed painful electrical stimuli were given until the animals no longer reacted and there was total abolition of reflexes. The chamber was then ventilated and the animals stimulated until recovery. During exposure a mean exposure time of 731.5 sec for the first signs of hind paw paralysis to appear and 2570.5 sec to proceed to total abolition of response to pain was necessary. The recovery time was 500.0 sec. The anaesthetic properties of a toluene/ xylene mixture were also studied, with toluene giving a reduction in mean times. Xylene acted as an anaesthetic of protracted time course and long recovery. The addition of toluene changed the profile to that more like toluene eg shorter anaesthetic period and shorter recovery.

44

Table 1: ACUTE TOXICITY OF XYLENES TO ANIMALS
Table 1.1 Inhalation Studies

Species	Concentration/dose/ duration	Observations
Rat (95) F 344 Males		Study of the effect on fixed ratio (FR 24) liquid reinforcement (RIF), the animals being tested during exposure.
4 animals/group	a) 113, 216 and 430 ppm for 2 h each, in a 6 h session.	a) There was a significant decrease in the reinforcement rate, during hours 1, 3 and 5 of exposure, which was concentration dependent.
5 animals/group	b) 113, 212 and 447 ppm for 2 h on separate days, with at least 7 d between exposures to prevent the development of tolerance.	b) There was a significant decrease in the reinforcement rate during the 4th 15 min exposure period (45-60 min) at all concentrations. At 446 ppm there was a marked decrease in reinforcement rate during the 6th and 8th 15 min exposure periods (75-90 min and 105-120 min respectively).
4 animals/group	c) 99 ppm for 5 h. Xylene undefined.	c) The reinforcement rate was not significantly changed at any period during the 5 h exposure. This study demonstrates that at 113 ppm and above there was a transient decrease in reinforcement rate followed by the development of acute tolerance. No cumulative effects were seen during prolonged exposure to 99 ppm.
Rat (96) F 344 4 males/group	116, 214 and 442 ppm for 2 h on separate days, with at least 7 d between exposures to prevent the development of tolerance. Xylene undefined.	Study of the effect on fixed ratio (FR 24) liquid reinforcement (RIF), the animals being tested during exposure. There was a significant decrease in the reinforcement rate during the second 15 min testing period (45-60 min) at all concentrations. In addition, this decrease in reinforcement rate was not significantly different from that given by toluene.
Rat (93, 97) Strain, sex and numbers not given		Study to examine the effect of xylene on fixed ratio (FR 24) liquid reinforcement (RIF) with or without intracranial self-stimulation, the animals being tested during exposure.
	a) 3 graded concentrations (not stated) for 2 h each, in a 6 h session.	a) A decrease in RIF was seen during 1, 3 and 5 h, with improved behavioural performance during 2, 4 and 6 h indicating development of tolerance.
	b) 139 ppm for 5 h. Xylene undefined.	b) Decreased RIF seen at 1 and 2 h, with subsequent improvement indicating the development of tolerance.

Table 1: ACUTE TOXICITY OF XYLENES TO ANIMALS
Table 1.1 Inhalation Studies

Species	Concentration/dose/duration	Observations
		Decreases in RIF were also reported in rats subjected to intracranial self-stimulation.
		Incomplete details, relating to exposure concentrations, limits the value of this study, which was reported in summary form only.
Rat (286) Fisher F344		Study of the effect on intracranial self-stimulation behaviour.
a) 5 males/group	a) 0, 102, 192, 419 and 623 ppm for 2 h on separate days, with at least 7 d between exposures to prevent the development of tolerance.	a) At 623 ppm there was a significant decrease in response rate throughout the exposure period. At 419 ppm a significant decrease was seen only in the second hour, and at 192 ppm a significant decrease was seen only in one 20 min period. There was no effect at 102 ppm.
b) 4 males/group	b) 0 or 106 ppm for 4 h. Xylene undefined.	b) The rate of response was not significantly altered at any period during the 4 h exposure.
		This study demonstrates decreased intracranial self-stimulation behaviour at 192 ppm and above. No cumulative effect was seen during prolonged exposure.
Rat (98) Fisher F344 12 males/group		Study of the effect on hearing loss as assessed by a behavioural (conditioned avoidance) method.
	a) 0 or 1700 ppm for 4 h.	a) There was no effect noted.
	b) 0 or 1450 ppm for 8 h.	b) There was a slight increase (approximately 5 dB) in the auditory response threshold at 20 kHz.
	About 35 d after exposure the animals were trained to perform a multisensory conditioned avoidance response (CAR) task (Visual, auditory and somatosensory stimuli), followed by the behavioural audiometric tests. Xylene used was; 10% *o*-xylene 80% *m*-xylene 10% *p*-xylene.	These results demonstrate some evidence of ototoxicity in the rat.

Table 1: ACUTE TOXICITY OF XYLENES TO ANIMALS
Table 1.1 Inhalation Studies

Species	Concentration/dose/ duration	Observations
Rat (287) CFY 5 males/group	Concentration not stated. Exposure period not stated. All animals anaesthetised with pentobarbital (40 mg/kg i.p.) before treatment. Xylene undefined.	Study to observe the effect on ECG. Xylene induced moderate repolarisation disturbance and occasionally arrhythmia at the beginning of anaesthesia. Atrial fibrillation, brady-arrhythmia and asystole later developed at the onset of respiratory paralysis.
Mouse (6) Swiss-Webster 6 males/group	ca 460, 1300, 2500, 6500 or 12 000 ppm for 60 sec. Xylene used was; 7.63% o-xylene 65.01% m-xylene 7.84% p-xylene 19.27% ethylbenzene.	A study of concentrations required for a depression of the respiratory rate by 50% or more. There was a concentration-dependent increase in the number of animals with a respiratory rate depressed by at least 50%. There was no effect at 460 ppm. An inhibition of 50% or more was not observed in any animals tested during the 15 min post exposure period.
Mouse (79) CD-1		Study on the effects on a) behavioural test for milk reinforcement (Inter Response Time, IRT>10sec) and on b) a motor coordination test (inverted screen).
a) 15 males	a) A range of concentrations from 500 to 7000 ppm. Animals exposed for 30 mins to ascending concentrations on Tuesday and Friday of each week, and to air (control) on Thursday.	a) the animals were trained and then tested (for 15 min) immediately after each exposure. There was an increase in response rate at intermediate concentrations (1400-2000 ppm) and a marked decrease at 7000 ppm, due to gross ataxia and prostration in the animals. There was a concentration-dependent decrease in reinforcement rate. There was a moderate disruption of response patterning, with an increase in IRT less than 10 sec at 1400-4000 ppm, and an increase in IRT after 22 sec at 7000 ppm.
b) 2 x 6 males	b) At least 3 concentrations from 2000 to 7000 ppm. Exposure period not stated. Xylene undefined.	b) The animals were tested at 1, 5, 15, 30, 45 and up to 60 min after exposure. The animals required 5 to 15 min recovery for normal test performance. These studies indicate that xylene gave a biphasic response with excitation at low concentrations and depression at higher concentrations. These effects were reversible.

Table 1: ACUTE TOXICITY OF XYLENES TO ANIMALS
Table 1.1 Inhalation Studies

Species	Concentration/dose/duration	Observations
Rabbit (288) 5 animals/group Strain and sex not given	5740, 6900 or 9200 ppm for up to 6 h. Xylene undefined.	Study of the time to onset of narcosis with organic solvents. There were no deaths reported. At 5740 ppm 1 animal developed mild narcosis. At 6900 ppm 4 animals developed mild narcosis, with 3 proceeding to deep narcosis. At 9200 ppm 4 animals developed mild narcosis all proceeding to deep narcosis. Trembling was not observed and there was no effect on rectal temperature. Wide individual variation in the time of onset, and severity, of effects obscured any possible concentration-dependence.
Dog (6) Beagle Sex and numbers not given.	ca 530 or 1200 ppm for 4 h. Xylene used was; 7.63% o-xylene 65.01% m-xylene 7.84% p-xylene 19.27% ethylbenzene.	Study to determine the level at which there were no signs of toxicity. 1200 ppm caused lacrimation. There was no noticeable effect at 530 ppm.
Dog (289) 'Several' males/group Breed not given	Concentration not stated. Administered through a tracheal cannula under pentobarbital anaesthesia. Xylene undefined.	Qualitative study of adrenaline induced ventricular fibrillation in xylene exposed animals. Xylene reported to enhance the action of adrenaline in inducing ventricular fibrillation. However, study is of limited value as exposure concentration is not given.
Cat (6) 4 males/group	ca 9500 ppm for up to 2 h. Xylene used was; 7.63% o-xylene 65.01% m-xylene 7.84% p-xylene 19.27% ethylbenzene.	General acute toxicity study. The animals responded in a time related pattern of salivation, ataxia, clonic and tonic spasms, narcosis and death. All animals died within 2 h. There were no treatment related histopathological abnormalities in the respiratory tract, liver, kidney, brain, bone marrow, skeletal muscle or peripheral nervous system.

Table 1: ACUTE TOXICITY OF XYLENES TO ANIMALS
Table 1.1 Inhalation Studies

Species	Concentration/dose/duration	Observations
Cat (288) 5 animals/group Sex not given.	5740, 6900 or 9200 ppm for up to 6 h. Xylene undefined.	Study of the time to onset of narcosis with organic solvents. There were no deaths reported. There was an apparent concentration-dependent decrease in time to onset of staggering, lying down and mild narcosis, though wide individual variation was reported. Deep narcosis was seen in at least 4 animals at 9200 ppm. There was no effect on rectal temperature.

Table 1: ACUTE TOXICITY OF XYLENES TO ANIMALS
Table 1.2: Oral Studies

Species	Concentration/dose/ duration	Observations
o-Xylene		
Rat (100) CFY Sex and numbers not given	3608 mg/kg.	LD_{50} value. 95% confidence limits 3142-4145 mg/kg. A 1:1 mixture, by volume, with toluene gave an LD_{50} of 5504 mg/kg, 95% confidence limits 4839-6256 mg/kg.
Rat (123) 10 animals Strain and sex not given	4350 mg/kg in olive oil.	There were 7 deaths. Signs of toxicity were not reported. A number of gross lesions were reported in a wide range of organs, including hyperaemia, haemorrhage and congestion. It is unclear which target organs relate to o-xylene.
m-Xylene		
Rat (100) CFY Sex and numbers not given	5011 mg/kg.	LD_{50} value. 95% confidence limits 4476-5616 mg/kg. A 1:1 mixture, by volume, with toluene gave an LD_{50} of 5095 mg/kg, 95% confidence limits 4714-5510 m/kg.
Rat (101) Carworth-Wistar 5 males/group	6660 mg/kg.	LD_{50} value. ±1.96 Standard Deviations 5390-8230 mg/kg.

Table 1: ACUTE TOXICITY OF XYLENES TO ANIMALS
Table 1.2 Oral Studies

Species	Concentration/dose/ duration	Observations
Rat (123) 10 animals Strain and sex not given	4350 mg/kg in olive oil.	There were 3 deaths. Signs of toxicity not reported. A number of gross lesions were reported in a wide range of organs, including hyperaemia, haemorrhage and congestion. It is unclear which target organs relate to m-xylene.

p-Xylene

Species	Concentration/dose/ duration	Observations
Rat (100) CFY Sex and numbers not given	4029 mg/kg.	LD_{50} value. 95% confidence limits 3392-4779 mg/kg. An 1:1 mixture, by volume, with toluene gave an LD_{50} of 6202 mg/kg, 95% confidence limits 5268-7301 mg/kg.
Rat (123) 10 animals Strain and sex not given	4350 mg/kg in olive oil.	There were 6 deaths. However signs of toxicity not reported. A number of gross lesions were reported in a wide range of organs, including hyperaemia, haemorrhage and congestion. It is unclear which target organs relate to p-xylene.
Rat (283) Long Evans All animals were surgically prepared		Study of the effect of p-xylene on the functional integrity of the visual system using flash-evoked potentials (FEP)
a) 10-11 males per group	0, 500, 1,000 or 2,000 mg/kg	The animals were tested 75 mins after treatment. There was a slight hypothermia (rectal temperature in the 2,000 mg/kg group was never more than 1^0C below that of the control group). Of the 6 FEP peaks measured (P1, N1, P2, N2, P3, N3) only N3 was significantly affected (peak amplitude reduced at all dose levels).
	0, 125 or 250 mg/kg	The animals were tested 45 mins after treatment. Only FEP peak N3 was measured. The peak amplitude was reduced significantly to 53% of control at 250 mg/kg (non significantly to 73% at 125 mg/kg).
	0 or 500 mg/kg	The animals were tested 0.75, 1.5, 3 or 6 hours after treatment. Peak amplitude of FEP peak N3 was reduced significantly at all test times. There was little significant change in the magnitude of the

Table 1: ACUTE TOXICITY OF XYLENES TO ANIMALS
Table 1.2 Oral Studies

Species	Concentration/dose/ duration	Observations
		reduction throughout this period.
		In this study the peak amplitude of FEP peak P2 was significantly increased (with little change in magnitude) throughout the period.
d) 16 males per group	0 or 500 mg/kg	The animals were tested 4, 8, 16 or 30 hours after treatment.
		In this study peak amplitude of FEP peak N3 was depressed 8 hours after treatment. By 16 hours after treatment recovery appeared to be complete.
		Thus in these studies xylene has been shown to reversibly alter the processing of visual information. The authors suggest that this may be secondary to changes in arousal or excitability.
Xylene		
Rat (102) F 344/N a) 5 males/group	0, 500, 1000, 2000, 4000 or 6000 mg/kg in corn oil, by gavage.	An acute toxicity study. a) LD_{50} 3523 mg/kg. 95% confidence limits 2707-4587 mg/kg.
b) 5 females/group	Xylene used was; 9.1% o-xylene 60.2% m-xylene 13.6% p-xylene 17.0% ethylbenzene.	b) All survived at doses up to and including 4000 mg/kg. All died at 6000 mg/kg. All deaths occurred within 48 h of dosing. Signs reported in both sexes in the top two dose groups were lack of co-ordination, prostration, loss of hind leg movement and hunched posture which were seen within 24 h. No clinical signs seen in survivors at end of week 1.
Rat (103) Wistar 20 males	4300 mg/kg. Xylene used was; 19% o-xylene 52% m-xylene 24% p-xylene.	LD_{50} value. No confidence limits given.
Rat (100) CFY Sex and numbers not given	5846 mg/kg. Xylene used was; 34% o-xylene 33% m-xylene 33% p-xylene.	LD_{50} value. 95% confidence limits 5142-6638 mg/kg. The LD_{50} was reported to be higher than that predicted from the toxicity of the individual isomers.

Table 1: ACUTE TOXICITY OF XYLENES TO ANIMALS
Table 1.2 Oral Studies

Species	Concentration/dose/duration	Observations
Rat (92) Long-Evans 6 males/group	8700 mg/kg. Xylene undefined.	LD_{50} value. 95% confidence limits 6500-11 600 mg/kg. Most deaths occurred within the first 72 h after dosing.
Rat (104) Wistar-CFT 6 females/group	0, 3400, 4250, 5100, 5950, 6800, 8500 or 10 200 mg/kg by gavage. Xylene undefined.	Minimum Lethal Dose 5950 mg/kg LD_{90} 9987 mg/kg. There were no deaths up to 5100 mg/kg, but 5950 mg/kg produced 67% mortality within 168 h. At higher doses mortality was dose-dependent, maximum mortality occurring within 72 h. At fatal doses sluggishness appeared within 4-6 h, followed by dullness, stupor, narcosis and coma. At histology the only findings were congestion of cells in liver, kidney and spleen.
Mouse (102) B6C3F$_1$ a) 5 males/group b) 5 females/group	a) 5627 mg/kg. b) 5251 mg/kg. In corn oil, by gavage. Xylene used was; 9.1% o-xylene 60.2% m-xylene 14.6% p-xylene 17.0% ethylbenzene.	An acute toxicity study. a) LD_{50} value. 95% confidence limits 4765-6646 mg/kg. b) LD_{50} value. 95% confidence limits 4583-6014 mg/kg. Deaths occurred within 32 h of dosing. Signs reported in both sexes were tremors, prostration and/or slowed breathing at 4000 or 6000 mg/kg within 48 h.

Table 1: ACUTE TOXICITY OF XYLENES TO ANIMALS
Table 1.3: Dermal Studies

Species	Concentration/dose/ duration	Observations
***o*-Xylene**		
Rabbit (105) New Zealand White 1 or 2 animals/group Sex not given	>20 000 mg/kg. 24 h exposure, under a sleeve.	LD_{50} value. Marked irritant effects were reported. No deaths reported. Narcosis evident but diminishing at 24 h.
***m*-Xylene**		
Rabbit (101) New Zealand White 4 males/group	12 180 mg/kg. 24 h exposure, under a sleeve.	LD_{50} value.
Xylene		
Rabbit (92) New Zealand White 3 males/group	A range of concentrations (not stated) up to 4350 mg/kg, under occlusion, for 4 h. Xylene undefined.	Acute dermal study. At 4350 mg/kg there was one death on day 5. Survivors showed discomfort and prostration during observation. No deaths at 1700 mg/kg.

Table 1: ACUTE TOXICITY OF XYLENES TO ANIMALS
Table 1.4: Parenteral Studies

Species	Concentration/dose/ duration	Observations
INTRAVENOUS		
o-Xylene		
Rat (110) Sprague-Dawley 6 females/group	5.3 mg/kg/min, as a continuous intravenous infusion, dissolved in 'Intralipid', for 60 min.	A study of the effect on the vestibulo-oculomotor reflex. *o*-Xylene increased the duration of post rotatory nystagmus. The threshold for this effect was at a blood level of 170 ppm, at which no signs of general toxicity were reported.
m-Xylene		
Rat (110) Sprague-Dawley 10 females/group	6.4 mg/kg/min, as a continuous intravenous infusion, dissolved in 'Intralipid', for 60 min.	A study of the effect on the vestibulo-oculomotor reflex. *m*-Xylene increased the duration of post rotatory nystagmus. The threshold for this effect was at a blood level of 200 ppm at which no signs of general toxicity were reported.
Rabbit(111, 112, 113, 114, 115, 116, 117) Strain, sex and numbers not given	2.2 to 12.0 mg/kg min as a continuous i.v. infusion, dissolved in 'Intralipid'.	Studies of the effect on the vestibulo-oculomotor system. Some animals died at a blood concentration of 100 µg/ml, showing signs of respiratory distress. A positional nystagmus, in lateral positions, was shown in all animals at 30 µg/ml, the no effect level being 10 ppm. There was some evidence of a biphasic nystagmus response. There was an exaggerated nystagmus response to rotation and an increased duration of post rotatory nystagmus. Both the positional and rotatory nystagmus were dose-dependent. There was an increased opticokinetic fusion limit. No findings on spontaneous nystagmus were reported.

Species	Concentration/dose/duration	Observations
		The authors suggest that the positional nystagmus effects may have been due to blockage of the inhibitory action of the cerebellum, on the vestibulo-oculomotor pathways.
Dog (34) Mongrel 5 animals/group Sex not given	0 or 50 mg/kg was injected into the femoral vein of pentobarbital anaesthetised animals.	A study of the effect on the liver. There was no significant effect on bile secretion. There was a marked increase in serum aspartate aminotransferase (AST) activity, and a slight increase in serum alanine aminotransferase (ALT) activity.
Dog (290) Mongrel 5 animals/group Sex not given	0 or 50 mg/kg was injected into the femoral vein of pentobarbital anaesthetised animals.	Study of the effect on superoxide dismutase (SOD) activity in the erythrocytes and various organs. There were no significant changes in SOD activity in the erythrocytes, heart, lungs, liver, kidneys, spleen, cerebrum, cerebellum, muscle, intraperitoneal fat, small intestine or pancreas.

***p*-Xylene**

Species	Concentration/dose/duration	Observations
Rat (110) Sprague-Dawley 7 females/group	5.3 mg/kg/min, as a continuous intravenous infusion, dissolved in 'Intralipid', for 60 min.	A study of the effect on the vestibulo-oculomotor reflex. *p*-Xylene increased the duration of post rotatory nystagmus. The threshold for this effect was at a blood level of 170 ppm, at which no signs of general toxicity were reported.

Xylene

Species	Concentration/dose/duration	Observations
Rabbit (291) 10 animals Strain and sex not given	130 mg/kg. Xylene undefined.	9 animals died. The signs of toxicity were not given. However death was reported to be rapid.
Rabbit (292) Strain, sex and numbers not given	ca 260 or 410 mg/kg.	At 260 mg/kg death occurred after 20 min with haemolysis. At 410 mg/kg death occurred within 3 min with very severe haemolysis.

Table 1: ACUTE TOXICITY OF XYLENES TO ANIMALS
Table 1.4: Parenteral Studies

Species	Concentration/dose/ duration	Observations
INTRAPERITONEAL		
o-Xylene		
Rat (29) Wistar 4 males/group		Study to determine the effect on hepatic glutathione levels.
	a) 0 or 425 mg/kg in 0.5 ml arachis oil. 3 h after dosing, rats were killed and liver glutathione assayed.	a) Treatment with *o*-xylene led to a decrease in liver glutathione (2.0± 0.2, cf 7.6 ± 0.3 µmol/g liver control).
	b) 0, 50, 160, 425 or 850 mg/kg (approximately) in 0.5 ml arachis oil. 3 h after dosing, rats were killed and liver glutathione assayed.	b) A dose-dependent decrease in liver glutathione levels was observed with almost maximal depletion reported after 425 mg/kg.
		24 h after administration of the highest dose, the liver glutathione had returned to the normal range.
Rat (119) Sprague-Dawley 8 males/group	0 or 531 mg/kg, in corn oil.	A study of the effect on pulmonary and hepatic cytochrome P-450.
		There was no effect on liver and lung weights.
		There was a significant decrease in the P-450 concentration in the lung. There was no significant effect on the P-450 concentration in the liver.
		There was no significant effect on aryl hydrocarbon hydroxylase activity in the liver or lung.
		There was a significant increase in liver 7-ethoxycoumarin O-deethylase activity, and a significant decrease in the lung activity. There was a significant increase in liver 7-ethoxyresorufin O-deethylase activity, and a marked increase in the lung activity.
		There was no significant effect on cytochrome b_5 or NADPH-cytochrome c reductase in the liver or lung.
		The destruction of pulmonary cytochrome P-450 was a common effect elicited by a number of aromatic hydrocarbons.

Table 1: ACUTE TOXICITY OF XYLENES TO ANIMALS
Table 1.4: Parenteral Studies

Species	Concentration/dose/ duration	Observations
Mouse (109) NMRI 6 males/group	1364 ± 3 mg/kg.	LD_{50} value.
m-Xylene		A study of acute behavioural effects.
Rat (106) CFY 10 males/group	a) 2236 mg/kg.	a) LD_{50} value. 95% confidence limits 2003-2494 mg/kg.
	b) At least 5 dose levels between approximately 150 and 2100 mg/kg.	b) There was a significant, dose-dependent, decrease in activity in both open field ambulation and rearing. The minimum effective doses were 892 and 393 mg/kg respectively.

There were significant, dose-dependent changes in the response to the tilted plane and tube test. The minimum effective doses were 265 and 892 mg/kg respectively. There was no significant effect on wheel running activity.

The authors ascribed these findings to the predominantly CNS depressant action of m-xylene. |
| **Rat** (29) Wistar 4 males/group | 0 or 425 mg/kg in 0.5 ml arachis oil. 3 h after dosing, rats were killed and liver glutathione assayed. | Study to determine the effect on hepatic glutathione levels.

Treatment with m-xylene led to a decrease in liver glutathione (4.3 ± 0.2, cf 7.6 ± 0.3 µmol/g liver control) |

Table 1: ACUTE TOXICITY OF XYLENES TO ANIMALS
Table 1.4: Parenteral Studies

Species	Concentration/dose/ duration	Observations
Rat (119) Sprague-Dawley 8 males/group	0 or 531 mg/kg, in corn oil.	A study of the effect on pulmonary and hepatic cytochrome P-450. There was no effect on liver and lung weights. There was a significant decrease in the P-450 concentration in the lung. There was no significant effect on the P-450 concentration in the liver. There was a significant increase in liver and lung aryl hydrocarbon hydroxylase activity. There was a significant increase in liver 7-ethoxycoumarin O-deethylase activity, and a slight decrease in the lung activity. There was a significant increase in liver and lung 7-ethoxyresorufin O-deethylase activity. There was no significant effect on cytochrome b_5 and NADPH - cytochrome c reductase activity in the liver or lung. The destruction of pulmonary cytochrome P-450 was a common effect elicited by a number of aromatic hydrocarbons.
Mouse (109) NMRI 6 males/group	1731 ± 9 mg/kg.	LD_{50} value.
Mouse (293) Swiss (Cr 1:CD-1) Male Numbers not given	0, 200, 300 or 400 mg/kg, in polyoxyethylated vegetable oil, prior to subcutaneous injection of 200 mg/kg pentylenetetrazol.	Study of the effect on pentylenetetrazol induced convulsions. m-Xylene gave a dose-dependent, significant prolongation of the time to onset of convulsions. The ED_{50} for prevention of tonic extension was 394.1 mg/kg (confidence limits 338.5 - 458.9 mg/kg).

Table 1: ACUTE TOXICITY OF XYLENES TO ANIMALS
Table 1.4: Parenteral Studies

Species	Concentration/dose/ duration	Observations
p-Xylene		
Rat (51, 87)		A study of the effect of inducers on acute toxicity.
Sprague-Dawley Female Numbers not given	3280 mg/kg.	LD_{50} value. 95% confidence limits 2880-3680 mg/kg.
	Some of the animals were pretreated, i.p., as follows:	Pretreatment with 3-methylcholanthrene increased the LD_{50} (26%) whereas both other inducers gave marginal decreases (<5%).
	a) 75 mg/kg phenobarbital.	
	b) 15 mg/kg chlorpromazine.	
	c) 20 mg/kg 3-methylcholanthrene.	
	for 3 d prior to exposure.	
Rat (29) Wistar 4 males/group	0 or 425 mg/kg in 0.5 ml arachis oil. 3 h after dosing, rats were killed and liver glutathione assayed.	Study to determine the effect on hepatic glutathione levels. Treatment with p-xylene led to a decrease in liver glutathione (4.6 ± 0.1, cf 7.6 ± 0.3, µmol/g liver control).
Rat (91, 294) Sprague-Dawley 4 females/group	0 or 1000 mg/kg. Some of the animals were pretreated as follows: a) 3 d prior exposure to drinking water containing 1 mg/ml sodium phenobarbital. b) 2 h prior to study, a single, i.p. dose of the alcohol dehydrogenase inhibitor pyrazole (180 mg/kg).	Study of the effect on hepatic alcohol and aldehyde dehydrogenase activities. There was no effect on alcohol or aldehyde dehydrogenase activities in the hepatic cytosol, due to p-xylene alone. a) Phenobarbital significantly increased aldehyde dehydrogenase activity to similar levels in both the presence and absence of p-xylene. There was no effect on alcohol dehydrogenase activity. b) Pyrazole significantly decreased alcohol dehydrogenase activity to similar levels in both the presence and absence of p-xylene. There was no effect on aldehyde dehydrogenase activity.

Table 1: ACUTE TOXICITY OF XYLENES TO ANIMALS
Table 1.4: Parenteral Studies

Species	Concentration/dose/duration	Observations
Rat (119) Sprague-Dawley 8 males/group	0 or 531 mg/kg, in corn oil.	A study of the effect on pulmonary and hepatic cytochrome P-450. There was no effect on liver and lung weight. There was a significant decrease in the P-450 concentration in the lung. There was no significant effect on the P-450 concentration in the liver. There was a slight increase in liver and lung aryl hydrocarbon hydroxylase activity. There was a significant increase in liver 7-ethoxycoumarin O-deethylase activity, and a decrease in the lung activity. There was a significant increase in liver and lung 7-ethoxyresorufin O-deethylase activity. There was no significant effect on cytochrome b_5 and NADPH - cytochrome c reductase activity in the liver or lung. The destruction of pulmonary cytochrome P-450 was a common effect elicited by a number of aromatic hydrocarbons.
Rat (236) Sprague -Dawley Male Numbers not given	0,1000 mg/kg in soybean oil, with sacrifice at 1 hour.	A study of the effect of p - xylene on lung microsomes. (Microsomal metabolism of benzo-[a]-pyrene). p-Xylene caused an inhibition of *in vitro* benzo-[a]-pyrene metabolism to 3-hydroxy benzo-[a]-pyrene. Aryl hydrocarbon hydroxylase activity was decreased by approximately 40%. The concentration of pulmonary cytochrome P450 was reduced to below the limit of detection and total phospholipid and phosphatidylcholine were decreased 28% and 17%. Membrane fluidity was slightly decreased (5%) in the microsomes.

Species	Concentration/dose/ duration	Observations
Rat (295, 296) Sprague-Dawley Male		Study of the effect of *p*-xylene on the lung metabolism of benzo-(a)-pyrene, (B(a)P).
a) Numbers not given	a) 0 or 1000 mg/kg Sacrifice at 24 h.	a) The P-450 content of lung microsomes was significantly reduced together with aryl hydrocarbon hydroxylase (AHH) activity (41%). There was no effect on P-450 content of liver microsomes. There was a significant decrease in the formation of 3-OH B(a)P (32%) and of B(a)P-4,5-diol (50%), as well as a marked decrease in 9-OH B(a)P formation (27%). There was no effect on the formation of B(a)P-7,8-diol, B(a)P-9,10-diol or quinone formation. The B(a)P-9,10-diol/3-OH B(a)P ratio was significantly increased, the B(a)P-7, 8-diol/3-OH B(a)P ratio was significantly increased, and the B(a)P-4,5-diol/3-OH B(a)P ratio was significantly decreased.
b) 7 animals/group	b) 0 or 1000 mg/kg Sacrifice at 15 min, 30 min, 1 h or 4 h.	b) The formation of 3-OH B(a)P was significantly reduced at all time points (27-43%)
c) 6 animals/group	c) 0, 100, 500 or 1000 mg/kg. Sacrifice at 1 h.	c) There was no change in 3-OH B(a)P formation at the 100 mg/kg level. However at 500 and 1000 mg/kg there was a significant, dose-dependent inhibition (27 and 46% respectively).
d) 7 animals/group	d) 0 or 1000 mg/kg, with or without ethanol (5 g/kg, oral). Sacrifice at 1 h. *p*-Xylene in soyabean 5 g/kg oil (1:1).	d) Ethanol had no effect on AHH activity, and in combination with xylene decreased the magnitude of the inhibition due to *p*-xylene alone (25 and 42% respectively). This study indicates that *p*-xylene causes a dose-dependent inhibition in the lung microsomal metabolism of B(a)P. This effect occurs rapidly and persists for at least 24 h. It is suggested that this effect is due to P-450 destruction by the *p*-tolualdehyde metabolite, ethanol decreasing the effect by competitive inhibition of alcohol dehydrogenase. It is suggested that inhibition of 3-OH B(a)P formation may shift the metabolic profile towards toxicification.
Mouse (109) NMRI 6 males/group	2109 ± 174 mg/kg.	LD_{50} value.

Table 1: ACUTE TOXICITY OF XYLENES TO ANIMALS
Table 1.4: Parenteral Studies

Species	Concentration/dose/ duration	Observations
Xylene		
Rat (99, 108) Sprague-Dawley Female		A study to determine LD_{50} values and the relative hepatotoxicity of some organic solvents using sorbitol dehydrogenase (SDH) activity.
a) 6 per group	a) A geometric range of concentrations. 24 h and 14 d observations.	a) 24 h, LD_{50} = 2608 mg/kg. No fractional mortality was observed and so no confidence limits. Doses closest to LD_{50} were 1944 and 3499 mg/kg. 14 d, LD_{50} = 2459 mg/kg. 95% confidence limits 2136-2832 mg/kg.
b) 5 per group	b) 326 or 652 mg/kg. A group was then sacrificed at 3 h intervals from 3 to 36 h after injection.	b) Dose related increases in SDH activity were reported, with maximal activity occurring at 18 h after administration.
c) 6 per group	c) 0, 81.5, 163 or 326 mg/kg. Animals sacrificed 18 h after injection. a)/b)/c) Xylene diluted in peanut oil to give final volume of 0.1 to 1 ml.	c) There was no significant increase in SDH activity.
d) 6 per group	d) 652 mg/kg, undiluted, 10% or 20% solution in peanut oil. Animals sacrificed 18 h after injection. Xylene undefined.	d) The increase in SDH activity was significantly reduced on dilution to 10% in peanut oil.

Table 1: ACUTE TOXICITY OF XYLENES TO ANIMALS
Table 1.4: Parenteral Studies

Species	Concentration/dose/duration	Observations
Rat (107) Sprague-Dawley Female Numbers not given		An acute study, using serum sorbitol dehydrogenase (SDH) and aspartate aminotransferase (AST) activities as markers for liver damage.
	a) 2608 mg/kg.	a) LD_{50} (24 h) value. 95% confidence limits 1944-3499 mg/kg.
	b) 2459 mg/kg.	b) LD_{50} (14 d) value. 95% confidence limits 2136-2832 mg/kg.
	c) 0,81.5, 163 or 326 mg/kg. Animals sacrificed 18 h after injection. Xylene undefined.	c) There was no effect on enzyme activities.
Rat (144) Strain, sex and numbers not given	Single dose. Dose range not stated. Xylene undefined.	Early toxicity study. At doses up to 653 mg/kg no effects were seen except slight apathy. At higher doses, deranged equilibrium and weakness, culminating in loss of power of movement and finally complete narcosis, with a fall in body temperature was reported. The lethal dose was 1740 - 2175 mg/kg.
Rat (287) CFY 5 males/group	a) 2 x 435 mg/kg b) 2 x 870 mg/kg c) 1740 mg/kg d) 3480 mg/kg. With 20 min interval between repeat doses. Controls received saline, 2 x 4000 mg/kg. All animals anaesthetised with pentobarbital (40 mg/kg, i.p.) before treatment. Xylene undefined.	Study to observe the effects on ECG pattern. Most animals died within a few hours of the administration of 1740 mg/kg. There were no observed changes in ECG at any dose level.

Table 1: ACUTE TOXICITY OF XYLENES TO ANIMALS

Table 1.4: Parenteral Studies

Species	Concentration/dose/ duration	Observations
Mouse (94) Approximately 100/ group Strain and sex not given	1610 mg/kg. Xylene undefined.	LD_{50} value. 95% confidence limits 1559-1679 mg/kg. The LD_{50} for a toluene/xylene mixture (2:1) 1357 mg/kg. 95% confidence limits 1287-1436 mg/kg.
Guinea Pig (297) 6 animals/group Sex and strain not given	0, 350 or 520 mg/kg. Electrical stimulation was applied to the zone of motor projection for flexion of the contralateral forelimb. Injections were administered and then a series of threshold determinations were performed with time. Xylene undefined.	Study to determine the effect on the cortical motor stimulus thresholds. After the injection the animals exhibited a typical posture, consisting of declined head, arched back, increased tonus of front limbs with impaired locomotion. Later, slight to average narcosis was observed (lateral position with declined head, corneal reflex positive). Still later, clonic muscle twitching and tremor were seen in some animals. At both 350 and 520 mg/kg there was a significant, dose-dependent initial elevation of threshold values which appeared to return to normal by about 2 h in all but one animal. The action of xylene on the CNS initially manifested as narcosis which then proceeded to a phase of elevated excitability characterized by behavioural changes (tremor, muscle twitching).
Guinea pig (118) 4 males/group Strain not given	0, 1000 or 2000 mg/kg. Xylene undefined.	Study to assess the hepatotoxic effects of solvents, using serum activity of ornithine carbamyl transferase (OCT) at 24 h. At 1000 mg/kg there were no deaths reported. At 2000 mg/kg 3 animals died. At 1000 mg/kg and 2000 mg/kg some accumulation of lipid was reported (Oil Red O Stain). No necrosis was seen. At both 1000 mg/kg and 2000 mg/kg (surviving animal) increased serum OCT activity was reported (18.4 i.u., 25.2 i.u. respectively, cf control value 2.02 ± 1.61 i.u.). Thus evidence was presented of hepatotoxic effects at 1000 mg/kg.

65

Table 1: ACUTE TOXICITY OF XYLENES TO ANIMALS
Table 1.4: Parenteral Studies

Species	Concentration/dose/ duration	Observations
SUBCUTANEOUS		
o-Xylene		
Rat (298) Strain, sex and numbers not given	0 or 4350 mg/kg.	A blue discolouration of the tissues and/or urine was reported for a number of 'chromogenic' hydrocarbons, including *o*-xylene.

Subsequent work has shown that for one chemical the chromogenic properties are linked to neurotoxicity.

The significance of these findings with respect to *o*-xylene is unclear. |
| **Rabbit** (85) Strain, sex and numbers not given | Single dose. Dose range not stated. | Lethal dose was between 2200-4400 mg/kg.

Necropsy of dead animals revealed no macroscopic or microscopic organ lesions. However a limited range of tissues was examined. |
| *m*-Xylene | | |
| **Mouse** (299) Velaz Albino 16 females/group | 0 or 360 mg/kg in an emulsion, given 2 h prior to a subcutanous injection of acrylonitrile (60 mg/kg). | Study to determine the effect of *m*-xylene on the acute toxicity of acrylonitrile.

8 deaths in co-exposed animals within 2 h and 3 more deaths within 2 d.

m-Xylene significantly potentiated acrylonitrile toxicity compared to controls (no deaths).

It was claimed that this effect was due to enhanced acrylonitrile absorption. |
| **Rabbit** (85) Strain, sex and numbers not given | Single dose. Dose range not stated. | Lethal dose was between 4400-8700 mg/kg.

Necropsy of dead animals revealed no macroscopic or microscopic organ lesions. However a limited range of tissues was examined. |

Table 1: ACUTE TOXICITY OF XYLENES TO ANIMALS
Table 1.4: Parenteral Studies

Species	Concentration/dose/ duration	Observations
_p_-Xylene		
Rabbit (85) Strain, sex and numbers not given	Single dose. Dose range not stated.	Lethal dose was between 4400-8700 mg/kg. Necropsy of dead animals revealed no macroscopic or microscopic organ lesions. However a limited range of tissues was examined.
INTRAMUSCULAR		
_p_-Xylene		
Rabbit (156) 1 or 2 males/group Strain not given	2580 mg/kg, with sacrifice at 1, 3 and 7 d.	Study of the effects on the pathology of a limited number of organs. No deaths were reported. Some congestion and/or infiltration of polymorphonuclear leukocytes was seen in the liver, kidneys, lungs and spleen. After 7 days slight haemosiderosis was noted in the splenic pulp. The presence of schistocytes was noted in the seminal glands as well as a decrease in spermatogenesis. Evidence of an acute inflammatory response and increased reticulocyte turnover was seen in the bone marrow, and a local inflammatory reaction was seen at the site of injection. No definite conclusions may be drawn from this study since full details were not presented.
INTRAOCULAR		
_p_-Xylene		
Rat (300) CFY Sex and numbers not given	0.11, 0.21 or 0.42 mg/kg injected into the anterior chamber of the right eye.	Study of the effect on the sympathetic, adrenergic nerve plexus of the eye. 0.42 mg/kg induced significant hyperinnervation.

Table 1: ACUTE TOXICITY OF XYLENES TO ANIMALS
Table 1.5: *In Vitro* Studies

Species	Concentration/dose/ duration	Observations
o-Xylene		
Rat (120) Sprague-Dawley Male Numbers not given	At least seven concentrations between 1.062 and 10 620 mg/ml.	An *in vitro* study of the effect of o-xylene on the activity of rat liver microsomal aryl hydrocarbon hydroxylase (AHH) and 7-ethoxycoumarin O-deethylase (ECD). o-Xylene caused an inhibition of both enzyme activities with an IC_{50} of 660 and 117 mg/ml for AHH and ECD respectively. Evidence of an inverse correlation was reported between inhibition and water solubility, for a series of structurally related aromatic compounds.
Rat (122) Strain, sex and numbers not given	Concentration range not given.	Study to determine the potency of organic solvents in protecting erythrocytes undergoing hypotonic haemolysis. The antihaemolytic ED_{50} was 0.029 mg/ml. The antihaemolytic ED_{100} was 0.096 mg/ml. For a range of organic solvents the antihaemolytic potency correlated with the iso-octane: water partition co-efficient. The antihaemolytic effect was associated with an increase in the critical cell volume.
Rat (123) Strain, sex and numbers not given	87 mg was added to 2 ml of oxalated rat blood.	This, briefly reported, study examined hydrocarbons as stromatolytic agents. o-Xylene was a potent agent compared to other alkyl and alkenylbenzenes.
Mouse (301) NMRI Sex and numbers not given	0 or approximately 0.1 mg/ml.	Study on the effect of solvents on adrenergic transmitter mechanisms *in vitro*. The mechanical response of the mouse vas deferens, to electric stimulation, was increased to $173 \pm 23\%$ of controls. This effect was given by a variety of structurally unrelated organic solvents.

Table 1: ACUTE TOXICITY OF XYLENES TO ANIMALS
Table 1.5: *In Vitro* Studies

Species	Concentration/dose/duration	Observations

m-Xylene

Species	Concentration/dose/duration	Observations
Rat (120) Sprague-Dawley Male Numbers not given	At least seven concentrations between 1.062 and 10 620 mg/ml.	An *in vitro* study of the effect of *m*-xylene on the activity of rat liver microsomal aryl hydrocarbon hydroxylase (AHH) and 7-ethoxycoumarin O-deethylase (ECD). *m*-Xylene caused an inhibition of both enzyme activities with an IC_{50} of 637 and 96 mg/ml for AHH and ECD respectively. Evidence of an inverse correlation was reported between inhibition and water solubility, for a series of structurally related aromatic compounds.
Rat (122) Strain, sex and numbers not given	Concentration range not stated.	Study to determine the potency of organic solvents in protecting erythrocytes undergoing hypotonic haemolysis. The antihaemolytic ED_{50} was 0.039 mg/ml. The antihaemolytic ED_{100} was 0.086 mg/ml. For a range of organic solvents the antihaemolytic potency correlated with the iso-octane: water partition co-efficient. The antihaemolytic effect was associated with an increase in the critical cell volume.

p-Xylene

Species	Concentration/dose/duration	Observations
Rat (120) Sprague-Dawley Male Numbers not given	At least seven concentrations between 1.062 and 10 620 mg/ml.	An *in vitro* study of the effect of *p*-xylene on the activity of rat liver microsomal aryl hydrocarbon hydroxylase (AHH) and 7-ethoxycoumarin O-deethylase (ECD). *p*-Xylene caused an inhibition of both enzyme activities with an IC_{50} of 616 and 117 mg/ml for AHH and ECD respectively. Evidence of an inverse correlation was reported between inhibition and water solubility, for a series of structurally related aromatic compounds.
Rat (122) Strain, sex and numbers not given	Concentration range not stated.	Study to determine the potency of organic solvents in protecting erythrocytes undergoing hypotonic haemolysis. The antihaemoloytic ED_{50} was 0.044 mg/ml. The antihaemoloytic ED_{100} was 0.107 mg/ml.

Table 1: ACUTE TOXICITY OF XYLENES TO ANIMALS
Table 1.5: *In Vitro* Studies

Species	Concentration/dose/ duration	Observations
		For a range of organic solvents the antihaemolytic potency correlated with the iso-octane: water partition co-efficient.
		The antihaemoloytic effect was associated with an increase in the critical cell volume.
Xylene		
Rat (302) Wistar Males Numbers not given	0 or 500 ppm for 18 h. Xylene undefined.	Study to observe the effect of organic solvents on Ca^{2+} uptake into brain synaptosomes.
		Xylene exposure stimulated $^{45}Ca^{2+}$ uptake by potassium stimulated synaptosomes.
		Similar effects were seen with toluene. However the relevance of these findings is not clear.
Rat (303) Strain, sex and numbers not given	Concentration range not given. Xylene undefined.	Study, reported as a summary, to observe toxicity to alveolar macrophages *in vitro*.
		O_2 consumption of macrophages, stimulated by zymosan particles, could be decreased approximately 70% (ED_{50} = 9.9 mM).
		O_2^- release could be completely blocked (ED_{50} = 6.2 mM). Only slight cell leakiness was observed (87% cells exclude trypan blue).
		Xylene observed to inhibit both O_2 uptake and O_2^- release, and thus suggested to diminish the antibacterial activity of these cells.

70

Table 2: SUB-ACUTE TOXICITY OF XYLENES TO ANIMALS
Table 2.1: Inhalation Studies

Species	Concentration/dose/ duration	Observations
o-Xylene		
Rat (134) Sprague-Dawley or Long-Evans 15 animals/group Males and females	a) 0 or 780 ppm, 8 h/d, 5 d/week for 6 weeks.	Study to determine the effect of repeated inhalation exposure. a) 2 deaths on day 3 and another death on day 7. There was no effect on body weight gain. There was no effect on leukocyte count, haemoglobin level or haematocrit. Histopathological examination of the liver, kidney, heart, spleen and lung revealed no effects.
	b) 0 or 78 ppm continuously for 90 d.	b) 1 death on day 56. There was no effect on body weight gain. There was no effect on leukocyte count, haemoglobin level or haematocrit. Histopathological examination of the liver, kidney, heart, spleen and lung revealed no effects. Study reported in limited detail only.
Rat (135) Sprague-Dawley 6 males/group	0 or 2000 ppm, 6 h/d for 3 d. Animals killed 16-18 h after final exposure.	Study of the effect on levels of noradrenaline and dopamine in various parts of the forebrain and hypothalamus. No clinical signs of toxicity were noted. There was a significant increase in catecholamine levels in various parts of the hypothalamus (subependymal layer of the median eminence, the anterior periventricular hypothalamic region and the parvocellular part of the paraventricular hypothalamic nucleus). There was also a significant increase in catecholamine turnover in various parts of the hypothalamus (subependymal layer, the lateral and medial palisade zones of the median eminence and the parvocellular part of the paraventricular hypothalamic nucleus).

Species	Concentration/dose/duration	Observations
		There was no effect on dopamine levels in the forebrain.
		There was a significant decrease in dopamine turnover in various parts of the forebrain (marginal zone and medial part of the nucleus caudatus, the anterior and posterior nucleus accumbens and the medial posterior tuberculum olfactorium).
		There was a significant decrease in serum prolactin levels. There was no effect on serum levels of growth hormone, thyroid-stimulating hormone, corticosterone or follicle-stimulating hormone.
Rat (136) CFY Females Number not given	0 or 3500 ppm, 8 h/d, for 4 weeks. Some animals were also exposed to ethanol.	Study of the effect of ethanol on o-xylene hepatotoxicity. There was a significant rise in relative liver weight, a slight proliferation of smooth endoplasmic reticulum, increased cytochrome P-450 and b_5 concentrations, increased aniline hydroxylase and aminopyrine N-demethylase activities, as well as increased numbers of peroxisomes. Coexposure to ethanol was reported to give an additive induction effect. However there was no effect on the hepatotoxicity of ethanol. Reported in summary form only.
Rat (133) CFY 30 males/group	0 or 3500 ppm, 8 h/d, for; a) 1 week	Study of the effect on the liver. The final body weight was significantly decreased and there was a marked increase in water consumption. There was no effect on food consumption. There was a significant increase in relative liver weight, but no effect on absolute liver weight. No treatment related macroscopic or microscopic hepatic lesions were noted at necropsy. Only slight changes were noted in enzyme histochemical studies. Electron microscope studies revealed that the intracellular levels of peroxisomes were significantly increased and intracellular glycogen significantly decreased.

Table 2: SUB-ACUTE TOXICITY OF XYLENES TO ANIMALS
Table 2.1: Inhalation Studies

Species	Concentration/dose/duration	Observations
		There was no effect on the amount of rough or smooth endoplasmic reticulum or mitotic index.
	b) 6 weeks.	The final body weight was significantly decreased and there was a marked increase in both food and water consumption.
		There was a significant increase in both absolute and relative liver weight.
		No treatment related macroscopic or microscopic hepatic lesions were noted at necropsy.
		Only slight changes were noted in enzyme histochemical studies.
		Electron microscope studies revealed a significant decrease in the number of cells per unit area, as well as significant increases in the nuclear volume and the amount of rough endoplasmic reticulum. There was no effect on the amount of smooth endoplasmic reticulum, peroxisomes, or glycogen or on mitotic index.
Rat (138) Sprague-Dawley 4 males/group	0 or 2000 ppm, 6 h/d for 3 d.	Study of the effect on cytochrome P-450 and enzyme activities in the liver, kidney and lung.
		There were significant increases in relative liver weight, cytochrome P-450 content (with particular increases in two forms), NADPH-cytochrome c reductase activity and 7-ethoxyresorufin 0-deethylase activity.
		There were significant increases in the hepatic hydroxylation of n-hexane.
		There were significant increases in the hepatic 6β and 7α-hydroxylation of 4-androstene-3,17-dione. There was no effect on 16-hydroxylation.
		There was a significant increase in the hepatic formation of benzo(a)pyrene [B(a)p] 4,5 - dihydrodiol. There was no effect on the formation of B(a)P-7,8-diol, B(a)P-9,10-diol, phenols, or quinones.
		There were significant increases in the relative kidney weight, cytochrome P-450 content, 7-ethoxyresorufin 0-deethylase activity and the 1-hydroxylation of n-hexane. There was no effect on

73

Species	Concentration/dose/duration	Observations
		NADPH-cytochrome c reductase or on the 2 or 3-hydroxylation of n-hexane.
		There was a marked decrease in pulmonary cytochrome P-450 and a significant decrease in the hydroxylation of n-hexane. The authors claimed a small decrease in 7-ethoxyresorufin 0-deethylase activity.
		Increased enzyme activity in the liver (phenobarbital-type induction) and kidney, and decreased activity in the lung were observed.
Rat (137) Sprague-Dawley 4 males/group	0 or 2000 ppm, 6 h/d for 3 d.	Study of the effect on rat liver microsomal P-450.
		There was a significant increase in cytochrome P-450 levels, 7-ethoxyresorufin 0-deethylase activity and n-hexane hydroxylase activity, for 1, 2 and 3 hydroxylation. There was a significant increase in *in vitro* benzo(a)pyrene metabolism for B(a)P-4, 5-diol. Levels of B(a)P-9, 10-diol, B(a)P-7, 8-diol, phenols and quinones were also increased.
Rat (85) Wistar 10 animals Sex not given	1531 ppm, 8 h/d for 14 d.	No deaths occurred and no other results were reported.
Guinea Pig (134) Princeton derived 15 animals/group Males and females		Study to determine the effect of repeated inhalation exposure.
	a) 0 or 780 ppm, 8 h/d, 5 d/week for 6 weeks	a) No deaths reported.
		There was a marked decrease in body weight gain.
		There was no effect on leukocyte count, haemoglobin level or haematocrit.
		Histopathological examination of the liver, kidney, heart, spleen and lung revealed no effects.
	b) 0 or 78 ppm continuously for 90 d.	b) No deaths reported.
		There was no effect on body weight gain.
		There was no effect on leukocyte count, haemoglobin level or haematocrit.

Table 2: SUB-ACUTE TOXICITY OF XYLENES TO ANIMALS
Table 2.1: Inhalation Studies

Species	Concentration/dose/ duration	Observations
		Histopathological examination of the liver, kidney, heart, spleen and lung revealed no effects.
		Study reported in limited detail only.
Dog (134) Beagle 2 males/group		Study to determine the effects of repeated inhalation exposure.
	a) 0 or 780 ppm, 8 h/d, 5 d/week for 6 weeks	No deaths reported.
		One dog exhibited tremors of varying severity throughout the exposure period.
		There was no effect on body weight gain.
		There was no effect on leukocyte count, haemoglobin level or haematocrit.
		Histopathological examination of the brain, spinal cord, liver, kidney, heart, spleen and lung revealed no effects.
	b) 0 or 78 ppm continuously for 90 d.	No deaths reported.
		There was no effect on body weight gain.
		There was no effect on leukocyte count, haemoglobin level, or haematocrit.
		Histopathological examination of the brain, spinal cord, liver, kidney, heart, spleen and lung, revealed no effects.
		Study reported in limited detail only.
Monkey (134) (Squirrel Monkey) 3 males/group		Study to determine the effects of repeated inhalation exposure.
	a) 0 or 780 ppm, 8 h/d, 5 d/week for 6 weeks.	One death on day 7.
		There was no effect on body weight gain.
		Histopathological examination of the brain, spinal cord, liver, kidney, heart, spleen and lung revealed no effects.
	b) 0 or 78 ppm continuously for 90 d.	No deaths reported.
		There was no effect on body weight gain.
		Histopathological examination of the brain, spinal cord, liver, kidney, heart, spleen and lung revealed no effects.
		Study reported in limited detail only.

Table 2: SUB-ACUTE TOXICITY OF XYLENES TO ANIMALS
Table 2.1: Inhalation Studies

Species	Concentration/dose/ duration	Observations
m-Xylene		
Rat (135) Sprague-Dawley 6 males/group	0 or 2000 ppm, 6 h/d for 3 d. Animals killed 16-18 h after final exposure	Study of the effect on levels of noradrenaline and dopamine in various parts of the forebrain and hypothalamus. No clinical signs of toxicity were noted. There was a significant increase in catecholamine levels in various parts of the hypothalamus (subependymal layer, medial and lateral palisade zones of the median eminence, the nucleus dorsomedialis hypothalami, and the parvocellular and magnocellular parts of the paraventricular/ hypothalamic nucleus). There was also a significant increase in catecholamine turnover in various parts of the hypothalamus (subependymal layer, the medial and lateral palisade zones of the median eminence, the nucleus dorsomedialis hypothalami, and the parvocellulalar and magnocellular parts of the paraventricular hypothalamic nucleus). There was no effect on dopamine levels or turnover in the forebrain. There was a significant decrease in serum corticosterone levels. There was no effect on serum levels of thyroid-stimulating hormone, growth hormone, prolactin or follicle-stimulating hormone.
Rat (140) Wistar 8 males/group		Study of behavioural impairment using tests of motor activity and acoustic startle reflex.
	a) 0 or 300 ppm, 7 h/d for 4 d. Some animals were exposed to mixtures with ethylbenzene;	There was no effect on motor activity, startle reactivity or prepulse inhibition.
	i) 220 ppm m-xylene and 80 ppm ethylbenzene.	i) There was a slight increase in motor activity and a slight decrease in startle reactivity at 5 d. There was no effect on prepulse inhibition.
	ii) 150 or 300 ppm of both m-xylene and ethylbenzene. Testing was performed on the day prior to exposure, 3 h after the first	ii) There was a significant increase in motor activity and a significant decrease in startle reactivity at 5 d. There was no effect on prepulse inhibition.

Table 2: SUB-ACUTE TOXICITY OF XYLENES TO ANIMALS
Table 2.1: Inhalation Studies

Species	Concentration/dose/duration	Observations
	exposure, and 24 h after the last exposure.	
	b) 0 or 300 ppm, 7 h/d, 4 d/week for 16 weeks. Some animals were exposed to a mixture with ethylbenzene;	There was a significant impairment in the inhibitory impact of an acoustic prepulse to the startle reflex at week 16. There was no effect on motor activity or startle reactivity.
	i) 220 ppm *m*-xylene and 80 ppm ethylbenzene	i) No effects were noted.
	Testing was performed prior to exposure, then at weeks 4, 8, 12 and 16, at 48-72 h from the last exposure day of the month.	There was some evidence of CNS dysfunction presenting following exposure to *m*-xylene alone. Combined exposure with ethylbenzene gave a different pattern of effects.
Rat (138) Sprague-Dawley 4 males/group	0 or 2000 ppm, 6 h/d for 3 d.	Study of the effects on cytochrome P-450 and enzyme activities in the liver, kidney and lung. There were significant increases in relative liver weight, cytochrome P-450 content (with particular increases in two forms), NADPH-cytochrome c reductase activity and 7-ethoxyresorufin O-deethylase activity. There were significant increases in the hepatic 2 and 3-hydroxylation of *n*-hexane. There was no effect on 1-hydroxylation. There were significant increases in the hepatic 6β, 7α and 16-hydroxylation of 4-androstene-3,17-dione. There were significant increases in the hepatic formation of benzo(a)pyrene-4,5-diol, B(a)P-7,8-diol, B(a)P-9,10-diol, phenols and quinones. There were significant increases in renal cytochrome P-450 content, NADPH-cytochrome c reductase activity and 7-ethoxyresorufin O-deethylase activity. There was no effect on relative kidney weight or the hydroxylation of *n*-hexane. There was a marked decrease in pulmonary cytochrome P-450 and a significant decrease in the hydroxylation of *n*-hexane. There was no effect on 7-ethoxyresorufin activity. Increased enzyme activity in the liver (phenobarbital-type induction) and kidney,

Table 2: SUB-ACUTE TOXICITY OF XYLENES TO ANIMALS
Table 2.1: Inhalation Studies

Species	Concentration/dose/ duration	Observations
		and decreased activity in the lung were observed.
Rat (137) Sprague-Dawley 4 males/group	0 or 2000 ppm, 6 h/d for 3 d.	Study of the effect on rat liver microsomal cytochrome P-450.
		There was a significant increase in P-450 levels, 7-ethoxyresorufin 0-deethylase activity and n-hexane hydroxylase activity for 2 and 3 hydroxylation. 1 hydroxylation activity was also increased.
		There was a significant increase in *in vitro* benzo(a)pyrene metabolism for B(a)P-9,10-diol, B(a)P-4,5-diol, B(a)P-7,8-diol, phenols and quinones.
Rat (141) Wistar 10 males/group	0, 50, 400 or 750 ppm, 6 h/d, 5 d/week for;	Study of the effect on hepatic and renal xenobiotic metabolism.
	a) 1 week.	a) There was a significant increase in hepatic microsomal protein and NADPH-cytochrome c reductase levels, at 400 and 750 ppm. There was no effect on cytochrome P-450 levels.
		Hepatic 7-ethoxycoumarin 0-deethylase was significantly raised at all dose levels (dose-dependent) whereas ethoxyresorufin 0-deethylase and UDP-glucuronyl transferase activities were significantly raised at 400 and 750 ppm.
		There was a significant decrease in hepatic glutathione at 400 and 750 mg/kg.
		There was no effect on serum alanine aminotransferase activity.
		There were no abnormalities on histopathological examination of the liver.
		There was a significant increase in renal cytochrome P-450, 7-ethoxycoumarin 0-deethylase and UDP-glucuronyl transferase activities at all dose levels (the former dose-dependent). There was no effect in renal microsomal protein.
		There was no effect in renal glutathione.
	b) 2 weeks.	b) There was a significant increase in hepatic microsomal protein and NADPH-cytochrome c reductase levels, at 400 and 750 ppm, as well as a significant increase in cytochrome P-450 at 750 ppm.

Species	Concentration/dose/ duration	Observations
		Hepatic 7-ethoxycoumarin O-deethylase, ethoxyresorufin O-deethylase and UDP-glucuronyl transferase activities were significantly, dose-dependently raised at all dose levels.
		There was a significant, dose-dependent decrease in hepatic glutathione at 400 and 750 ppm.
		There was no effect on serum alanine aminotransferase activity.
		There were no abnormalities on histopathological examination of the liver.
		There was a significant increase in renal microsomal protein and cytochrome P-450, at 400 and 750 ppm. There was a significant, dose-dependent increase in 7-ethoxycoumarin O-deethylase and UDP-glucuronyl transferase activities at all dose levels.
		There was no effect in renal glutathione.
		Significant changes in hepatic and renal enzyme activities thus occurred at all dose levels. However no evidence of hepatic damage was noted.
Rat (16) Wistar 20 males/group	0 or 300 ppm, 6 h/d, 5 d/week, for;	Study of the effect on hepatic and renal xenobiotic metabolism.
	a) 1 week	a) There was a significant increase in hepatic 7-ethoxycoumarin O-deethylase activity and a significant decrease in reduced glutathione.
		There was no effect on hepatic cytochrome P-450, NADPH-cytochrome c reductase or UDP-glucuronyl transferase activities.
		There was no effect on hepatic aldehyde dehydrogenase activity.
		There was a significant increase in renal 7-ethoxycoumarin O-deethylase and UDP-glucuronyl transferase.
		There was no effect on renal cytochrome P-450 or reduced glutathione.
	b) 2 weeks	b) There was a significant increase in hepatic cytochrome P-450, NADPH-cytochrome c reductase, 7-ethoxycoumarin O-deethylase and UDP-glucuronyl transferase activities. There was a significant decrease in

79

Table 2: SUB-ACUTE TOXICITY OF XYLENES TO ANIMALS
Table 2.1: Inhalation Studies

Species	Concentration/dose/duration	Observations
		hepatic reduced glutathione.
		There was no effect on hepatic aldehyde dehydrogenase activity.
		There was a significant increase in renal 7-ethoxycoumarin O-deethylase activity.
		There was no effect on renal cytochrome P-450, UPD-glucuronyl transferase activity or reduced glutathione.
Rat (15) Wistar 6 males/group	0 or 300 ppm, 7 h/d, 4 d/week for 5 weeks.	Study of the effect on lung cytochrome P-450.
		No overt clinical signs of toxicity or effect on body weight gain were observed.
		There was no effect on liver or kidney weights.
		There was a significant decrease in cytochrome P-450 content and 7-ethoxycoumarin O-deethylase activity.
		There was no effect on the content of cytochrome b_5 and non-protein thiol groups, or in the activities of NADPH-cytochrome c reductase, m-methylbenzaldehyde dehydrogenase, propionaldehyde dehydrogenase or glutathione S-transferase.
Rat (17) Wistar 15 males/group	0, 50, 400 or 750 ppm, 6 h/d, 5 d/week for 1 or 2 weeks.	Study of the effect on cerebral biochemistry.
		There was a significant decrease in glutathione levels, at weeks 1 and 2 at all concentrations.
		There was a dose-dependent decrease in superoxide dismutase activity, at week 2, reaching significance at 400 and 750 ppm. There was no effect at week 1.
		There was a significant increase in NADPH-diaphorase activity, at week 2, at all concentrations. There was no effect at week 1.
		There was a significant increase in azoreductase activity, at week 2, at the two higher concentrations. There was no consistent effect at week 1.
		There was no effect on RNA levels or acid proteinase activity, at weeks 1 and 2.

Table 2: SUB-ACUTE TOXICITY OF XYLENES TO ANIMALS
Table 2.1: Inhalation Studies

Species	Concentration/dose/ duration	Observations
		After a two week recovery period RNA levels were significantly increased at the two higher concentrations and azoreductase activity was significantly increased at 400 ppm. All other parameters, at each concentration level, were within the control range.
Rat (304) Wistar 6 females/group	0 or 300 ppm, 8 h/d for 7 d.	Study of the effect on leukocyte and serum alkaline phosphatase activities. There was a significant decrease in serum alkaline phosphatase activity. There was no significant effect on leucocyte alkaline phosphatase activity.
Rat (85) Wistar 10 animals Sex not given	1005 ppm, 8 h/d for 14 d.	No deaths occurred and no other results were reported.
Mouse (139) NMRI-BOM	0 or 1600 ppm, 4 h/d, 5 d/week for;	Study of the effect on feeding and drinking behaviour, as well as central adrenergic receptor binding.
a) 8 females/group	7 weeks	There was no effect on overall mean body weight. However there was a significant difference between the changes in mean weight of the control and exposed groups over the 4 h exposure period. Controls lost weight during exposure whereas test animals only lost weight in the first few days, and thereafter showed no consistent effect. There was increased mean food and water consumption in test animals over controls during the 4 h exposure period, except during the first few days. There was significantly increased mean food consumption in controls, during the 20 h period between exposures. There was no effect on mean water consumption over the same period, or on food/water consumption during the weekends. The test animals were reported to demonstrate increased motor activity and profuse sweating. These effects ceased "about 30 min after exposure". There was significantly decreased binding of ^{3}H-clonidine to *alpha*-adrenergic

Table 2: SUB-ACUTE TOXICITY OF XYLENES TO ANIMALS
Table 2.1: Inhalation Studies

Species	Concentration/dose/duration	Observations
		receptors in the hypothalamus region of the brain. There was no effect on binding in the diencephalon, cortex or cerebellum.
b) 7 females/group	2 weeks.	The effects on mean body weight, as well as mean food and water consumption were broadly consistent with those seen in the previous study.
		There was no effect on the binding of ^{3}H-clonidine to *alpha*-adrenergic receptors in the hypothalamus, diencephalon, cortex or cerebellum.
		The authors suggest that the increase in food and water consumption may be related to the decreased *alpha*-receptor binding in the hypothalamus.
Guinea Pig (305) Strain, sex and numbers not given	a) 450 ppm for 4 h on day one, then 300 ppm for 4 h/d 6 d/week for a total of 65 exposures.	One animal died, on day 1, and the other animals were prostrate. Histological examination revealed slight degeneration in the liver and evidence of an inflammatory reaction in the lungs.
	b) 300 ppm for 4 h/d, 6 d/week for a total of 58 exposures.	No deaths reported. Histological examination revealed small areas of catarrhal inflammation in the lungs of 2 animals and scattered, moderate tubular degeneration in the kidneys. Few details reported in this early study.
Rabbit (306) Chinchilla 9 animals/group Sex not given	a) 0 or 46 ppm, 2 h/d for 10-12 months.	Study of the effect of low exposure concentrations.
	b) 0 or 11 ppm, 4 h/d for 10-12 months.	There was significant leukocytosis reported at both concentrations, with a shift towards increased neutrophil numbers. Insufficient data was provided to permit any firm conclusions to be drawn.

p-Xylene

Species	Concentration/dose/duration	Observations
Rat (135) Sprague-Dawley 6 males/group	0 or 2000 ppm 6 h/d for 3 d. Animals killed 16-18 h after final exposure.	Study of the effect on levels of noradrenaline and dopamine in various parts of the forebrain and hypothalamus. No clinical signs of toxicity were noted. There was a significant increase in catecholamine levels in various parts of the hypothalamus (subependymal layer,

82

Species	Concentration/dose/ duration	Observations
		medial and lateral palisade zones of the median eminence, the nucleus dorsomedialis hypothalami, and the parvocellular and magnocellular parts of the paraventricular hypothalamic nucleus).
		There was also a significant increase in catecholamine turnover in various parts of the hypothalamus (subependymal layer, medial and lateral palisade zones of the median eminence, the nucleus dorsomedialis hypothalami, the anterior periventricular hypothalamic region, and the parvocellular and magnocellular parts of the paraventricular hypothalamic nucleus).
		There was no effect on dopamine levels or turnover in the forebrain.
		There was a significant decrease in serum levels of corticosterone and prolactin. There was no effect on serum levels of thyroid-stimulating hormone, growth hormone or follicle-stimulating hormone.
Rat (138) Sprague-Dawley 4 males/group	0 or 2000 ppm, 6 h/d for 3 d.	Study of the effect on cytochrome P-450 and enzyme activities in the liver, kidney and lung.
		There were significant increases in relative liver weight, cytochrome P-450 content (with particular increases in two forms) and NADPH-cytochrome c reductase activity. There was no effect on hepatic 7-ethoxyresorufin O-deethylase activity.
		There were significant increases in the hepatic 2 and 3-hydroxylation of n-hexane. There was no effect on 1-hydroxylation.
		There were significant increases in the hepatic 6β and 7α-hydroxylation of 4-androstene-3,17-dione. There was no effect on 16-hydroxylation.
		There were significant increases in the hepatic formation of benzo(a)pyrene-4,5-diol, B(a)P-9,10-diol and phenols. There was no effect on B(a)P-7,8-diol formation or quinones.
		There were significant increases in renal NADPH-cytochrome c reductase and 7-ethoxyresorufin O-deethylase activities. There was no effect on relative kidney weight, cytochrome P-450 content, or the hydroxylation of n-hexane.
		There was a marked decrease in pulmonary

Species	Concentration/dose/ duration	Observations
		cytochrome P-450 and a significant decrease in the hydroxylation of n-hexane. There was no effect on 7-ethoxyresorufin O-deethylase.
		Increased enzyme activity in the liver (phenobarbital-type induction) and kidney, and decreased activity in the lung were observed.
Rat (137) Sprague-Dawley 4 males/group	0 or 2000 ppm, 6 h/d for 3 d.	Study of the effect on rat liver microsomal cytochrome P-450.
		There was a significant increase in P-450 levels and in n-hexane hydroxylase activity for 2 and 3 hydroxylation. 1-hydroxylation and 7-ethoxyresorufin O-deethylase activity were also increased.
		There was a significant increase in *in vitro* benzo(a)pyrene metabolism for B(a)P-9,10-diol, B(a)P-4,5-diol, and a phenol fraction. Levels of B(a)P-7,8-diol a phenol fraction and quinones were also increased.
Rat (307) CFY Females Numbers not given	0 or 700 ppm, 6 h/d, for 3 d.	Study of the effect on intravenously administered progesterone.
		The plasma clearance of progesterone was significantly enhanced.
Rat (85) Wistar 10 animals Sex not given	1226 ppm, 8 h/d for 14 d	No deaths occurred and no other results were reported.
Mouse (85) 10 animals Strain and sex not given	1226 ppm, 8 h/d for 14 d.	No deaths occurred and no other results were reported.
Rabbit (91) New Zealand White 4 males/group	0 or 1000 ppm, 4 h/d, for 2 d.	Study of the effect on lung microsomal activity.

Table 2: SUB-ACUTE TOXICITY OF XYLENES TO ANIMALS
Table 2.1: Inhalation Studies

Species	Concentration/dose/ duration	Observations
		There was a significant decrease in microsomal cytochrome P-450 concentration.
		There was a significant decrease in NADPH cytochrome c reductase activity, but no effect on NADH cytochrome c reductase activity.

Xylene

Species	Concentration/dose/ duration	Observations
Rat (143) Strain, sex and numbers not given	620, 980 or 1600 ppm, 18-20 h/d for 7 d. Xylene undefined.	Instability and incoordination were reported at 1600 and 980 ppm, leading to narcosis and death at the higher concentration. Signs of mucous membrane irritation were reported at 1600 and 980 ppm. At 980 ppm the bone marrow and the spleen were reported to be hyperplastic, with the kidneys showing acute congestion with moderate cloudy swelling. From this study it appears that 620 ppm was a No Effect Level. However this early study was only reported in limited detail.
Rat (144) Strain, sex and numbers not given	620, 980 or 1600 ppm, 18-20 h/d, for 7 d. Xylene undefined.	Early toxicity study. At 1600 ppm deaths were reported. There was a dose-dependent decrease in body weight gain and increase in severity of narcosis, with no effects at 620 ppm. There was a small, dose-dependent decrease in leukocyte count.

Rat (85) Harlan-Wistar 25 males/group	0, 180, 460 or 810 ppm, 6 h/day, 5 d/week for 13 weeks.
	
	At 3, 7 and 13 weeks, 3, 3 and 4 animals respectively were sacrificed.
	
	At 13 weeks 10 animals/group were challenged with 6700 ppm for 4 h.
	
	Xylene used was;
	  7.63% o-xylene
	65.01% m-xylene
	  7.84% p-xylene
	19.27% ethylbenzene.
		General toxicology study.
		
		No treatment related deaths and no effect on body weight gain.
		
		There were no consistent, significant effects reported in haematological parameters or clinical chemistry.
		
		There were no treatment related effects reported at histopathological examination.
		
		At challenge no significant differences were seen in the median time to death for any dose group.

85

Table 2: SUB-ACUTE TOXICITY OF XYLENES TO ANIMALS
Table 2.1: Inhalation Studies

Species	Concentration/dose/duration	Observations
Rat (135) Sprague-Dawley 6 males/group	0 or 2000 ppm, 6 h/d for 3 d. Animals killed 16-18 h after final exposure. Xylene used was; 2.0% *o*-xylene 64.5% *m*-xylene 10.0% *p*-xylene 23.0% ethylbenzene.	Study of the effect on levels of noradrenaline and dopamine in various parts of the forebrain and hypothalamus. No clinical signs of toxicity were noted. There was a significant increase in catecholamine levels in various parts of the hypothalamus (subependymal layer and lateral palisade zone of the median eminence, as well as the parvocellular part of the paraventricular hypothalamic nucleus). There was also a significant increase in catecholamine turnover in various parts of the hypothalamus (subependymal layer, the medial and lateral palisade zones of the median eminence, and the parvocellular and magnocellular parts of the paraventricular hypothalamic nucleus). There was a significant increase in dopamine levels in various parts of the forebrain (central and marginal parts of the caudate nucleus, as well as the posterior nucleus accumbens and the medial posterior tuberculum olfactorium). There was also a significant increase in dopamine turnover in various parts of the forebrain (marginal zone, medial and central part of the nucleus caudatus, the anterior nucleus accumbens and the medial posterior tuberculum olfactorium). There was a significant decrease in serum thyroid-stimulating hormone level. There was no effect on serum levels of growth hormone, corticosterone, prolactin or follicle-stimulating hormone.
Rat (145) Sprague-Dawley 5-6 males/group	0, 200, 400 or 800 ppm, for 30 d. Xylene undefined.	Study of the effect on levels of neurotransmitters, putative second messengers and amino acids in the brain. Acetylcholine levels in the striatum were decreased in a concentration dependent manner at 400 ppm and above, reaching significance at 800 ppm. Noradrenaline levels in the hypothalamus were increased, reaching significance at 800 ppm. cAMP levels in the striatum were decreased in a concentration dependent manner at 400 ppm and above.

Table 2: SUB-ACUTE TOXICITY OF XYLENES TO ANIMALS
Table 2.1: Inhalation Studies

Species	Concentration/dose/ duration	Observations
		Glutamine levels in the midbrain were significantly increased at 800 ppm.
		Glycine and GABA levels in the midbrain were consistently increased at all exposure concentrations.
Rat (286) Fisher F344 4 males/group	0 or 444 ppm, 2 h/d for 5 d. Xylene undefined.	Study of the effect on intracranial self-stimulation behaviour.
		There was a significant decrease in response rate during the second hour of exposure on day 2 and during the whole 2 h period on day 3. The response on day 3 was not a cumulative effect, since the pre-exposure response rate on that day was within normal limits.
		Thus the animals demonstrated increasing sensitivity to the depressant effect of xylene, up to day 3, followed by the development of tolerance.
Rat (98) Fischer F344 12 males/group		Study of the effect on hearing loss, as assessed by behavioural (conditioned avoidance) and/or electrophysiological (brainstem auditory-evoked response) methods.
	a) 0 or 1450 ppm, 8 h/d, for 3 d. About 35 d after the last exposure the animals were trained to perform a multisensory conditioned avoidance response (CAR) task (visual, auditory and somatosensory stimuli), followed by the behavioural audiometric test.	There was a marked increase (approximately 20 dB) in the auditory response threshold at 12 and 20 kHz.
	b) 0, 800, 1000 or 1200 ppm, 14 h/d, 7 d/week for 6 weeks. 2 d after the last exposure the animals were trained to perform the multisensory CAR task, followed by testing. Brainstem auditory- evoked response (BAER) thresholds were measured 2 weeks after the last exposure.	At 1200 ppm there was slight impairment of the auditory, but not visual or somatosensory, CAR. There was no effect at lower concentrations.
		All animals had increased auditory response thresholds relative to controls at the same frequencies. At 1200 ppm there was an impairment of about 10-30 dB at 2 kHz and above, at 1000 ppm about 10-30 dB at and above 8 kHz and at 800 ppm about 20 dB at 12 kHz and above.
		At 1200 ppm BAER thresholds were markedly

Table 2: SUB-ACUTE TOXICITY OF XYLENES TO ANIMALS
Table 2.1: Inhalation Studies

Species	Concentration/dose/ duration	Observations
	Xylene used was: 10% o-xylene 80% m-xylene 10% p-xylene.	elevated at 4, 8 and 16 kHz tone frequency. At 1000 and 800 ppm the thresholds were elevated markedly at 16 kHz and slightly at 8 kHz.
		These results clearly demonstrate that xylene is ototoxic to the rat.
Rat (146) Sprague-Dawley Males		Study of the effect on the liver and hepatic cytochrome P-450.
a) 8-12 animals/group	0, 75, 250, 500, 1000 or 2000 ppm, 6 h/d for 3 d.	There was a dose-dependent increase in the concentration of liver microsomal P-450, significant at all concentrations.
		There was a dose-dependent increase in the activities of 7-ethoxyresorufin 0-deethylase and NADPH-cytochrome c reductase, significant at all concentrations.
b) Numbers not given	0, 1000 or 2000 ppm, 6 h/d for 5 d. Xylene used was: 2.0% o-xylene 64.5% m-xylene 10.0% p-xylene 23.0% ethylbenzene	There was a dose-dependent increase in the surface area of smooth endoplasmic reticulum (80-100% increase over controls, at 2000 ppm) but no change in the area of rough endoplasmic reticulum. There was no apparent increase in the size or number of mitochondria or peroxisomes. Staining with toluidine blue showed no hepatocytomegaly, fatty accumulation or necrosis.
		Further studies showed that the inducing effects of xylene are relatively similar in male and female rats.
		On the basis of isozyme analysis and the observed morphological changes, the authors concluded that xylene caused phenobarbital-type induction in the liver.
Rat (137) Sprague-Dawley 4 males/group		Study of the effect on hepatic cytochrome P-450.
	a) 0, 75, 250, 500, 1000 or 2000 ppm, 6 h/d for 3 d.	There was a dose-dependent increase in P-450 levels and 7-ethoxyresorufin 0-deethylase activity, significant at 250 ppm and above. At 2000 ppm there was a significant increase in n-hexane hydroxylase activity for 1, 2 and 3 hydroxylation. At 2000 ppm there was a significant increase in *in vitro* benzo(a) pyrene-4,5-diol and B(a)P-7,8-diol. Levels of B(a)P-9,10-diol, phenols and quinones were also increased.
	b) 0 or 600 ppm, 6 h/d,	There was an increase in P-450 levels,

Table 2: SUB-ACUTE TOXICITY OF XYLENES TO ANIMALS
Table 2.1: Inhalation Studies

Species	Concentration/dose/ duration	Observations
	5 d/week for 4 weeks. Xylene used was; 2.0% *o*-xylene 64.5% *m*-xylene 10.0% *p*-xylene 23.0% ethylbenzene.	and significant increases in *in vitro* benzo(a)pyrene metabolism for B(a)P-9,10-diol B(a)P-4,5-diol and quinones. Levels of B(a)P-7,8-diol and phenols were also increased.
Rat (147) Sprague-Dawley 4 males/group	0 or 630 ppm, 6 h/d, 5 d/week for 4 weeks. Animals were killed the morning after the last day of exposure. Xylene used was; 2.0% *o*-xylene 64.5% *m*-xylene 10.0% *p*-xylene 23.0% ethylbenzene.	Study of the effects on hepatic cytochrome P-450 and enzyme activities. There was a significant decrease in body weight gain. Absolute and relative liver weights were significantly increased. There was a marked increase in hepatic cytochrome P-450, with particular increases in two forms noted. There were significant increases in the *in vitro* 2- and 4- hydroxylation of biphenyl. There was no effect on 3-hydroxylation. There were changes in the *in vitro* metabolism of benzo(a)pyrene with significantly increased formation of B(a)P-9,10-diol, B(a)P-4,5-diol and quinones. There were no significant effects on formation of B(a)P-7,8-diol or phenols. There were changes in the *in vitro* metabolism of 4-androstene-3,17-dione, with significantly increased formation of the 16-hydroxy metabolite. There were no significant effects on the formation of 7α- or 6β- hydroxy metabolites. There were changes in the *in vitro* metabolism of 5α-androstene-$3\alpha,17\beta$-diol with significantly increased formation of the 3α, 7β, 17β-triol, and the 3α, 17β, 18-triol metabolites, and significantly decreased formation of the $2\alpha,3\beta$, 17β-triol metabolite. Thus xylene was shown to act as a phenobarbital - like inducer of cytochrome P-450.

Table 2: SUB-ACUTE TOXICITY OF XYLENES TO ANIMALS
Table 2.1: Inhalation Studies

Species	Concentration/dose/ duration	Observations
Rat (138) Sprague-Dawley 4 males/group	0 or 2000 ppm, 6 h/d for 3 d.	Study of the effect on cytochrome P-450 and enzyme activities in the liver, kidney and lung.
	Xylene used was; 2.0% o-xylene 64.5% m-xylene 10.0% p-xylene 23.0% ethylbenzene	There were significant increases in hepatic cytochrome P-450 (with particular increases in two forms), NADPH-cytochrome c reductase activity and 7-ethoxyresorufin 0-deethylase activity. There was no effect on relative liver weight.
		There were significant increases in the hepatic 2 and 3-hydroxylation of n-hexane. There was no effect on 1-hydroxylation.
		There were significant increases in the hepatic 6β, 7α and 16-hydroxylation of 4-androstene-3, 17-dione.
		There were significant increases in the hepatic formation of benzo(a)pyrene-4,5-diol and B(a)P-7,8-diol. There was no effect on B(a)P-9,10-diol, phenol or quinone formation.
		There were significant increases in renal cytochrome P-450 content, NADPH-cytochrome c reductase, 7-ethoxyresorufin 0-deethylase activities and the 1-hydroxylation of n-hexane. There was no effect on relative kidney weight.
		There was a marked decrease in pulmonary cytochrome P-450 content and a significant decrease in the hydroxylation of n-hexane. There was no effect on 7-ethoxyresorufin 0-deethylase activity.
		Increased enzyme activity in the liver (phenobarbital-type induction) and kidney and decreased activity in the lung were observed.
Rat (148) Sprague-Dawley 4 males/group	600 ppm, 6 h/d, 5 d/week for 4 weeks.	Study of the effect on *in vitro* hepatic microsomal metabolism of biphenyl and benzo(a)pyrene.
	Xylene undefined.	There was a 20% increase in the total liver microsomal concentration of cytochrome P-450, as well as a significantly increased metabolism of biphenyl and benzo(a) pyrene.

Table 2: SUB-ACUTE TOXICITY OF XYLENES TO ANIMALS
Table 2.1: Inhalation Studies

Species	Concentration/dose/ duration	Observations
		Electrophoresis revealed a significant change in the forms of cytochrome P-450 with an observed increase in two forms of apparent molecular weight of 50,000 and 54,000.
		The *in vitro* metabolism and electrophoresis pattern were reported to be changed in a manner similar to that following phenobarbital exposure.
		Thus xylene can induce cytochrome P-450 activity in a phenobarbital like manner.
Rat (18) Wistar 20 males/group	0 or 300 ppm, 6 h/d, 5 d/week for 1-2 weeks. 10 animals per group had 15% v/v ethanol in the drinking water (equivalent to approximately 6-9 g/kg/day). Xylene used was; 80% *m*-xylene 12% *p*-xylene.	Study of the effect on the nervous system, liver and kidney. There was a significant decrease in motor activity, in an open field situation, 17 h after the 4 d exposure. There was no effect on motor activity at 1 h, or on rearing, preening frequency, preening time, defaecation or urinary frequency. There was a significant increase in brain DT-diaphorase activity, at week 2, and in acid proteinase, at week 1. There was no effect on brain levels of protein or RNA, or on the activity of superoxide dismutase at weeks 1 and 2. There was a significant increase in hepatic 7-ethoxycoumarin O-deethylase activity at week 2. There was no effect on hepatic cytochrome P-450 or NADPH-cytochrome c reductase levels or on the activity of 2,5-diphenyloxazole hydroxylase or DT-diaphorase at week 2. There was a significant increase in renal 7-ethoxycoumarin O-deethylase activity at week 2. There was no effect on renal UDP-glucuronyltransferase activity. There was a significant decrease in serum non-specific cholinesterase activity at week 2. There was no effect at week 1, or on serum creatine kinase at weeks 1 or 2. Concurrent dosing with ethanol had a marked synergistic effect on hepatic and renal 7-ethoxycoumarin O-deethylase activity (205 and 551% respectively).
Rat (19) Wistar 60 males/group	0 or 300 ppm, 6 h/d, 5 d/week for up to 18 weeks.	Study of the effect on the liver and kidney.

Table 2: SUB-ACUTE TOXICITY OF XYLENES TO ANIMALS
Table 2.1: Inhalation Studies

Species	Concentration/dose/ duration	Observations
	30 animals/group had 15% ethanol in the drinking water, for the first 9 weeks, then 20% ethanol (equivalent to approximately 10 g/kg/day). Xylene used was; 19.2% o-xylene 43.0% m-xylene 19.5% p-xylene 18.3% ethylbenzene.	In the liver there was a significant increase in diphenyloxazole hydroxylase activity from week 5 onwards. There was also a significant increase in UDP-glucuronyl transferase activity at 5 and 18 weeks. Ethoxycoumarin 0-deethylase activity was markedly increased in two phases, initially to the end of week 2 and then from week 9 onwards. There were no significant effects reported on the levels of cytochrome P-450 or reduced glutathione, or on the activities of NADPH-cytochrome c reductase, epoxide hydratase or aldehyde dehydrogenase. In the kidney there was a significant increase in ethoxycoumarin 0-deethylase activity at 5 and 18 weeks. There was no significant effect on reduced glutathione levels. At histopathological examination of the liver, no treatment-related abnormalities were observed. Concurrent ethanol ingestion increased hepatic and renal microsomal enzyme activities. Fatty change in the liver was more marked in co-exposed animals than for animals exposed to ethanol alone.
Rat (149) Wistar 5 males/group	0, 50 400 or 750 ppm, 6 h/d, 5 d/week, for 2 weeks. Xylene undefined.	Study of the effect on hepatic and renal xenobiotic metabolism. Hepatic cytochrome P-450, the activities of 7-ethoxycoumarin 0-deethylase and UDP-glucuronyl transferase as well as glutathione levels were reported to be only moderately changed. Renal 7-ethoxycoumarin 0-deethylase activity was markedly increased (up to approximately 400% of controls) in a dose-dependent manner. Renal cytochrome P-450, UDP-glucuronyl transferase activity and glutathione levels were reported to be only moderately changed. Study reported in summary form only.
Rat (308, 309) 15 males/group Strain not given	0, 0.05 or 3.4 ppm, continuously for 85 d. There was a 13 d partial starvation period in the second half of the exposure period. Xylene undefined.	Study to examine the effects of very low concentrations of xylene during and for up to 30 d post exposure. There were no deaths reported and there were no significant effects on body weight gain.

Species	Concentration/dose/ duration	Observations
		The animals exhibited increased excitability, restlessness and aggression at 3.4 ppm.
		There was an increased leukocyte count at 3.4 ppm which was significant by day 30 and which continued to increase throughout the exposure period. The leukocytosis was associated with neutropenia, monocytosis, absolute lymphocytosis and the appearance of stab cells.
		There was a decrease in whole blood cholinesterase activity, at 3.4 ppm, which was significant during the first half of the exposure period.
		There were marked, progressive decreases in the ratio of motor chronaxies for antagonist muscles, at 3.4 ppm, from which recovery was slow.
		There was no effect on organ weights for the lung, heart, liver, kidney, spleen and brain.
		A number of histological changes were noted, including partial tigrolysis of neurons and haemosiderin deposition in the spleen. However these effects were unclearly reported.
		No effects were observed at 0.05 ppm.
Rat (310) 18 animals/group Strain and sex not given		Study of the effects of continuous versus intermittent exposure.
	a) 5 concentrations ranging from 3 to 230 ppm. Duration of this continuous exposure not stated.	No deaths were reported. Decreased body weight gain and behavioural changes were reported above 23 ppm. Decreased antagonist muscle chronaxie ratio and blood cholinesterase activity were reported, as well as leukocytosis. The magnitude of these effects, and the time of onset, was dependent on both concentration and duration of exposure.
	b) Intermittent exposure at 230 ppm. Exposure duration and intervals between exposures not stated. Xylene undefined.	The time to appearance of the above described effects increased with length of the intervals between exposures. The author reports that over the same period of time and with an identical mean exposure concentration, continuous exposure produces more pronounced toxicity than intermittent exposure. However this study is reported in only limited detail.

Table 2: SUB-ACUTE TOXICITY OF XYLENES TO ANIMALS
Table 2.1: Inhalation Studies

Species	Concentration/dose/ duration	Observations
Rat (311) 6 males/group Strain not given	0 or 800 ppm, 4 h/d, 5 d/week for 3 weeks. Xylene undefined.	Experiment to study the effect of xylene on acquisition and extinction of an avoidance reponse, undertaken 2 h after commencing exposure. No deaths occurred, there was no effect on body weight gain, and no conspicuous behavioural abnormalities were noted. Neither acquisition (1st week of exposure) nor extinction (3rd week) of the avoidance response were significantly affected. Thus xylene had no effect on learning or performance.
Rat (312) Sprague-Dawley Males a) 8 animals/group	0 or 320 ppm, continuously for: 30 d	Study of the effect on the brain lipid composition. There was no effect on mean body weights. There was no effect on the mean weights of the whole brain, cerebral cortex, brain stem, hippocampus, or cerebellar vermis. There was a significant increase in the mean liver/body weight ratio. There was no effect on the total content of phospholipids or cholesterol in the cerebral cortex. There was a significant decrease in linoleic acid in cerebral cortex ethanolamine phosphoglyceride.
b) 6 animals/group	90 d. Xylene undefined.	There were no significant effects on any of the above parameters. Thus xylene exposure produced only limited, transient changes.
Rat (20) Wistar 20 males/group	0 or 300 ppm, 6 h/d, 5 d/week for 5 to 18 weeks. 10 animals/group were also exposed to ethanol in the drinking water (15% v/v). Xylene used was; 7.5% o-xylene 85.0% m-xylene 7.5% p-xylene.	Study of the effect on the brain both with and without simultaneous ethanol intake. There was no effect on body weight gain. A transient reduction in preening time and frequency was recorded in an open-field test. There was no effect on cerebral protein or RNA levels.

Table 2: SUB-ACUTE TOXICITY OF XYLENES TO ANIMALS
Table 2.1: Inhalation Studies

Species	Concentration/dose/ duration	Observations
		There was a significant increase in cerebral microsomal superoxide dismutase activity by week 18. There were no consistent effects on acid proteinase, NADPH-diaphorase or cytosolic glutathione peroxidase activities.
		There was no effect on serum non-specific cholinesterase activity.
		Co-exposure to ethanol reduced the effects of xylene exposure.
Rat (313) Wistar 5 animals/group Sex not given	0 or 300 ppm, 6 h/d, 5 d/week for 18 weeks. Xylene undefined.	Study of the effect on spinal cord axon membrane lipid composition. There was an apparent decrease in membrance lipid per mg of protein. However there was no apparent change in the cholesterol/lipid phosphorus ratio. Combined exposure with ethanol (15% v/v in the water) enhanced the decrease in membrane lipids and decreased the cholesterol/lipid phosphorus ratio.
Rat (314) Sprague-Dawley		Study of the effect on antipyrine metabolism, both *in vitro* and *in vivo*, as a marker for enzyme induction.
a) 4-5 males/group	0, 75, 250, 500, 1000 or 2000 ppm, 6 h/d for 3 d.	There was a dose-dependent increase in the *in vitro*, liver microsomal metabolism of antipyrine, which was significant at 250 ppm and above.
b) 6-8 males/group	0, 75, 500 or 1000 ppm 6 h/d for 3 d. Xylene used was: 2.0% *o*-xylene 64.5% *m*-xylene 10.0% *p*-xylene 23.0% ethylbenzene.	There was a significant decrease in the antipyrine t½ at 1000 ppm. In addition, antipyrine clearance was significantly increased at 500 and 1000 ppm. Thus xylene exposure increases the metabolism of antipyrine both *in vitro* and *in vivo*.
Rat (23) Wistar 9 animals/group Sex not given	690 ppm, 8 h/d, 6 d/week, for 110 to 130 d. Xylene undefined.	General toxicology study. No deaths reported. Clinical signs were ambiguously reported. There was a slight fall in leukocyte count reported. There was no effect on other haemotological parameters. There was a marked increase in blood urea levels. The presence of blood and albumen in the urine was noted.

Table 2: SUB-ACUTE TOXICITY OF XYLENES TO ANIMALS
Table 2.1: Inhalation Studies

Species	Concentration/dose/ duration	Observations
		Marked renal lesions were reported at hisopathological examination. Changes associated with the glomerulae included swelling of the capillaries and cell desquamation. In the convoluted tubule there were signs of cell necrosis and the appearance of blood 'cylinders'. Hyperplasia of the bone marrow and widespread congestion were also reported.

The limited reporting of this study (including no clear reference to a concurrent control group) restricts the conclusions that may be drawn. |
| **Rat** (307) CFY Females Numbers not given | 0 or 700 ppm, 6 h/d, for 3 d.

Xylene undefined. | Study of the effect of xylene on intravenously administered progesterone.

Xylene has no effect on the plasma clearance. |
| **Rat** (315) Wistar Males Numbers not given | 0, 5747 or 6897 ppm 5 h/d for 7, 14 and 21 d.

Xylene undefined. | Study of the effect on:

i) Response to a previously learnt conditioned reflex.

ii) Motor activity in an open field test.

The animals exhibited ruffled fur, hypersensitivity to noise, lethargy and ataxia.

There was no effect on response to a conditioned reflex.

There was no consistent effect on motor activity.

The absence of more severe toxic signs is unexpected given the high levels of exposure. |
| **Rat** (316) 10 males/group Strain not given | 0 or 69 ppm, 4 h/d, 5 d/week for 45 days.

Animals were simultaneously exposed to noise of intensity 0, 85 or 95 dB.

Xylene undefined. | Study of the effect of simultaneous exposure to noise and xylene on metabolic activity in the lung.

Xylene alone gave a significant increase in pulmonary lactate dehydrogenase (LDH) as well as increases in glucose 6-phosphate dehydrogenase(G_6PD), alkaline phosphatase (ALP) and acid phosphatase (AcP) activities. |

Table 2: SUB-ACUTE TOXICITY OF XYLENES TO ANIMALS
Table 2.1: Inhalation Studies

Species	Concentration/dose/duration	Observations
		Co-exposure to noise, which alone had no effect on the above parameters, gave further increases in the activity of these enzymes.
		Xylene alone decreased levels of thiol groups, as did co-exposure to 85 or 95 dB (9, 10 or 13% respectively) but all values were within normal limits.
		Thus co-exposure to noise enhanced the effects associated with xylene alone. However the significance of these findings is unclear.
Rat (317) Male Strain and numbers not given	0 or 69 ppm, 4 h/d, 5 d/week for 6 weeks. Animals were simultaneously exposed to noise of intensity 0, 46, 85 or 95 dB. Xylene undefined.	Study of the effect of simultaneous exposure to noise and xylene on metabolic activity in the myocardium. Xylene alone gave an increase in ATPase (25%) and diphosphoglycerate mutase (41%) as well as a decrease in glucose 6-phosphatase (35%) activities. Simultaneous exposure to 95 dB gave a marked increase in glucose 6-phosphate dehydrogenase (102%) and lactate dehydrogenase (97%) activities. Exposure to xylene and xylene/noise produced changes in the activities of different enzymes. However no firm conclusions can be drawn since this study was only briefly reported.
Mouse (142) White 10 animals/group Sex not stated	1150, 1725 or 2300 ppm, 7 h/d for 6 d. Xylene undefined.	At 2300 ppm there were 7 deaths reported. Transient weight loss was reported. All mice adopted an abnormal body position and exhibited ataxia of the rear limbs and waddling gait leading to paralysis. Distention of the abdomen was observed, along with shallow, irregular breathing. The animals seemed cold to touch, after exposure. Of the animals that died, 3 showed sub-pleural bleeding at necropsy. At 1725 ppm there were no effects reported. At 1150 ppm 2 animals adopted an abnormal body position and exhibited ataxia.

Table 2: SUB-ACUTE TOXICITY OF XYLENES TO ANIMALS
Table 2.1: Inhalation Studies

Species	Concentration/dose/ duration	Observations
Mouse (318) NMRI 10 males and 10 females per group	0 or 150 ppm for 30 d. Xylene used was; 18% o-xylene 70% m-xylene 12% p-xylene.	A study to examine the effect of xylene on butylcholinesterase (BuChE) activity. There were no significant changes in body weight gain, liver or kidney weight, for both sexes. In females there was a significant decrease in spleen weight. There was a minor increase in BuChE activity in females, but this was not considered to be toxicologically significant.
Rabbit (319) New Zealand White 8 males/group	0 or 750 ppm, 12 h/d for 7 d. Xylene undefined	Study to determine the effects on levels of dopamine, homovanillic acid and noradrenaline in the rabbit brain. Xylene had no effect on levels of dopamine or homovanillic acid in the striatum of the tuberoinfundibular area. There was no effect on noradrenaline levels in the hippocampus or the tuberoinfundibular area. Dosing with methylhippuric acid, the major xylene metabolite (773 mg/kg/day, ip for 3 days), also had no effect on any of the above parameters.
Rabbit (320) New Zealand White 8 males per group	0 or 750 ppm, 12 h/d for 7 d Xylene undefined	Study of the effect of xylene on striatal and tubero-infundibular dopamine levels. Xylene had no effect. Intraperitonal administration of methylhippuric acid, the major xylene metabolite, (750 mg/kg/d) for 3 days also had no effect.
Rabbit (321) Chinchilla 6-8 animals/group Sex not given	a) 0 or 46 ppm, 2 h/d for 7-8 months. b) 0 or 11 ppm, 4 h/d for 7-8 months. Xylene undefined.	Study of the effect of low exposure concentrations. There was significant leukocytosis, significantly decreased antibody formation, increased urinary excretion of neutral 17-ketosteroids and a clear reduction in the serum albumin-globulin ratio reported at both concentrations. Insufficient data was provided to permit any firm conclusions to be drawn.

Table 2: SUB-ACUTE TOXICITY OF XYLENES TO ANIMALS
Table 2.1: Inhalation Studies

Species	Concentration/dose/ duration	Observations
Rabbit (322) 9 animals Strain and sex not given	0 or 299 ppm, 5-6 h/d, for 4-7 months. Xylene undefined.	Study of the influence on the immune response to injection with dysenteric vaccine. There was a significant decrease in the specific antibody titre and in the bactericidal action of the serum. There was no effect on the total or differential leukocyte count.
Rabbit (23) Strain and sex not given a) 6 animals/group	1150 ppm, 8 h/d, 6 d/week for 40 to 55 d.	General toxicology study. No deaths reported. Clinical signs were ambiguously reported. There was a marked decrease in erythrocyte count and leukocyte count as well as a marked increase in platelet count. These effects were reported to be reversible. There was no effect on the differential leukocyte count or coagulation time. There was a marked increase in blood urea levels. The presence of blood and albumin in the urine was noted.
b) 12 animals/group	690 ppm, 8 h/d, 6 d/week, for 110 to 130 d. Xylene undefined.	No deaths reported. Clinical signs were ambiguously reported. There was a slight fall in leukocyte count. No other haematological effects were noted. Other effects were as reported above. At both concentrations marked renal lesions were reported at histopathological examination. Changes associated with the glomerulae included swelling of the capillaries and cell desquamation. In the convoluted tubules there were signs of cell necrosis and the appearance of blood 'cylinders'. Hyperplasia of the bone marrow was reported. Widespread congestion, presumably at both exposure levels, was also reported. The limited reporting of this study (including no clear reference to a concurrent control group) restricts the conclusions that may be drawn.

Table 2: SUB-ACUTE TOXICITY OF XYLENES TO ANIMALS
Table 2.1: Inhalation Studies

Species	Concentration/dose/ duration	Observations
Gerbil (323) Mongolian 4 males and 4 females/group	0 or 160 or 320 ppm continuously for 3 months, followed by a 4 month exposure-free period. Xylene used was; 18% o-xylene 70% m-xylene 12% p-xylene <3% ethylbenzene.	Study of neurotoxicity using two astroglial cell marker proteins and DNA. There were no deaths or significant differences in body weights between test and control animals at 3 or 7 months. There was no effect on the weight of either the whole brain or any of the dissected brain regions. There was a significant increase in the concentration of glial fibrillary acidic (GFA) protein in the anterior cerebellar vermis at 160 and 320 ppm. In addition significant increases were seen in the posterior cerebellar vermis and the frontal cerebral cortex at 320 ppm. No significant effects were seen in other areas of the brain. There was a significant increase in the concentration of S-100 protein in the frontal cerebral cortex at 320 ppm. No significant effects were seen in other areas of the brain. There was a significant increase in the concentration of DNA in the posterior cerebellar vermis at 160 and 320 ppm. No significant effects were seen in other areas of the brain. There was no effect on protein concentrations in any area of the brain. The authors suggest that exposure to xylene resulted in brain damage which was manifest as a hypertrophic/hyperplastic response by astroglial cells. The response would appear to be irreversible or only slowly reversible. Effects were seen in particular areas of the brain at 160 and 320 ppm but the only significant overall brain response (increased GFA) was noted at 320 ppm.
Dog (6) Beagle 4 males/group	0, 180, 460 or 810 ppm, 6 h/d, 5 d/week for 13 weeks. Xylene used was; 7.63% o-xylene 65.01% m-xylene 7.84% p-xylene 19.27% ethylbenzene.	General toxicology study. No treatment related deaths were reported and there was no effect on body weight gain. There were no significant effects on haematological parameters or clinical chemistry. Normal ECG's were reported. Liver and kidney weights were not affected. There were no treatment related effects reported on histopathological examination.

Table 2: SUB-ACUTE TOXICITY OF XYLENES TO ANIMALS
Table 2.2: Oral Studies

Species	Concentration/dose/ duration	Observations
***o*-Xylene**		
Rat (150, 152) CFY Males and Females 8 animals/group	0 or 2166 mg/kg for 4 d.	Study of the effects on the liver. Decreased body weight and/or body weight gain was reported. There was a significant increase in liver weight. There was a significant increase in the hepatic cytochrome P450 concentration. There were significant increases in the activities of hepatic NADPH-cytochrome c reductase, aniline hydroxylase and aminopyrine N-demethylase. Hypertrophy of the centrilobular hepatocytes, and a widening of the centrilobular zone, was observed, with decreased staining for succinate dehydrogenase and glucose-6-phosphatase activity. Ultrastructural examination revealed minimal proliferation of the smooth endoplasmic reticulum in the centrilobular hepatocytes. Other effects, including mortality, were reported. However it is not made clear as to which of the solvents tested were responsible.
Rat (151) Sprague-Dawley 8-10 males/group	1062 mg/kg for 3 d.	Study to determine the effect on microsomal enzymes in rat liver, kidney and lung. No deaths were reported. Body weight loss was significantly greater than in controls. Liver weight was significantly increased, but there was no effect on kidney and lung weights. Cytochrome b_5 levels were significantly increased in the liver and kidneys. No results given for lung.

Table 2: SUB-ACUTE TOXICITY OF XYLENES TO ANIMALS
Table 2.2: Oral Studies

Species	Concentration/dose/ duration	Observations
		There were no significant effects reported on cytochrome P-450 or NADPH-cytochrome c reductase levels.
		There were significant increases in liver aminopyrine N-demethylase and kidney aniline hydroxylase activity.
Rat (153) Long-Evans hooded 5-10 males/group	0 and 200 ppm, feed concentration, for 1, 2, 3 or 6 months.	Study conducted to examine effects on liver histology.
		The livers appeared normal on macroscopic examination.
		Electron microscopy revealed the presence of 2 distinct types of membrane bound vacuoles in the hepatocytes. These structures were observed at one month and continued administration up to 6 months did not increase, or alter the appearance, of the structure. The 1st type was bound by a double unit membrane, the outer unit membrane appearing to be derived from SER. The 2nd type was single membrane bound, peripherally located in the hepatocytes and possibly derived from plasmalemma.
		Sub-chronic oral ingestion can cause vacuolar degeneration in aging rat hepatocytes.
Rat (324) Sprague - Dawley 10 males and females/group	0,250,1000 or 2000 mg/kg daily for 10d. In corn oil, by gavage One untreated control group as well.	General toxicology study (no organs examined for pathological change) No compound - related deaths. Body weight gain was apparently reduced at 2000 mg/kg (males). Haematology, serum chemistry and urinalysis revealed no compound-related effects.
		Relative liver weight was increased at 1000 mg/kg (females) and 2000 mg/kg (both sexes)

_m_-Xylene

Species	Concentration/dose/ duration	Observations
Rat (154) Fischer F344 10 males/group	0, 500 or 2000 mg/kg, 5 d/week for 4 weeks.	Study to determine the nephrotoxicity of various gasoline components.
		At 2000 mg/kg there were 6 deaths. None occurred at 500 mg/kg.
		The mean terminal body weights were found to be significantly reduced in both treatment groups.
		At necropsy, the mean kidney weights, for both treatment groups, were not significantly different from controls.

Table 2: SUB-ACUTE TOXICITY OF XYLENES TO ANIMALS
Table 2.2: Oral Studies

Species	Concentration/dose/ duration	Observations
Rat (151) Sprague-Dawley 8-10 males/group	1062 mg/kg for 3 d.	Study to determine the effect on microsomal enzymes in rat liver, kidney and lung.
		No deaths were reported.
		Body weight loss was significantly greater than in controls.
		Liver and kidney weights were significantly increased, but there was no effect on lung weight.
		There were significant increases in cytochrome P-450, cytochrome b_5 and NADPH-cytochrome c reductase in the liver and kidney.
		There was no significant effect on lung NADPH-cytochrome c reductase and results for lung cytochrome P-450 and cytochrome b_5 were not given.
		There were significant increases in liver aminopyrine N-demethylase and in liver and kidney aniline hydroxylase activity.
Rat (150, 152) CFY Males and females 8 animals/group	0 or 2166 mg/kg for 4 d.	Study of the effect on the liver.
		Decreased body weight and/or body weight gain was reported.
		There was a significant increase in liver weight.
		There was a marked increase in the hepatic cytochrome P450 concentration, significant in males.
		There were significant increases in the activities of hepatic NADPH-cytochrome c reductase, aniline hydroxylase and aminopyrine N-demethylase.
		Hypertrophy of the centrilobular hepatocytes, and a widening of the centrilobular zone, was observed, with decreased staining for succinate dehydrogenase and glucose-6-phosphatase activity.
		Ultrastructural examination revealed proliferation of the smooth endoplasmic reticulum and the appearance of variably shaped mitochondria in the centrilobular hepatocytes.

Table 2: SUB-ACUTE TOXICITY OF XYLENES TO ANIMALS
Table 2.2: Oral Studies

Species	Concentration/dose/ duration	Observations
		Other effects, including mortality, were reported. However it is not made clear as to which of the solvents tested were responsible.
Rat (15) Wistar 2 males	0 or 1728 mg/kg for 3 d.	Study of the effect on lung morphology using a scanning electron microscope. One animal died. Scanning electron microscopy revealed no lung abnormalities in the remaining animal.
Rat (324) Sprague - Dawley 10 males and 10 females/ group.	0,250,1000 or 2000 mg/kg daily for 10 d. In corn oil, by gavage One untreated control group as well.	General toxicology study (no organs examined for pathological change). No compound - related deaths. Body weight gain was apparently reduced at 2000 mg/kg (males). Haematology, serum chemistry, and urinalysis revealed no compound-related effects. Relative liver weight showed a dose-related increase at 1000 and 2000 mg/kg in both sexes. Relative spleen weight was decreased at 2000 mg/kg (males).

Table 2: SUB-ACUTE TOXICITY OF XYLENES TO ANIMALS
Table 2.2: Oral Studies

Species	Concentration/dose/ duration	Observations

p-Xylene

Species	Concentration/dose/ duration	Observations
Rat (150, 152) CFY Males and females 8 animals/group	0 or 2166 mg/kg for 4 d.	Study of the effect on the liver. Decreased body weight and/or body weight gain was reported. There was a significant increase in liver weight. There was a marked increase in the hepatic cytochrome P450 concentration. There were significant increases in the activities of hepatic NADPH-cytochrome c reductase, aniline hydroxylase and aminopyrine N-demethylase. Hypertrophy of the centrilobular hepatocytes, and a widening of the centrilobular zone, was observed, with decreased staining for succinate dehydrogenase and glucose-6-phosphatase activity. Ultrastructural examination revealed proliferation of the smooth endoplasmic reticulum and the appearance of variably shaped mitochondria in the centrilobular hepatocytes. Other effects, including mortality, were reported. However it is not made clear as to which of the solvents tested were responsible.
Rat (151) Sprague-Dawley 8-10 males/group	1062 mg/kg for 3 d.	Study to determine the effect on microsomal enzymes in rat liver, kidney and lung. No deaths were reported. Body weight loss was significantly greater than in controls. There were no significant effects on liver, kidney or lung weights. There were significant increases reported in levels of cytochrome b_5 in liver and kidneys, cytochrome P-450 in kidneys, and NADPH-cytochrome c reductase in the liver. There were significant increases in liver aminopyrine N-demethylase and kidney aniline hydroxylase activity.

Table 2: SUB-ACUTE TOXICITY OF XYLENES TO ANIMALS
Table 2.2: Oral Studies

Species	Concentration/dose/ duration	Observations
Rat (324) Sprague - Dawley 10 males and 10 females/group	0,250,1000 or 2000 mg/kg daily for 10 d. In corn oil, by gavage. One untreated control group as well.	General toxicology study, (no organs examined for pathological change). Deaths occurred at 2000 mg/kg (2 females). Body weight gain was apparently reduced at 2000 mg/kg (males). Haematology, clinical chemistry, and urinalysis revealed no compound - related effects. Relative liver weight was increased and relative thymus weight decreased at 2000 mg/kg.

Xylene

Species	Concentration/dose/ duration	Observations
Rat (102) F 344/N Males and females a) 5 animals/group	0, 125, 250, 500, 1000 or 2000 mg/kg, for 14 d.	General toxicology study. 3 males and 5 females died at 2000 mg/kg. Mean body weight gain was reduced in males by 23-29% at 250 mg/kg and above, and in females at 1000 mg/kg. Shallow, laboured breathing and prostration were reported immediately after dosing at 2000 mg/kg. No macroscopic, treatment related abnormalities were observed at necropsy.
b) 10 animals/group	0, 62.5, 125, 250, 500 or 1000 mg/kg, 5 d/week for 13 weeks. In corn oil, by gavage. Xylene used was; 9.1% o-xylene 60.2% m-xylene 13.6% p-xylene 17.0% ethylbenzene	No deaths reported. Mean body weight gain was reduced at 1000 mg/kg by 15% in males and 8% in females. There was no clinical signs of toxicity. No macroscopic or microscopic, treatment-related abnormalities were observed at necropsy.
Mouse (102) B6C3F$_1$ Males and females a) 5 animals/group	0, 250, 500, 1000, 2000, or 4000 mg/kg for 14 d.	General toxicology study. At 4000 mg/kg all animals died on the second day of dosing. Mean body weight gain was reduced in males by 25-90%. No consistent effects were noted in females. Shallow breathing and prostration were reported, during the first week, in mice at 2000 mg/kg. No macroscopic, treatment-related abnormalities were observed at necropsy.

Table 2: SUB-ACUTE TOXICITY OF XYLENES TO ANIMALS
Table 2.2: Oral Studies

Species	Concentration/dose/duration	Observations
b) 10 animals/group		At 2000 mg/kg 2 females died, however these deaths may be gavage related.
	0, 125, 250, 500, 1000 or 2000 mg/kg, 5 d/week for 13 weeks.	Mean body weight was reduced at 2000 mg/kg by 7% in males and 17% females.
	In corn oil, by gavage.	Weakness, lethargy, short and shallow breathing, unsteadiness, tremors and paresis were reported at 2000 mg/kg. These signs occurred within 5-10 min of dosing and lasted 15-60 min.
	Xylene used was; 9.1% *o*-xylene 60.2% *m*-xylene 13.6% *p*-xylene 17.0% ethylbenzene	No macroscopic or microscopic, treatment-related abnormalities were observed at necropsy.
Rat (324) Sprague - Dawley 10 males and 10 females/group.	0,150,750,1500 mg/kg daily for 90d. In corn oil, by gavage.	General toxicology study with microscopic examination of liver and kidneys only. No deaths occurred. Reduced body weight gain and increased aggressiveness noted in males at 1500 mg/kg.
	Xylene used was: 17.6% *o*-xylene 62.3% (*m*-xylene (*p*-xylene 20.0% ethylbenzene.	Haematology, clinical chemistry and urinalysis revealed no effects of clear toxicological significance.
		Relative liver weight showed a dose-related increase in males (150 mg/kg and above) and females (750 mg/kg and above). Relative kidney weight showed a dose-related increase in males (750 mg/kg and above) and an increase in females at 1500 mg/kg. Relative spleen and heart weights increased slightly in females at 1500 mg/kg. In kidneys, dose-related increased (all dose levels) noted for the incidence of slight to mild hyaline droplet formation in tubules of males and of minimal chronic nephropathy in females (scattered tubular dilation and atrophy, with occasional regeneration).

Table 2: SUB-ACUTE TOXICITY OF XYLENES TO ANIMALS
Table 2.3: Dermal Studies

Species	Concentration/dose/ duration	Observations
Xylene		
Rat (325) Wistar 80 pregnant females	0, 100, 200 or 2000 mg/kg, "throughout gestation". Xylene undefined.	A briefly reported study of neurotoxicity on pregnant animals and fetuses, using brain enzyme activities. The pregnant females exhibited reduced motor activity, in an open field test, significant at 2000 mg/kg. There was a dose-dependent decrease in maternal brain activities of cytochrome oxidase and cholinesterase, significant at all doses. DNA concentration and soluble proteins were reported to be decreased at the higher doses, with glucose-6-phosphate dehydrogenase activity increased at 2000 mg/kg only. There was a decrease in fetal brain activity of cytochrome oxidase and cholinesterase. There was a dose-dependent increase in the activities of malate dehydrogenase, isocitric dehydrogenase and glucose-6-phosphate dehydrogenase, significant at 200 and 2000 mg/kg.

Table 2: SUB-ACUTE TOXICITY OF XYLENES TO ANIMALS
Table 2.4: Parenteral Studies

Species	Concentration/dose/ duration	Observations
INTRAPERITONEAL		
o-Xylene		
Rat (153) Long-Evans 5-10 males/group	0 or 73 mg/kg for 3 d, in corn oil.	Study conducted to examine effects on liver histology.
		There were white, raised nodular lesions along the free margins of the liver (near the injection site).
		Electron microscopy revealed the lesions to be comprised of lipid droplets surrounded by macrophages and fibroblasts. Some fibroblasts appeared active in collagen synthesis. Mast cells and eosinophils were occasionally seen. Hepatocytes appeared morphologically normal.
		This exposure did not cause untrastructurally observable abnormalities in hepatocytes of young rats.
Mouse (326) North Carolina Dept of Health Strain 4 males/group	0 or 100 mg/kg for 3 d, in corn oil.	Study of the effect on the liver.
		There were no effects on relative liver weight, the specific activity of cytochrome P450 or the activities of p-nitroanisole O-demethylase and aminopyrene N-demethylase.
m-Xylene		
Rat (327) Sprague - Dawley females	0 or 750 mg/kg 5 d/week for 2 weeks.	Study to examine nephrotoxicity.
		No significant effects on urinary excretion of albumin or β_2-microglobulin.
	0 or 500 mg/kg 5 d/week for 2 weeks.	No significant effects on urinary excretion of albumin, β_2 microglobulin or N-acetyl-β-glucosaminidase.
		Thus no evidence of glomerular or tubular damage was seen in this study.

Table 2: SUB-ACUTE TOXICITY OF XYLENES TO ANIMALS
Table 2.4: Parenteral Studies

Species	Concentration/dose/ duration	Observations
Mouse (326) North Caroline Dept of Health Strain 4 males/group	0 or 100 mg/kg for 3 d, in corn oil.	Study of the effect on the liver. There was no effect on relative liver weight, the specific activity of cytochrome P450 or the activities of p-nitroanisole O-demethylase and aminopyrene N-demethylase.

p-Xylene

Rat (51) Sprague-Dawley Female Numbers not given	86 mg/kg for 3 d. Sacrifice 24 h after final injection.	Study of the effect on the organs. Histopathological examination of tissues (not stated) was reported to reveal moderate fatty infiltration of the liver and dilation of the smaller blood vessels of the lung. The study is briefly reported such that n firm conclusions to be drawn.

o

Mouse (326) North Caroline Dept of Health Strain 4 males/group	0 or 100 mg/kg for 3 d, in corn oil.	Study of the effect on the liver. There were no effects on relative liver weight, the specific activity of cytochrome P450 or the activities of p-nitroanisole O-demethylase and aminopyrene N-demethylase.

Table 2: SUB-ACUTE TOXICITY OF XYLENES TO ANIMALS
Table 2.4: Parenteral Studies

Species	Concentration/dose/ duration	Observations
Xylene		
Rat (43) Sprague-Dawley 8 males/group	0 or 2123 mg/kg, for 3 d, in corn oil. Xylene used was; 30% o-xylene 55% m-xylene 15% p-xylene.	Study of the effect on liver enzyme activities. There was no effect on body weight gain and no clinical signs of toxicity were noted. There was a significant increase in relative liver weight, microsomal protein content, cytochrome P450 content and the activities of NADPH-cytochrome c reductase, aminopyrine N-demethylase and aniline hydroxylase. There was a significant decrease in cytosolic glutathione levels and a significant increase in the glutathione S-transferase conjugation of 1, 2-dichloro-4-nitrobenzene. There was no effect on the glutathione S-transferase conjugation of 1-chloro-2, 4-dinitrobenzene and 1, 2-epoxy-3-(p-nitrophenoxy) propane. There was no effect on UDP glucuronyl transferase activity to phenol and o-aminophenol. There was a significant increase in the *in vitro* metabolism of benzene and toluene.
SUBCUTANEOUS		
o-**Xylene** **Rat** (328) Holtzman or Charles River Male. Numbers not given.	0 or 6370 mg/kg, in peanut oil, for 7 d.	Study of the effects of hydrocarbons on liver regeneration after partial hepatectomy. There was no effect on liver weight restoration.
Rabbit (85) Strain, sex and numbers not given	880 mg/rabbit for 3 d.	Study of effect on haematology. No clear effect was observed on a variety of haematological parameters, in this poorly reported study.

Table 2: SUB-ACUTE TOXICITY OF XYLENES TO ANIMALS
Table 2.4: Parenteral Studies

Species	Concentration/dose/ duration	Observations
_m_-Xylene		
Rat (328) Holtzman or Charles River Male Numbers not given	0 or 6370 mg/kg for peanut oil, for 7 d.	Study of the effects of hydrocarbon on liver regeneration after partial hepatectomy. There was no effect on liver weight restoration.
Rabbit (85) Strain, sex and numbers not given	864 mg/rabbit for 3 d.	Study of effect on haematology. No clear effect was observed on a variety of haematological parameters, in this poorly reported study.
_p_-Xylene **Rat** (328) Holtzman or Charles River Male. Numbers not given	0 or 9555 mg/kg in peanut oil for 7 d.	Study of the effects of hydrocarbon on liver regeneration after partial hepatectomy. There was no effect on liver weight restoration.
Rabbit (85) Strain, sex and number not given	861 mg/rabbit for 3 d.	Study of effect on haematology. No clear effect was observed on a variety of haematological parameters, in this poorly reported study.
Xylene **Rat** (155) Strain not given		Study of the effect on conditioned behaviour, and food reinforcement, using a maze.
a) 9 males/group	0, 174, 435 or 870 mg/kg, 7 d/week for 4 weeks. Exposure occurred after the 4 week training period.	At 870 mg/kg slight ataxia was noted for days 16-18 onwards and on day 20 there were 4 deaths. There was a marked decrease in body weight gain at 435 and 870 mg/kg. There was no significant effect on the performance of learnt activity.

Table 2: SUB-ACUTE TOXICITY OF XYLENES TO ANIMALS
Table 2.4: Parenteral Studies

Species	Concentration/dose/duration	Observations
b) 16 males/group	0 or 435 mg/kg, 7 d/week for 6 weeks. Exposure occurred one week prior to the initiation of training/testing. Xylene undefined.	There was a marked decrease in body weight gain. The mean running time was significantly higher from the start and decreased at a slower rate, attaining the 10-12 sec mean control time, 4 weeks after the last control animal. The mean error frequency was significantly higher than controls. Successful, error-free performance was markedly delayed compared to controls (Day 41/42 cf Day 27). Thus there was no significant effect on learnt behaviour. However there was a significant decrease in learning rate.
Rat (144) Stain, sex and numbers not given	870 or 1740 mg/kg, daily, for 4-22 d (average of 10 d). Xylene undefined.	Early toxicity study. A slight weight loss and decreased motor activity were reported. A slight, transient decrease in erythrocyte count was noted and there was reported to be no permanent effect on leukocyte count.
Rat (143) 10 males/group Strain not given	870 or 1740 mg/kg for 10 d. Xylene undefined	Early toxicity study. There was reported to be no effect on body weight, general condition or motor activity. A moderate reduction on erythrocyte count was noted and there was reported to be no effect on leukocyte count. There were no gross abnormalities reported at necropsy. Microscopically bone marrow hyperphasia, mild central hepatic necrosis, mild diffuse nephritis and moderate pigmentation of the spleen were reported.
Rat (287) CFY 5 males/group	 a) 2 x 435 mg/kg, daily b) 2 x 870 mg/kg, daily 7 h between doses, dosing for 7 months. Xylene undefined.	Study of effects on the heart using ECG. a) Repolarization disorders were seen in 2 animals after 3 months. b) One death reported. Repolarization disorders were seen in 3 animals after 6 weeks. After 3 months disorders in repolarization and atrial fibrillation were seen in the surviving animals, with low voltage in 2 of them.

Table 2: SUB-ACUTE TOXICITY OF XYLENES TO ANIMALS
Table 2.4: Parenteral Studies

Species	Concentration/dose/duration	Observations
Rat (329) Female Strain and numbers not given	0 or 87 mg/kg, twice per week for 4 months. Xylene undefined.	Effect on the thyroid gland and adrenal cortex during and up to two months after exposure. There appeared to be a reduction in size and activity (structural and histochemical changes) of the thyroid gland in immature rats, however the lack of quantitative data makes appraisal of this study difficult. The authors concluded that no marked effects or non-reversible structural changes occurred.
Rabbit (330) a) 5 animals/group b) 5 animals/group c) 21 animals/group Strain and sex not given.	 a) 300 mg/kg for 6 weeks b) 700 mg/kg for 9 weeks c) 300 mg/kg and busulphan (10 mg/kg, route not given), both for 2 weeks. Xylene undefined.	Study of the effect on peripheral blood cell counts. a)/b) There was no effect on peripheral blood cell counts. c) Study of the effect on busulphan myelotoxicity. All animals died due to gastroenteric side effects. There was no effect on busulphan myelotoxicity, as seen in peripheral blood cell counts and bone marrow DNA synthesis.

INTRAMUSCULAR

_p_-Xylene

Species	Concentration/dose/duration	Observations
Rabbit (156) a) 3 males/group b) 11 males/group	a) 0 or 860 mg/kg, daily until death. b) 0 or 86 mg/kg, daily for more than 4 weeks. Xylene undefined.	Study of the effect on the pathology of a limited number of organs. In the low dose group, 8 animals died. A minimal decrease in body weight gain was reported in both dose groups. A steady increase in leukocyte count was reported in the low dose group. In the high dose group a decrease was observed up to 2 days, followed by an increase. Some congestion and/or infiltration of polymorphonuclear leukocytes was reported in the liver, kidneys, lungs and spleen. A reduction in spermatogenesis was also reported. Evidence of an acute inflammatory response, with increased granulocyte turnover, was seen in the bone marrow. The limited data presented in this study prevent any definite conclusions being drawn.

114

Table 3: GENOTOXICITY OF XYLENES

Test system	Concentration/dose/duration	Observations
o-Xylene		
In vitro assays for point mutations with *Salmonella typhimurium*		
TA 98, TA 100,(157, 158) TA 1535, TA 1537	10000 µg/plate in DMSO.	Spot test. Negative both with and without metabolic activation (Rat and mouse S9). No positive control data were reported.
TA 98, TA 100,(159) TA 1535, TA 1537, TA 1538	0, 8.8, 88, 880, 4400, 8800 or 88000 µg/plate in acetone.	Plate incorporation assay. Negative both with and without mammalian metabolic activation. Toxicity was reported in all strains at the highest dose level. The positive controls gave an appropriate response.
TA 98, TA 100,(160) TA 1535, TA 1537, TA 1538	0, 20, 50, 100, 200 or 500 µg/plate in DMSO.	Plate incorporation assay. Negative both with and without metabolic activation (S9 from rats untreated or pretreated with Aroclor 1254). Bacterial toxicity was observed at the highest concentrations. The positive controls gave an appropriate response.
TA 98, TA 100, (157, 158) TA 1535, TA 1537	0.6, 2.4, 12, 60, 180 or 600 µg/plate in DMSO.	Plate incorporation assay. Negative both with and without metabolic activation (Rat S9) Toxicity was observed in strains TA 98 and TA 100 at the highest dose level. The positive controls gave an appropriate response.

115

Table 3: GENOTOXICITY OF XYLENES

Test system	Concentration/dose/duration	Observations
TA 98, TA 100,(161) UTH 8413, UTH 8414.	A range of concentrations from 10-1000 μg/plate in DMSO.	Plate incorporation assay. Negative both with and without metabolic activation (S9 from rats pretreated with Aroclor). No bacterial toxicity was reported. The positive controls gave an appropriate response.
TA 98, TA 100,(162) TA 1535, TA 1537.	0, 1, 3.3, 10, 33, 100 or 333 μg/plate, in DMSO.	Preincubation assay. Negative both with and without metabolic activation (S9 from rats or hamsters pretreated with Aroclor 1254). Slight bacterial toxicity was observed, at the highest dose, in all strains. The positive controls gave an appropriate response.

Other assays

Test system	Concentration/dose/duration	Observations
Mouse (109) NMRI 5 males/group	0, 106, 220, 326 or 440 mg/kg, ip. Two doses were given 24 h apart. Animals sacrificed 30 h after the first dose.	Micronucleus test. There was no increase in the incidence of micronucleated polychromatic erythrocytes. The ratio of polychromatic to normochromatic erythrocytes was not reported. No signs of toxicity were reported. However dose selection was based on an acute sighting study (LD_{50}, ip = 1364 mg/kg). The positive controls gave an appropriate response.
Rat (163) Sprague-Dawley Males Numbers not given	0, 440 or 1320 mg/kg, ip, for 2 d. Animals were maintained at $20-24^{0}C$ (all dose levels) or $24-32^{0}C$ (0 or 440 mg/kg).	Sperm head abnormality assay. There was no effect on the incidence of abnormal sperm in animals housed at $20-24^{0}C$. There was a significant increase in the incidence of abnormal sperm in animals housed at $24-30^{0}C$ and administered 440 mg/kg.

Test system	Concentration/dose/ duration	Observations
		Since the incidence of abnormal sperm increased with temperature, the authors proposed that o-xylene and temperature might act in a synergistic manner.

m-Xylene

In vitro assays for point mutations with *Salmonella typhimurium*

Test system	Concentration/dose/ duration	Observations
a) TA 98, TA 100,(164) TA 1535, TA 1537.	0, 3.2, 32, 318 or 3183 μg/plate, in ethanol.	Spot test.
		Negative both with and without metabolic activation (S9 from rats pretreated with Aroclor 1254).
		Bacterial toxicity was observed at the highest dose.
		The positive controls gave an appropriate response.
b) TA 98, TA 100.	0, 3.2, 32, 318 or 3183 μg/plate, in ethanol.	Assay type not stated.
		Negative both with and without metabolic activation (S9 from rats pretreated with 3-methylcholanthrene).
		Bacterial toxicity was observed at the highest dose.
		Positive controls were used.
TA 98, TA 100,(159) TA 1535, TA 1537, TA 1538	0, 8.6, 86, 864, 4320, 8640 or 86400 μg/plate in acetone.	Plate incorporation assay.
		Negative both with and without mammalian metabolic activation.
		Toxicity was observed in all strains, except TA 1538, at the highest dose level.
		The positive controls gave an appropriate response.

Table 3: GENOTOXICITY OF XYLENES

Test system	Concentration/dose/ duration	Observations
TA 98, TA 100,(160) TA 1535, TA 1537, TA 1538.	0, 20, 50, 100, 200, or 500 μg/plate in DMSO.	Plate incorporation assay. Negative both with and without metabolic activation (S9 from rats untreated or pretreated with Aroclor 1254). Bacterial toxicity was observed at the highest concentrations. The positive controls gave an appropriate response.
TA 98, TA 100,(161) UTH 8413, UTH 8414.	A range of concentrations from 10-1000 μg/plate in DMSO.	Plate incorporation assay. Negative both with and without metabolic activation (S9 from rats pretreated with Aroclor). No bacterial toxicity was reported. The positive controls gave an appropriate response.
TA 98, TA 100,(162) TA 1535, TA 1537.	0, 0.3, 1, 3.3, 10 or 33 μg/plate, in DMSO.	Preincubation assay. Negative both with and without metabolic activation (S9 from rats or hamsters pretreated with Aroclor 1254). No bacterial toxicity was observed. The positive controls gave an appropriate response.

Table 3: GENOTOXICITY OF XYLENES

Test system	Concentration/dose/ duration	Observations
Other assays		
Mouse (109) NMRI 5 males/group	0, 320, 432, 536 or 648 mg/kg, ip. Two doses were given 24 h apart. Animals sacrificed 30 h after the first dose.	Micronucleus test. There was no increase in the incidence of micronucleated polychromatic erythrocytes. The ratio of polychromatic to normochromatic erythrocytes was not reported. No signs of toxicity were reported. However dose selection was based on an acute sighting study (LD_{50}, ip = 1731 mg/kg). The positive controls gave an appropriate response.

Table 3: GENOTOXICITY OF XYLENES

Test system	Concentration/dose/ duration	Observations

p-Xylene

In vitro assays for point mutations with *Salmonella typhimurium*

Test system	Concentration/dose/ duration	Observations
a) TA 98, TA 100, (164) TA 1535, TA 1537	0, 3.2, 32, 318 or 3183 µg/plate, in ethanol.	Spot test. Negative both with and without metabolic activation (S9 from rats pretreated with Aroclor 1254). Bacterial toxicity was observed at the highest dose. The positive controls gave an appropriate response.
b) TA 98, TA 100	0, 3.2, 32, 318 or 3183 µg/plate, in ethanol.	Assay type not stated. Negative both with and without metabolic activation (S9 from rats pretreated with 3-methylcholanthrene). Bacterial toxicity was observed at the highest dose. Positive controls were used.
TA 98, TA 100, (159) TA 1535, TA 1537, TA 1538	0, 8.6, 86, 861, 4305, 8610 or 86100 µg/plate in acetone.	Plate incorporation assay. Negative both with and without mammalian metabolic activation. Toxicity was observed in all strains at the two highest dose levels. The positive controls gave an appropriate response.
TA 98, TA 100, (160) TA 1535, TA 1537, TA 1538	0, 20, 50, 100, 200 or 500 µg/plate, in DMSO.	Plate incorporation assay. Negative both with and without metabolic activation (S9 from rats untreated or pretreated with Aroclor 1254). Bacterial toxicity was observed at the highest concentrations. The positive controls gave an appropriate response.

Table 3: GENOTOXICITY OF XYLENES

Test system	Concentration/dose/ duration	Observations
TA 98, TA 100, (161) UTH 8413, UTH 8414.	A range of concentrations from 10-1000 µg/plate, in DMSO.	Plate incorporation assay. Negative both with and without metabolic activation (S9 from rats pretreated with Aroclor). No bacterial toxicity was reported. The positive controls gave an appropriate response.
TA 98, TA 100, (162) TA 1535, TA 1537.	0, 1, 3.3, 10, 33, 100 or 200 µg/plate, in DMSO.	Preincubation assay. Negative both with and without metabolic activation (S9 from rats or hamsters pretreated with Aroclor 1254). Slight bacterial toxicity was observed, at the highest dose, in all strains. The positive controls gave an appropriate response.
TA 98, TA 100, (165) TA 1535, TA 1537, TA 1538.	0, 1, 5, 10, 50, 100, 500 or 1000 µg/plate, in DMSO.	Preincubation assay. Negative both with and without metabolic activation (S9 from rats pretreated with polychlorinated biphenyl). Bacterial toxicity was observed at the highest two dose levels. The positive controls gave an appropriate response.

In vitro assay for point mutations with *Escherichia coli*

WP2 uvr A (165)	0, 1, 5, 10, 50, 100, 500 or 1000 µg/plate, in DMSO.	Preincubation assay. Negative both with and without metabolic activation (S9 from rats pretreated with polychlorinated biphenyl). Bacterial toxicity was observed at the highest dose levels. The positive controls gave an appropriate response.

121

Table 3: GENOTOXICITY OF XYLENES

Test system	Concentration/dose/ duration	Observations
Other assays		
Mouse (109) NMRI 5 males/group	0, 319, 431, 534 or 646 mg/kg, ip. Two doses were given 24 h apart. Animals sacrificed 30 h after the first dose.	Micronucleus test. There was no increase in the incidence of micronucleated polychromatic erythrocytes. The ratio of polychromatic to normochromatic erythrocytes was not reported. No signs of toxicity were reported. However dose selection was based on an acute sighting study (LD$_{50}$, ip = 2109 mg/kg). The positive controls gave an appropriate response.

Xylene

In vitro assays for point mutations with _Salmonella typhimurium_

Test system	Concentration/dose/ duration	Observations
TA 98, TA 100. (172)	Concentration range not stated. In DMSO. Xylene undefined.	Spot test. Negative both with and without metabolic activation (S9 from phenobarbital pretreated rats). In one test with TA 98, a mutation frequency twice that of the negative control was observed. However the colonies did not assume a typical ring appearance and the response was considerably less than the positive control. The authors ascribe the finding to contamination. Bacterial toxicity was not reported. The positive controls gave an appropriate response.
TA 98, TA 100, (167) TA 1535, TA 1537, TA 1538.	0, 4.0, 8.1, 16.1 or 32.2 μ/ml in acetone Xylene used was; 11.40% o-xylene 52.07% m-xylene 0.31% p-xylene 36.08% ethylbenzene.	Suspension assay. Negative both with and without metabolic activation (S9 from rats pretreated with Aroclor 1254). The maximum dose tested was that which killed approximately 50% of the bacteria. The positive controls gave an appropriate response. Study reportng is unclear.

Table 3: GENOTOXICITY OF XYLENES

Test system	Concentration/dose/duration	Observations
TA 98, TA 100, (167) TA 1535, TA 1537, TA 1538.	0, 0.87, 8.7, 87, 870 or 4350 µg/plate, in acetone. Xylene used was; 11.40% o-xylene 52.07% m-xylene 0.31% p-xylene 36.08% ethylbenzene.	Plate incorporation assay. Negative both with and without metabolic activation (S9 from rats pretreated with Aroclor 1254). The maximum dose tested was that which killed approximately 50% of the bacteria. The positive controls gave an appropriate response.
TA 97, TA 98, TA 100, (168) TA 1535.	0, 3.3, 10, 33, 100 or 200 µg/plate, in DMSO. Xylene undefined	Preincubation assay. Negative both with and without metabolic activation (S9 from rats or hamsters pretreated with Aroclor 1254). Testing was performed with S9 mix containing either 10 or 30% S9. Slight bacterial toxicity was observed, at the highest dose, in all strains. The positive controls gave an appropriate response.

In vitro assays with other bacteriological systems

Photobacterium phosphoreum Strain PPL- (331)	Concentration range not stated. Xylene undefined.	Spot test. There was an increase in the incidence of light emitting clones. Thus xylene was classified, by the authors, as a "carcinogen/mutagen". Bacterial toxicity was not reported. The mutagen and carcinogen 3,6-bis(dimethylamino) acridine gave a positive response. The significance of this result for the genotoxicity of xylene is unclear.

In vitro assays with mouse L5178Y cells

TK +/-. (167)	0, 5.6, 10.9, 21.8, 43.5, 65.3 or 87 µg/ml without activation.	Negative both with and without metabolic activation (S9 from non-induced mice).

123

Table 3: GENOTOXICITY OF XYLENES

Test system	Concentration/dose/duration	Observations
	0, 21.8, 43.5, 65.3, 87.0 or 130.5 µg/ml with activation.	Viability was reduced to 7.0% of controls at 87 µg/ml, without activation, and 1.1% at 130.5 µg/ml with activation.
	Xylene used was; 11.40% o-xylene 52.07% m-xylene 0.31% p-xylene 36.08% ethylbenzene.	The positive controls gave an appropriate response.

Cytogenetic studies in mammalian cells
In vitro assays

Human lymphocytes (332)	0, 15.2, 152, 1520 µg/ml	Cytogenetics assay.
	Xylene undefined.	There was no increase in the incidence of chromosome aberrations without metabolic activation, in metaphases of the 1st, 2nd or 3rd mitosis after the start of culture.
		Growth inhibition was reported at the highest dose.
		No positive control data were presented.

In vivo assays

Rat (167) Charles River 15 males/group.	0, 39, 128 or 384 mg/kg, ip as a single dose or daily for 5 d.	Bone marrow cytogenetics.
		There was no increase in the incidence of cells with chromosome aberrations.
	Animals sacrificed 6, 24 and 48 h after dosing (single dose study) or 6 h after the last dose (repeat dose study).	There was no effect on the mitotic index. Signs of toxicity were not reported.
	Xylene used was; 11.40% o-xylene 52.07% m-xylene 0.31% p-xylene 36.08% ethylbenzene.	The positive control gave an appropriate response.
Mouse (169) SHK 5-8 males/group	0, 1, 5, 25, 125 or 625 mg/kg, by gavage, daily for 10 d.	Bone marrow cytogenetics.
		There was no increase in the incidence of cells with chromosome aberrations.
	Animals sacrificed 6 h after the last dose.	Effects on mitotic activity were not reported.
	Xylene undefined.	No positive control data were presented.
		Study reported in limited detail.

Table 3: GENOTOXICITY OF XYLENES

Test system	Concentration/dose/duration	Observations
Rat (333) Female Strain and numbers not given.	Concentration and duration of daily exposure not stated. 60 d exposure. Sacrifice time not stated. Xylene undefined.	Micronucleus test. There was no increase in the incidence of micronucleated peripheral lymphocytes or bone marrow polychromatic erythrocytes compared to pre-exposure values. The ratio of polychromatic to normochromatic erythrocytes was not reported. Signs of toxicity were not reported. Benzene gave a positive response. Study reported in limited detail.
Rat (333) Female Strain and numbers not given.	A single parenteral dose. Dose levels not stated. Animals sacrificed 2 h after dosing. Xylene undefined.	Micronucleus test. There was no increase in the incidence of micronucleated peripheral lymphocytes or bone marrow polychromatic erythrocytes. The ratio of polchromatic to normochromatic erythrocytes was not reported. Signs of toxicity were not reported. Benzene gave a positive response. Study reported in limited detail.
Mouse (171) ICR 10 males/group.	0 or 440 mg/kg, by gavage. Animals sacrificed 24 h after dosing. Xylene undefined.	Micronucleus test. There was no increase in the incidence of bone marrow micronucleated polychromatic erythrocytes. There was no effect on the ratio of polychromatic to normochromatic erythrocytes. No signs of toxicity were reported. Benzene gave a positive reponse.

Table 3: GENOTOXICITY OF XYLENES

Test system	Concentration/dose/ duration	Observations
Mouse (169) SHK 5-8 males/group.	0, 8, 40, 200 or 1000 mg/kg, by gavage. Two doses were given 24 h apart. Animals sacrificed 30 h after the first dose. Xylene undefined.	Micronucleus test. There was no increase in the incidence of bone marrow micronucleated polychromatic erythrocytes. The ratio of polychromatic to normochromatic erythrocytes was not reported. Signs of toxicity were not reported. Benzene gave a positive response. Study reported in limited detail.

Dominant lethal assays

Rat (172) Long-Evans 10 males/group.	0 or 870 mg/kg, ip, single dose. The treated males were then mated with untreated females (1 male to 2 females, each week for 10 weeks). Females sacrificed on the 17th day following first contact with males. Xylene undefined.	There were no adverse effects on the number of pregnant females, the ratio of implants to corpora lutea, or the ratio of total post-implantation deaths to implants. Signs of toxicity were not reported. The positive control gave an appropriate response.
Mouse (173) Swiss-Webster 10 males/group.	0 or 870 mg/kg, sc, single dose. The treated males were then mated with untreated females (1 male to 3 females, each week for 8 weeks). Females sacrificed on the 15th day following first contact with males. Xylene undefined.	There were no adverse effects on the number of pregnant females, or on the ratio of total post-implantation deaths to implants. Signs of toxicity were not reported. The positive control gave an appropriate response.

In vitro indicator tests for DNA damage

Bacillus subtilis ([173]) H 17 and the DNA repair deficient derivative M 45.	Concentration range not stated. Xylene undefined.	Microsuspension assay. Negative both with and without metabolic activation (S9 from rats pretreated with Aroclor 1254). A number of known genotoxic chemicals gave a positive response.

Table 3: GENOTOXICITY OF XYLENES

Test system	Concentration/dose/duration	Observations
Escherichia coli (174) WP 2 and the DNA repair deficient derivatives WP 2 uvr A, WP 67, CM 611, WP 100. Also W 3110 pol A$^+$ and its derivative p 3478 pol A$^-$.	Concentration range not stated. Xylene undefined.	Microsuspension assay. Negative both with and without metabolic activation (S9 from rats pretreated with Aroclor 1254). A number of known genotoxic chemicals gave a positive response.
Saccharomyces cerevisiae D4 (167)	0, 5.4, 10.9, 21.8 or 43.5 mg/ml. Xylene used was; 11.40% o-xylene 52.07% m-xylene 0.31% p-xylene 36.08% ethylbenzene	Mitotic recombination assay. Negative both with and without metabolic activation (S9 from rats pretreated with Aroclor 1254). The maximum dose tested was that which killed approximately 50% of the yeast. The positive controls gave an appropriate response. Study reporting is unclear.
Human lymphocytes (332)	0, 15.2, 152, 1520 µg/ml for 3 d. Xylene undefined.	Sister chromatid exchange (SCE) assay. There was no increase in the incidence of SCE's without metabolic activation. Growth inhibition was reported at the highest dose No positive control data were presented.

Table 4: CARCINOGENICITY STUDIES WITH XYLENES IN ANIMALS
Oral Studies

Species	Concentration/dose/duration	Observations
Xylene		
Rat (102) F 344/N 50 males and 50 females/group.	0, 250 or 500 mg/kg, 5 d/week for 103 weeks. Dosing in corn oil, by gavage, at 4 ml/kg. Xylene used was; 9.1% *o*-xylene 60.2% *m*-xylene 13.6% *p*-xylene 17.0% ethylbenzene.	Carcinogenicity study with full histopathological examination of all animals (excluding spinal cord and peripheral nervous system). Haematology and biochemistry were not investigated. Survival, excluding accidental deaths, was dose-dependently reduced in males, but only at 500 mg/kg was survival significantly reduced over controls (Survival to termination: 72% controls; 50% at 250 mg/kg; 40% at 500 mg/kg). There was no effect on female survival. Mean male bodyweights were decreased (4-8%) at 500 mg/kg from week 64. There was no significant effect on mean male bodyweights, at 250 mg/kg, or on mean female bodyweights in either dosed group. No clinical signs of toxicity were reported. There was no evidence of target organ toxicity at histopathological examination. There was no evidence of any treatment-related increase in the incidence of benign and/or malignant neoplasia. No forestomach tumours were seen in either males or females. Thus there was no evidence of systemic toxicity or carcinogenicity due to xylene in this study.
Rat (175, 176) Sprague-Dawley 40 males and 40 females/group. 50 males and 50 females in control group.	0 or 500 mg/kg, 4-5 d/week for 104 weeks. Animals then observed for remainder of lifespan (up to 141 weeks). Dosing in olive oil, by gavage. Xylene undefined.	Carcinogenicity study, with very limited reporting of data. 12.5% of test animals and 7% of controls were alive at 134 weeks. Oral carcinoma (10% test, 0% controls), as well as "acanthomas and dysplasias" of the forestomach (10% test, 0% controls) were reported at 134 weeks. Malignant neoplasms were noted in 45% of test animals and 21% of controls at 141 weeks. This study is so poorly reported that no assessment of the data is possible and thus no carcinogenicity evaluation may be made.

Table 4: CARCINOGENICITY STUDIES WITH XYLENES IN ANIMALS
        Oral Studies

Species	Concentration/dose/ duration	Observations
Mouse (102) B6C3F$_1$ 50 males and 50 females/group.	0, 500 or 1000 mg/kg, 5 d/week for 103 weeks. Dosing in corn oil, by gavage, at 8 ml/kg. Xylene used was; 9.1% *o*-xylene 60.2% *m*-xylene 13.6% *p*-xylene 17.0% ethylbenzene.	Carcinogenicity study, with full histopathological examination of all test animals and most controls (excluding spinal cord and peripheral nervous systems). Haematology and biochemistry were not investigated. There was no significant effect on survival. There was no significant effect on mean bodyweight. Hyperactivity, lasting 5-30 min, was reported in all animals after dosing at 1000 mg/kg. This effect was consistently observed over weeks 4-103. There was no evidence of target organ toxicity at histopathological examination. There was no evidence of any treatment related increase in the incidence of benign and/or malignant neoplasia. Squamous cell papillomas in the forestomach were seen in controls (2 males), at 500 mg/kg (1 male and 2 females) and at 1000 mg/kg (1 male). Thus there was no evidence of systemic toxicity or carcinogenicity due to xylene in this study.

Table 5: REPRODUCTIVE TOXICITY STUDIES WITH XYLENES IN ANIMALS

Species	Concentration/dose/duration	Observations
o-Xylene		
Rat (14, 181, 182, 183) CFY 15(control) and 20(treated) females per group	0, 34, 345 or 690 ppm, 24 h/d from days 7 to 14 of gestation.	The dams were killed on day 21 of gestation and their uteri and contents examined. There was a dose-related reduction in maternal food consumption and weight gain during the exposure period. No significant differences from control were observed on day 21. Routine histology and enzyme histochemistry revealed no treatment-related effects. Some ultrastructural changes in the liver (increased RER and SER) were observed in the dams exposed to 345 or 690 ppm. Exposure to *o*-xylene had no effect on post implantation loss or mean litter size.

At 345 and 690 ppm there was evidence of delayed development (reduced mean fetal weight and increased numbers of weight retarded fetuses and (at 690 ppm only) fetuses with delayed skeletal ossification (48 out of 121 examined). There was no increase in the incidence of fetuses with minor variations or malformations. There were no significant findings in the group exposed to 34 ppm.

Thus in this study exposure to *o*-xylene resulted in delayed fetal development only at exposure levels which resulted in some maternal toxicity. There was no evidence of teratogenicity. |
| **Mouse** (81, 184) CFLP 17 dams (treated) and 115 (air control) | 0 or 115 ppm for 4 h, 3 times per day, on days 6-15 of gestation | The dams were killed on day 18 of gestation and their uteri and contents examined.

The data were presented in summary form only. Maternal toxicity was not reported.

There was evidence of delayed development (increased incidence of weight-retarded fetuses and fetuses with delayed skeletal ossification). |

130

Table 5: **REPRODUCTIVE TOXICITY STUDIES WITH XYLENES IN ANIMALS**

Species	Concentration/dose/ duration	Observations
		There was no increase in the incidence of post-implantation loss, minor variants or malformations. In the absence of the reporting of any maternal toxicity the significance of the delayed development is unclear.
Rabbit (184) New Zealand White 9 dams (treated) and 60 (air control)	0 or 115 ppm continuously from days 7-20 of gestation.	The dams were killed on day 30 of gestation and their uteri and contents examined. The data were presented in summary form only. There was no effect on maternal weight gain or relative liver weight. In the treated group there were no significant effects on post-implantation loss, the incidence of delayed development, minor variants or malformations. As there was no maternal toxicity observed in this study, a maximum tolerated dose was not given. Thus this study is of limited value in assessing the teratogenic potential of *o*-xylene.
Mouse (185) CD-1 Number of animals used not stated	0, 261, 683 or 870 mg/kg, orally, from days 6-15 of gestation or 0 or 870 mg/kg from days 12-15 of gestation.	Report in abstract form only. Following administration over days 6-15 overt maternal toxicity, a significantly increased incidence of resorptions and an increased incidence of cleft palate were reported at 683 and 870 mg/kg. Following administration over days 12-15 there was a significant increase in the incidence of maternal mortality but no increase in the incidence of malformations. Thus in this study *o*-xylene administration resulted in an increased incidence of malformations only at a dose level causing maternal mortality.

Species	Concentration/dose/ duration	Observations

m-Xylene

Rat (14, 181, 182, 187)
CFY
25 (control)
20 (34, 345 ppm) or
30 (690 ppm) females
per group

0, 34, 345 or 690 ppm
24 h/d from days 7 to 14
of gestation.

The dams were killed on day 21 of gestation and their uteri and contents examined. 4 dams exposed to 690 ppm died and food consumption by this group was reduced during the exposure period. Maternal bodyweight gain was reduced at all exposure levels during the exposure period but only in the 690 ppm group on day 21. Routine histology and enzyme histochemistry revealed no treatment related effects.

In the group exposed to 690 ppm post implantation loss and litter size were not significantly affected. There was evidence of delayed development (reduced mean fetal weight and increased numbers of weight retarded fetuses). The incidence of fetuses with delayed skeletal ossification was not increased. An increased incidence of a minor variant (extra ribs) was observed in $^8/_{97}$. There was no increase in the incidence of fetuses with malformations.

There were no significant findings in the groups exposed to 34 or 345 ppm. Thus, in this study exposure to *m*-xylene resulted in delayed development and an increased incidence of a minor variant at an exposure level which resulted in some maternal mortality. There was no evidence of teratogenicity.

Mouse (181)
CFLP
18 dams (treated)
and 115 (air control)

0 or 115 ppm for 4 h, 3
times per day, on days
6-15 of gestation.

The dams were killed on day 18 of gestation and their uteri and contents examined.

The data were presented in summary form only. Maternal toxicity was not reported.

There was evidence of delayed development (increased incidence of weight-retarded fetuses and fetuses with delayed skeletal ossification). There was no increase in

Table 5:	REPRODUCTIVE TOXICITY STUDIES WITH XYLENES IN ANIMALS	
Species	Concentration/dose/ duration	Observations

		the incidence of post-implantation loss, minor variants or malformations.
		In the absence of the reporting of any maternal toxicity the significance of the delayed development is unclear.
Rabbit (181, 184) New Zealand White 9 dams (treated) and 60 (air control)	0 or 115 ppm continuously from days 7-20 of gestation.	The dams were killed on day 30 of gestation and their uteri and contents examined.
		The data were presented in summary form only.
		There was no effect on maternal weight gain or relative liver weight. In the treated group there were no significant effects on the incidence of delayed development, minor variants or malformations. A slightly increased incidence of post-implantation loss was observed.
		As there was no maternal toxicity observed in this study, a maximum tolerated dose was not given. Thus this study is of limited value in assessing the teratogenic potential of *m*-xylene.
Mouse (185) CD-1 Number of animals used not stated.	0, 261, 683 or 870 mg/kg, orally, from days 6-15 of gestation or 0 or 870 mg/kg from days 12-15 of gestation.	Report in abstract form only.
		Following administration over days 6-15, overt maternal toxicity and a significantly increased incidence of resorptions were reported at 870 mg/kg. In a repeat study, overt maternal toxicity was not observed but there was a statistically significant increase in the incidence of cleft palate at 870 mg/kg. Following administration over days 12-15 there was a significant increase in the incidence of both maternal mortality and of malformations (mostly cleft palates). In a repeat study no overt maternal toxicity was observed and there was no increase in the incidence of malformations. Thus in this study maternal toxicity and an increased incidence of malformations were reported but they were not consistently observed. In the absence of the full data no conclusions can be made.

Table 5: REPRODUCTIVE TOXICITY STUDIES WITH XYLENES IN ANIMALS

Species	Concentration/dose/ duration	Observations
Mouse (186) ICR/SIM 26 pregnant (control) and 27 (treated) animals	0 to 2000 mg/kg orally, from days 8 to 12 of gestation.	Study to validate a developmental toxicity screen. The dams delivered their young which were examined, counted and weighted on post natal days 1 and 3. Dead neonates were examined for external abnormalities. 1 treated dam died but there was no effect on weight gain in the remaining dams. m-Xylene administration had no effect on the number of litters born (100%), on the mean number of neonates per litter or mean neonate weight. Thus m-xylene administration had no effect in this developmental toxicity screen.
<u>p-Xylene</u>		
Rat (14, 181, 182, 188) CFY 20 females per group	0, 34, 345 or 690 ppm 24 h/d from days 7 to 14 of gestation.	The dams were killed on day 21 of gestation and their uteri and contents examined. There was a reduction in maternal food consumption and weight gain during the exposure period at 690 ppm. No significant differences from control were observed on day 21. Routine histology and enzyme histochemistry revealed no treatment related effects. At 690 ppm there were increased incidences of total resorptions and post implantation loss Mean litter size was significantly reduced There was evidence of delayed development (reduced mean fetal weight and increased number of weight retarded fetuses) at 690 ppm. The incidence of fetuses with delayed skeletal ossification was increased at all exposure levels. (control 16/116, 34 ppm 24/77, 345 ppm 38/100, 690 ppm 15/26) An increased incidence of a minor variant (extra ribs) was observed in 10/26 fetuses at 690 ppm. There was no increase in the incidence of fetuses with malformations. Thus in this study exposure to p-xylene resulted in post-implantation loss and delayed development and an increased incidence of a minor variant at exposure levels which resulted

Table 5 :

Table 5 :	REPRODUCTIVE TOXICITY STUDIES WITH XYLENES IN ANIMALS	
Species	Concentration/dose/ duration	Observations
		in some maternal toxicity. The incidence of delayed development (delayed skeletal ossification) was also increased at exposure levels having no significant maternal toxicity. There was no evidence of teratogenicity.
Rat (189) White 17 pregnant animals (control) and 29 (treated)	0 or 114 ppm continuously from days 1-20 of gestation.	The dams were killed on day 20 of gestation and their uteri and contents examined. There was no effect on the number of corpora lutea. There was a significant increase in the incidence of both pre-and post implantation losses in the treated group. There was no effect on the number of fetuses with delayed development or common variants and there were no malformed fetuses. Thus in this study *p*-xylene was fetotoxic causing an increased incidence of pre-and post-implantation losses. However, as maternal toxicity, if any, was not reported, this study is of limited value.
Rat (190) Sprague-Dawley 25 dams per group	0, 800 or 1600 ppm, 6 h/d from days 7-16 of gestation.	In this study the dams were allowed to deliver their young. The litters were counted, weighed and observed for external malformations on post-natal day (PD) 3 and the litters normalised to 8 pups (4 male and 4 female, ±1 on PD4. Behavioural testing was performed on PD13, 17, 21 and 63 (acoustic startle response) and on PD22 and 65 (locomotor activity in a figure-8 maze). Maternal weight gain was significantly reduced in the group exposed to 1,600 ppm. There was no effect on mean litter size or pup weight on PD1 or PD3. There were no effects on pup growth rate (to PD63) or on locomotor activity (to PD65) or the acoustic startle response (to PD63). Thus, in this study *p*-xylene had no effects on post-natal viability, growth or CNS development at an exposure level causing some maternal toxicity (reduced growth rate).

Table 5 :	REPRODUCTIVE TOXICITY STUDIES WITH XYLENES IN ANIMALS	
Species	Concentration/dose/ duration	Observations

Rat (300) CFY Number of animals used not stated	0 or 345 ppm, 8 h/d from days 8 to 10 of gestation.	Study of the effects of *p*-xylene on postganglionic noradrenergic nerves in the ovary and uterus of pregnant animals.
		The animals were killed on day 11 of gestation and their uteri and contents examined.
		Hyperinnervation was seen in the ovary, most pronounced periarterially but also around the corpora lutea. Increased numbers of mast cells were seen around blood vessels and corpora lutea.
		In the uterus occasional degeneration or hyperinnervation were observed.
		The authors suggest that possible disturbance in ovarian and uterine blood flow and in ovarian steroid production may be significant as an embryotoxicity mechanism for xylene.
Rat (334, 335. 336) CFY 20 pregnant females per group.	0 or 681 ppm for 24 h on day 10 or continuously on days 9 to 10 of gestation.	Study of the effect of xylene inhalation during pregnancy on sex steroids.
		The animals were killed on day 11 of gestation.
		Venous blood was obtained from one uterine horn and ovarian and uterine venous blood flow measured. Uterine and femoral vein progesterone and 17β - oestradiol were measured. The uterine contents were examined.
		No maternal toxicity was reported. Following exposure on days 9 to 10 fetal weight was reduced but there were no deaths. No effects on the placenta were observed.
		Ovarian blood flow decreased (not statistically significant) with increasing length of exposure. There was no effect on uterine blood flow.
		Ovarian progesterone and 17β-oestradiol secretion were not significantly affected by *p*-xylene treatment. However the levels of these 2 hormones in the uterine

Table 5 :   REPRODUCTIVE TOXICITY STUDIES WITH XYLENES IN ANIMALS

Species	Concentration/dose/duration	Observations
		and femoral veins were decreased following 48 (but not 24)h exposure. The authors conclude that p-xylene, by inducing hepatic monooxygenases, facilitates the biotransformation of progesterone and 17β-oestradiol. Decreased sex hormone levels may then play a role in the embryotoxicity of p-xylene.

No statistically significant changes were noted in a Hungarian language report of a similar study using exposure to 341 ppm. |
| **Mouse** (181, 184) CFLP 17 dams (treated) and 115 (air control) | 0 or 115 ppm for 4 h, 3 times per day, on days 6-15 of gestation | The dams were killed on day 18 of gestation and their uteri and contents examined.

The data were presented in summary form only. Maternal toxicity was not reported.

There was evidence of delayed development (increased incidence of weight-retarded fetuses and fetuses with delayed skeletal ossification).

There was no increase in the incidence of post-implantation loss, minor variants or malformations.

In the absence of the reporting of any maternal toxicity the significance of the delayed development is unclear. |
| **Rabbit** (181, 184) New Zealand White

8-10 dams per group (treated) and 60 **dams** (air control) | 0, 115, or 230 ppm continuously from days 7-20 of gestation. | The dams were killed on day 30 of gestation and their uteri and contents were examined.

The data were presented in summary form only.

At 230 ppm there were no live fetuses (1 dam died, 3 aborted and in 4 there was total resorption or fetal death *in utero)*.

At 115 ppm there was no effect on maternal weight gain or relative liver weight. There were no significant effects on post implantation loss, the incidence |

Table 5 :

REPRODUCTIVE TOXICITY STUDIES WITH XYLENES IN ANIMALS

Species	Concentration/dose/ duration	Observations
		of delayed development, minor variants or malformations. Thus in this study there were no live fetuses at 230 ppm and no significant findings at 115 ppm.
Mouse (185) CD-1 Number of animals used not stated	0, 261, 683 or 870 mg/kg, orally, from days 6-15 of gestation or 0 or 870 mg/kg from days 12-15 of gestation.	Report in abstract form only. Following administration over days 6-15 overt maternal toxicity, a significantly increased incidence of resorptions and an increased incidence of cleft palate were reported at 683 and 870 mg/kg. Following administration over days 12-15 there was a significant increase in the incidence of maternal mortality and in the incidence of malformations (mostly cleft palates). Thus in this study *p*-xylene administration resulted in an increased incidence of malformations only at a dose level causing maternal mortality.

Xylene

Rat (181, 184, 193) CFY 25 per group	0, 53, 437 or 772 ppm continuously from days 7-15 of gestation. Xylene used was; 10% *o*-xylene 50% *m*-xylene 20% *p*-xylene 20% Ethylbenzene	The dams were killed on day 21 of gestation and their uteri and contents examined. 1 dam exposed to 772 ppm died and food consumption and weight gain were reduced in this group during the exposure period. Group mean bodyweight remained significantly below control mean on day 21. Routine histology and enzyme histochemistry showed no treatment related effects. Post-implantation loss was increased in the group exposed to 772 ppm but there was no effect on mean litter size at any exposure level. Delayed development (retarded ossification) was observed at all exposure levels but there was no effect on mean fetal weight or the incidence of weight-retarded fetuses. At 772 ppm there was an increased incidence of a minor variant (extra ribs).

Table 5 :

Species	Concentration/dose/ duration	Observations
		There was no treatment related effect on the incidence of malformations.

Thus in this study there was evidence of delayed skeletal development and an increased incidence of a common variant at an exposure level causing maternal mortality. Delayed skeletal development was also observed at exposure levels not causing significant maternal toxicity. There was no evidence of teratogenicity.

The data presented in the original Hungarian language report (193) was represented, after apparent reassessment in a second Hungarian language report (181) and also as a summary in an English language report (184).
Following this reassessment an increased incidence of weight retarded fetuses was reported at 772 ppm. |
| **Rat** (192) CFY 26 controls and 20 treated females | 0 or 230 ppm continuously from days 9-14 of gestation.

Xylene used was; 10% o-xylene 50% m-xylene 20% p-xylene 20% Ethylbenzene | The dams were killed on day 21 of gestation and their uteri and contents examined.

There was no effect on maternal weight gain or post-implantation loss. There was no evidence of delayed development in the treated group, but there was an increased incidence of minor variants (fetuses with extra ribs or fused sternebrae). Malformations (^{2}/286 fetuses with agnathia and ^{1}/143 with fissura sterni) were observed in the treated group. None were observed in the controls.

Thus, in this study at an exposure level not resulting in significant maternal toxicity there was an increased incidence of minor variants. The significance of the 3 malformations observed is uncertain. |

Table 5 :	REPRODUCTIVE TOXICITY STUDIES WITH XYLENES IN ANIMALS	
Species	Concentration/dose/ duration	Observations
Rat (194) CFY 11-21 dams per group		The dams were killed on day 21 of gestation and their uteri and contents examined.
		The data were presented in summary form only.
	a) 0 or 138 ppm continuously from days 7-15 of gestation.	In the group exposed to xylene maternal weight gain was reduced and relative liver weight increased . There was no effect on post-implantation losses or malformations. There was an increased incidence of delayed development (weight retarded fetuses and fetuses with retarded skeletal ossification) and a minor variant (extra ribs).
	b) 0 or 138 ppm xylene, in conjunction with either 200 ppm benzene or 266 ppm toluene, continuously from days 7-15 of gestation.	In the co-exposure groups the effects on the fetuses were not additive.
c) 15 dams (xylene exposed) and 7-14 per per group (controls)	828 ppm xylene, continuously from days 10-13 of gestation. All animals received acetylsalicylic acid (ASA) (either 250 or 500 mg/kg) on day 12. Control animals were exposed to air and ASA (0, 250 or 500 mg/kg) as above.	Only 1 dam exposed to xylene and treated with 500 mg/kg ASA survived. In this animal all fetuses were resorbed. In the group treated with 250 mg/kg ASA no dams died. Decreased maternal weight gain was reported but no data were presented. Xylene increased the fetotoxic and teratogenic action of ASA by a mechanism which increased the plasma concentration of free salicylic acid.
d) 16-20 dams per group	0 or 333 ppm continuously from days 7-15 of gestation. In addition the drinking water contained either 5% sucrose or 5% sucrose and 10% ethanol. Xylene undefined	In the group exposed to xylene & sucrose there was no effect on post-implantation loss but there was evidence of delayed development (increased incidence of weight-retarded fetuses and fetuses with retarded skeletal ossification). There was no evidence of an increased incidence of malformations. In the group exposed to xylene & ethanol & sucrose the incidence of delayed development was increased but there was no evidence of teratogenicity. Thus, in these studies exposure to xylene resulted in delayed fetal development but no evidence of teratogenicity. In co-exposure studies xylene increased the

140

Table 5 :   REPRODUCTIVE TOXICITY STUDIES WITH XYLENES IN ANIMALS

Species	Concentration/dose/ duration	Observations

maternal toxicity, fetotoxicity and teratogenicity of ASA and the fetotoxicity of benzene.

Rat (191)
Sprague - Dawley
30 males and 60
females (control),
10 males and 20
females (60 or 250 ppm
groups) 20 males and 40
females (500 ppm). In
addition 10 males
exposed to 500 ppm were
mated with 20 untreated
females and 10 untreated
males were mated with 20
females exposed to
500 ppm.

0, 60, 250 or 500 ppm, 6 h/d, 7 d/week. Exposures continued for a 131 day pre-mating period after which males and unmated females continued to receive the appropriate exposures during the mating period. For the first 8 days of mating 1 male was housed with 2 females. For the remaining 13 days 1 male was randomly housed with 1 female. Mating continued until the female was considered mated (evidence of sperm in the vaginal smear).

Mated females were exposed daily during days 1-20 of gestation and days 5-20 of lactation.

Xylene used was;
20.4% o-xylene
44.2% m-xylene
20.3% p-xylene
12.8% Ethylbenzene

A single generation study with a teratology element. 20 control and 12 dams exposed to 500 ppm were killed on day 21 of gestation and their uteri and contents were examined. The remaining dams delivered their young.

Effects on F_0 generation

There were no mortalities among the treated animals. For the males, there was no effect on bodyweight gain during the premating, mating or post-mating (exposure-free) periods (50% of males killed on completion of the mating period).

For the females during the mating period mean bodyweight gain was significantly greater than controls in the groups exposed to 60 and 250 ppm. There were no differences in maternal bodyweight gain during gestation and no adverse effects on bodyweight were observed during lactation. There was no effect on food consumption during either gestation or lactation. For both males and females there were no other observations which were considered to be treatment related.

There were no treatment-related effects on mating, fertility or pregnancy indices.

Effects on F_1 generation (pups evaluated during lactation and into early adult life).

There were no treatment-related effects on mean duration of gestation or mean litter size (total or live pups) or mean pup

Table 5 :	REPRODUCTIVE TOXICITY STUDIES WITH XYLENES IN ANIMALS	
Species	Concentration/dose/ duration	Observations

weight on day 1. On day 4 of lactation litters where culled or cross-fostered where appropriate to give litters of 4 males and 4 females.

During the period of lactation there were no toxicologically important effects on mean pup weight or survival, mean litter size or survival or on pup sex distribution. On day 21, 1 pup/sex/ litter was killed and the gonads weighed. There was no effect on mean absolute or relative testis weights. No toxicologically important effects on mean relative or absolute ovary weights were noted.

On day 49 the pups were weighed and 1/sex/litter was killed and the gonads weighed. Mean pup weight (both male and female) in the group where both parents had been exposed to 500 ppm was significantly lower than for controls. There were no effects in any other group. There was no effect on mean absolute or relative testis or ovary weights.

Effects on F_1 generation (teratogenicity study)

There were no toxicologically important effects on the number of corpora lutea, implantation sites, live fetuses or live fetuses per implant or on mean fetal weight or sex distribution.

Examination of the fetuses showed that there was no increase in the incidence of fetuses with delayed development or malformations in the groups exposed to xylene.

Thus in this study xylene had no toxicologically important effects on male or female fertility or mating ability. There was similarly no effect on pregnancy or parturtion or on the pups during lactation and early post-natal life. In the teratogenicity study there was no evidence of delayed development or of an

Table 5 :   REPRODUCTIVE TOXICITY STUDIES WITH XYLENES IN ANIMALS

Species	Concentration/dose/ duration	Observations
		increased incidence of malformations in the groups exposed to xylene. However, no toxicity was observed in the parental animals during premating or mating or during gestation (females). Thus an MTD may not have been achieved and no conclusions can be drawn on the potential of xylene to have an adverse effect on reproduction.
Rat (191) Sprague-Dawley 26 females per group.	0, 100 or 400 ppm 6 h/d from days 6 to 15 of gestation. Xylene used was; 11.4% *o*-xylene 52.1% *m*-xylene 0.3% *p*-xylene 36.1% Ethylbenzene	The animals were killed on day 20 of gestation and their uteri and contents examined. There was no maternal mortality or effect on maternal weight gain or food consumption. There were no treatment-related effects on the number of implantation sites or live or dead fetuses, litter size or mean fetal weight. An increased incidence of fetuses with retarded skeletal ossification was noted at 400 ppm. However, as these were found predominantly in 3 litters this finding was not considered to be treatment-related. No malformations were observed. Thus, in this study xylene had no effect on various fetal parameters and no teratogenic potential was observed. However, as no maternal toxicity was observed the maximum exposure level was considered to be below the maximum tolerated dose.
Rat (196) Wistar 46 pregnant controls and 160 pregnant animals apparently divided between the 3 exposed groups.	0, 2, 11 or 114 ppm 6 h/d, 5 d/w from days 1-21 of gestation. Mixed xylene was tested but the isomer composition was not defined.	Some of the dams were killed on day 21 of gestation and their uteri and contents examined. The remaining dams delivered their young. Maternal toxicity, if observed, was not reported. Xylene exposure had no effect on the number of corpora lutea, pre-implantation loss, viable fetuses per litter or early resorptions. The incidence of post implantation loss and fetal death was significantly increased at both 11 and 114 ppm. At these exposure levels mean fetal weight was decreased and the incidence of fetuses with haemorrhages in the thoracic

Table 5 :   REPRODUCTIVE TOXICITY STUDIES WITH XYLENES IN ANIMALS

Species	Concentration/dose/ duration	Observations

and abdominal cavities was increased. Delayed skeletal development was observed at 11 and 114 ppm. At 114 ppm a significant increase in certain malformations was claimed but the incidence was not presented. In the groups which delivered their young there was no significant effect on post natal mortality. At 11 and 114 ppm pup bodyweights were significantly decreased on post-natal days 7 and 21 and not significantly on days 4 and 45.

At 11 and 114 ppm changes in behavioural activity and in enzyme activities of the brain, liver, myocardium and lungs were reported. However no data were presented. Thus in this study xylene exposure resulted in fetal death, reduced fetal weight and delayed skeletal development. However, in the absence of the reporting of maternal toxicity these effects are of uncertain significance. The significance of the claimed malformations and the changes in behavioural activity and enzyme levels cannot be assessed because no data were presented.

Rat ([337])
Wistar

a) 16 control and
   12 treated dams

0 or 36 mg/kg, orally from days 2 or 7 of gestation.

The animals were killed on day 8 of gestation. There was no effect on the number of corpora lutea or resorptions.

b) 13 control and 19
   treated dams

0 or 36 mg/kg orally from days 11 to 19 of gestation.

An undefined mixture of *o*-, *m*-, and *p*-xylene was used.

The animals delivered their young which were studied up to day 30 of post-natal life.

There was no effect on the mean duration of pregnancy, the number of live births, the newborn pup bodyweight or pup mortality up to post-natal day 2. After post-natal day 2 mortality in the treated group pups increased such that at post-natal day 30 overall mortality in the treated group was 56% and in the control group 16%. Pathological changes were noted in the tails of surviving treated animals. These changes were annular constrictions of the skin and muscles in the upper part of the tail which lead to

Table 5 :	REPRODUCTIVE TOXICITY STUDIES WITH XYLENES IN ANIMALS	
Species	Concentration/dose/ duration	Observations

		subsequent tail loss. The incidence of this observation (which was not seen in the control group) was not given.
		Thus in this study there was no effect on implantation rates, intra uterine death rates, gestation length or peri-natal pup weight or mortality. Increased mortality and pathological changes in the tail of survivors were noted during post-natal days 3-30.
Rat (338) White	0,150 or 400 mg/kg, subcutaneously, from either days 1 to 10 or 1 to 18 of gestation. Xylene undefined	The day on which the animals were examined was not stated. 5 out of 20 animals administered 400 mg/kg during days 1 to 18 died. In the groups treated over days 1 to 10 reduced maternal bodyweight gain, changes in kidney function, reduced haemoglobin level and increased leukocyte counts were observed. In the groups exposed over days 1 to 10 of gestation there was an increased incidence of preimplantation loss. In the group exposed to 400 mg/kg over days 1 to 18 total fetal losses were increased. Mean fetal weight was reduced in all treated groups.

Table 5 :	REPRODUCTIVE TOXICITY STUDIES WITH XYLENES IN ANIMALS	
Species	Concentration/dose/ duration	Observations
Mouse (197) ICR Number of pregnant animals per group not stated.	0, 500, 1000, 2000 or 4000 ppm 6 h/d, from days 6-12 of gestation. Xylene undefined.	Report available in abstract form only. $^2/_3$ of the dams were killed on day 17 of gestation and their uteri and contents examined. The remaining dams delivered their young. Maternal toxicity, if any, was not reported. There was no effect on the number of implantation sites, resorptions or number of live or dead fetuses. Fetal weight was significantly decreased at 2000 and 4000 ppm and there was a dose-related increase in the incidence of delayed ossification of the sternum and in the development of a 14th rib. No effect on the incidence of malformations was observed. In the groups which delivered their young, decreased bodyweight gain and delayed development of hair and teeth were observed in the pups of dams exposed to 4000 ppm. No differences were observed for the time of eye or ear opening or co-ordinated walking. Thus, in this study there was evidence of delayed fetal development (reduced weight and delayed sternal ossification) and increased incidence of a minor variant (extra ribs), although the authors report that this was a teratogenic response. In the absence of the reporting of maternal toxicity these findings are of uncertain significance.

Table 5 :

Table 5 :   **REPRODUCTIVE TOXICITY STUDIES WITH XYLENES IN ANIMALS**

Species	Concentration/dose/duration	Observations
Mouse (181, 184) CFLP 15 dams per group (treated) and 115 (air control group)	0, 115 or 230 ppm for 4 h, 3 times per day on days 6-15 of gestation. Xylene used was; 10% o-xylene 50% m-xylene 20% p-xylene 20% Ethylbenzene	The dams were killed on day 18 of gestation and their uteri and contents examined. The data were presented in summary form only. Maternal toxicity was not reported. At 230 ppm there was evidence of delayed development (increased incidence of weight-retarded fetuses and fetuses with delayed skeletal ossification). There was no increase in the incidence of post implantation loss, minor variants or malformations. No significant effects were observed at 115 ppm. Thus in this study there was evidence of delayed development but no evidence of teratogenicity. In the absence of reporting of any maternal toxicity the significance of the delayed development is unclear.
Mouse (339) White		Study of the effects of xylene on the oestrus cycle.
a) 10-15 females per group.	11-23, 23-45 or up to 227 ppm for 3 h. The controls and group exposed to 11-23 ppm were housed under laboratory conditions. The other groups were housed in cages located in industrial workshops where xylene concentrations, measured before, during and after exposure, were within the ranges given.	4 out of 15 mice in the group exposed to up to 227 ppm xylene were reported to have a disturbance in oestrus cycle. The nature of this disturbance was not stated.
b) 10-20 females per group.	23, 2.3-227 or 2.3-1150 ppm 3 h/d for 3 months. The group exposed to 23 ppm was housed under laboratory conditions. The other groups were housed in cages located in industrial workshops where the xylene concentrations during the study varied between the minimum and maximum quoted.	1 animal exposed to 2.3 - 1150 ppm died. Disturbances in the oestrus cycle were reported at all exposure levels ($^4/_6$ at 23 ppm, $^8/_{12}$ at 2.3 - 227 ppm and $^{15}/_{20}$ at 2.3 - 1150 ppm).

Species	Concentration/dose/ duration	Observations
c) 40 females	A control group housed under laboratory conditions. Xylene undefined.	No irregular oestrus cycles were observed. An extension of 1 day was observed in 5 animals.
d)		At the end of the exposure period all animals were killed and macroscopic and microscopic evaluation of the ovaries and uteri conducted. Glandular hyperplasia in the uterine horns was reported. No corpora lutea were seen in the ovaries, the follicles were in the early stage of development and there were atretic follicles. The incidence of these findings was not given. Thus in this study the authors report disturbances in the oestrus cycle and some pathological changes to the female sex organs.
Rabbit (181, 184) New Zealand White 10 dams per group (treated) and 60 dams (air control).	0, 115 or 230 ppm continuously from days 7-20 of gestation Xylene used was; 10% o-xylene 50% m-xylene 20% p-xylene 20% Ethylbenzene	The dams were killed on day 30 of gestation and their uteri and contents examined. The data were presented in summary form only. At 230 ppm there were no live fetuses (3 dams died, 6 aborted and in 1 there was total resorption or fetal death *in utero*). At 115 ppm there was no effect on maternal weight gain or relative liver weight. There were no significant effects on post-implantation loss, the incidence of delayed development (although mean female fetal weight was marginally reduced) minor variants or malformations. Thus, in this study there were no live fetuses at 230 ppm and no significant findings at 115 ppm.

Table 5 : REPRODUCTIVE TOXICITY STUDIES WITH XYLENES IN ANIMALS

Table 5 :	REPRODUCTIVE TOXICITY STUDIES WITH XYLENES IN ANIMALS	
Species	Concentration/dose/ duration	Observations

Mouse (198)
CD-1
66 (controls)
23-28 per group
(520, 1030, 2060
2580 mg/kg)
38 (3100 mg/kg)
15 (4130 mg/kg)

0, 520, 1030, 2060, 2580, 3100 or 4130 mg/kg, orally, on days 6-15 of gestation.

Xylene used was;
 9.1% o-xylene
60.2% m-xylene
13.6% p-xylene
17.0% Ethylbenzene

The animals were killed on day 18 of gestation and their uteri and contents were examined.

All animals (4130 mg/kg) and 12 (3100 mg/kg) died. Maternal bodyweight gain was significantly reduced at 3100 mg/kg. Maternal liver weight was significantly increased at 2060 and 2580 mg/kg.

At 3100 mg/kg there was a significant increase in the incidence of dams with complete resorptions. However, there was no effect on the number of implants per pregnant dam at any dose level.

Mean fetal weight was decreased significantly at 2060 mg/kg and above but the incidence of stunted fetuses was not increased. There was a significant increase in the incidence of cleft palate at 2060 mg/kg and above ($^{7}/_{227}$) at 2060, $^{11}/_{224}$ at 2580 and $^{7}/_{79}$ at 3100 mg/kg. Cleft palate was not observed in the 658 (control) or 208 (520 mg/kg) fetuses examined but was noted in $^{1}/_{232}$ fetuses at 1030 mg/kg. There was also a significant increase in the incidence of multiple bilateral wavy ribs at 2580 ($^{6}/_{227}$) and 3100 mg/kg ($^{3}/_{79}$). These observations were recorded in fetuses which were not stunted. No wavy ribs were observed in the 658 control, 208 (520 mg/kg) or 232 (1030 mg/kg) fetuses examined.

The authors concluded that xylene administration caused embryotoxicity (ie retarded fetal development) because of the observed decrease in mean fetal weight at 2060 and 2580 mg/kg. (Note - the incidence of delayed skeletal ossification, if any, was not reported).

It was also concluded that xylene was teratogenic at these dose levels because of the increased incidence of cleft palates. It was also considered that the multiple bilateral wavy ribs may also be indicative of teratogenicity. The fetal observations at 3100 mg/kg were considered to be possibly secondary to the maternal toxicity seen at this dose level.

Table 5 :	REPRODUCTIVE TOXICITY STUDIES WITH XYLENES IN ANIMALS	
Species	Concentration/dose/ duration	Observations
Hamster (199) No details of strain or number of animals used.	Dose levels not stated. Exposures (2 h/d) were from days 7-11 of gestation. Dermal exposure. Xylene mixture undefined.	The animals were killed on day 15 of gestation and their uteri and contents examined. In this summary report xylene was one of a number of reagents tested. Minimal embryotoxic effects were observed in the study, the effects generally limited to a decrease in fetal size and weight and an increase in the incidence of prenatal death. The malformations observed included haemorrhages and gastroschisis. It was not stated in which groups these malformations were observed. No conclusions can be made as only limited data are available.

APPENDIX: SUMMARY OF METABOLISM AND TOXICITY OF ETHYLBENZENE

The following summary is based on four published reviews and a 13-week inhalation study in mice, rats and rabbits[1, 340-343]. Ethylbenzene is well-absorbed by the respiratory route and is absorbed through skin at approximately the same rate as xylenes. The major metabolites are mandelic, phenylglyoxylic and hippuric acids, which are excreted in urine. Ethylbenzene is of low acute and sub-acute toxicity, with central nervous system effects being reported. Liquid ethylbenzene irritates animal skin and can cause some eye irritation. Induction of liver and kidney enzymes has been observed in animals following repeated exposure. No significant mutagenic effects have been noted and no animal carcinogenicity study is available. There is no clear evidence of an important reproductive effect in animals. Human exposure to concentrations of above 100 ppm caused fatigue, sleepiness and headache, as well as mild irritation of the eyes and respiratory tract. Repeated exposure to liquid ethylbenzene has resulted in dermatitis, probably because of its known defatting properties. No firm conclusions can be drawn about the effects of ethylbenzene in humans from the few workplace studies that have been conducted.

REFERENCES

1 Clayton G D and Clayton F E (Editors). *Patty's Industrial Hygiene and Toxicology,* Third Revised Edition. John Wiley and Sons, Inc, 1981.

2 Verschueren K. *Handbook of Environmental Data on Organic Chemicals.* Van Nostrand Reinhold Company, 1977. ISBN 0 44 229091 8

3 Sutton C and Calder J A. Solubility of alkylbenzenes in distilled water and sea water at 25.0°C. *Journal of Chemical and Engineering Data.* 1975, vol. **29**, 320-332.

4 Leo A, Hansch C and another. Dependence of hydrophobicity of apolar molecules on their molecular volume. *Journal of Medicinal Chemistry.* 1976, vol. **19**, 611-615.

5 Aldrich Chemical Co Ltd. Catalogue/Handbook of Fine Chemicals. 1985-1986. (Annual)

6 Carpenter C P, Rinkead E R and others. Petroleum hydrocarbon toxicity studies V. Animal and human response to vapours of mixed xylenes. *Toxicology and Applied Pharmacology.* 1975, vol. **33**, 543-558.

7 Bergman K. Whole-body autoradiography and allied tracer techniques in distribution and elimination studies of some organic solvents. *Scandinavian Journal of Work Environment and Health.* 1979, vol. **5**, Suppl. 1, 1-263.

8 Bergman R. Application and results of whole-body autoradiography in distribution studies of organic solvents. *CRC Critical Reviews in Toxicology.* 1983, vol. **12**, 59-118.

9 Gut I and Flek J. Effect of microsome enzyme induction by phenobarbitone on the metabolism of benzene, fluorobenzene, *m*-xylene and *p*-xylene. *Pracovni Lekarstvi.* 1981, vol. **33**, 124-127.

10 Mikulski P and Wiglusz R. Comparison of metabolism of benzene and its methyl derivatives in the rat and stimulatory effect of phenobarbital. *Bulletin of the Institute of Maritime and Tropical Medicine in Gdynia.* 1972, vol. **23**, 153-160.

11 Senczuk W and Winnicka A. Blood xylene content as a result of exposure to xylene vapours. *Bromatologia i Chemia Toksykologiczna.* 1978, vol. **11**, 367-372.

12 Tsuruta H. On the percutaneous absorption of aromatic hydrocarbons. Annual Meeting of the Japanese Industrial Hygiene Society. 1986, No. **59**, 46.

13 Carlsson A. Distribution and elimination of ^{14}C-xylene in rat. *Scandinavian Journal of Work Environment and Health.* 1981, vol. **7**, 51-55.

14 Ungvary G, Tatrai E and others. Studies on the embryotoxic effects of *ortho-, meta-* and *para-*xylene. *Toxicology.* 1980, vol. **18**, 61-74.

15 Elovaara E, Zitting A and others. *m*-Xylene inhalation destroys cytochrome P-450 in rat lung at low exposure. *Archives of Toxicology.* 1987, vol. **61**, 21-26.

16 Elovaara E, Pfaffli P and others. Marginal role of impaired aldehyde metabolism in *m*-xylene vapour-induced biochemical effects in the rat. *Journal of Applied Toxicology.*1982, vol. **2**, 27-32.

17 Savolainen H and Pfaffli P. Dose-dependent neurochemical changes during short-term inhalation exposure to *m*-xylene. *Archives of Toxicology.* 1980, vol. **45**, 117-122.

18 Savolainen H, Vainio H and others. Biochemical and toxicological effects of short-term, intermittent xylene inhalation exposure and combined ethanol intake. *Archives of Toxicology* 1978, vol. **41**, 195-205.

19 Elovaara E, Collan Y and others. The combined toxicity of technical grade xylene and ethanol in the rat. *Xenobiotica.* 1980, vol. **10**, 435-445.

20 Savolainen X, Pfaffli P and others. Neurochemical and behavioural effects of long-term intermittent inhalation of xylene vapour and simultaneous ethanol intake. *Acta pharmacologica et toxicologica.* 1979, vol. **44**, 200-207.

21 Ghantous H and Danielsson B R G. Placental transfer and distribution of toluene, xylene and benzene, and their metabolites during gestation in mice. *Biological Research in Pregnancy.* 1986, vol. **7**, 98-105.

22 Nawrot P S, Albro P W and others. Distribution and excretion of carbon-14 labelled *m*-xylene in pregnant mice. *Teratology.* 1980, vol. **21**, 58A.

23 Fabre R, Truhaut R and another. Toxicological studies on the replacement solvents for benzene. IV Study of the xylenes. *Archives Maladies Professionnelles.* 1960, vol. **21**, 301-313.

24 Sugihara R. High-performance liquid chromatography studies of toluene and xylene poisoning. Part II: Respiratory and urinary excretion of toluene and *m*-xylene following intraperitoneal administration to rats. *Acta Medica Okayama.* 1979, vol. **91**, 1433-1440.

25	Sugihara R and Ogata M. Quantitation of urinary *m*- and *p*-methylhippuric acids as indices of *m*- and *p*-xylene exposure. *International Archives of Occupational and Environmental Health*. 1978, vol **41**, 281-286.

26	Elovaara E, Engstrom K and another. Metabolism and disposition of simultaneously inhaled *m*-xylene and ethylbenzene in the rat. *Toxicology and Applied Pharmacology*. 1984, vol. **75**, 466-478.

27	Ogata M, Yamazaki Y and others. Quantitation of urinary *o*-xylene metabolites of rats and human beings by high performance liquid chromatography. *International Archives of Occupational and Environmental Health*. 1980, vol. **46**, 127-139.

28	Ogata M and Fujii T. Urinary excretion of hippuric acid and *m*-methylhippuric acid after administration of toluene and *m*-xylene mixture to rats. *International Archives of Occupational and Environmental Health*. 1979, vol. **43**, 45-51.

29	Van Doorn R, Bos R P and others. Effect of toluene and xylenes on liver glutathione and their urinary excretion as mercapturic acids in the rat. *Archives of Toxicology*. 1980, vol. **43**, 293-304.

30	Van Doorn R, Leijdekkers Ch-m and others. Alcohol and sulphate intermediates in the metabolism of toluene and xylenes to mercapturic acids. *Journal of Applied Toxicology*. 1981, vol. **1**, 236-242.

31	Bakke O M and Scheline R R. Hydroxylation of aromatic hydrocarbons in the rat. *Toxicology and Applied Pharmacology*. 1970, vol. **16**, 691-700.

32	Fabre R, Truhaut R and another. Research on the comparative metabolism of the xylenes or dimethylbenzenes. *Archives des Maladies Professionnelles*. 1960, vol. **21**, 314-328.

33	Bray H G, Humphris B G and another. Metabolism of derivatives of toluene. 3: *o*-, *m*- and *p*-Xylenes. *Biochemical Journal*. 1949, vol. **45**, 241-244.

34	Hobara T, Kobayashi H and others. Organic solvent levels in the bile, blood and livers of dogs following intravenous administration. *Nippon Eiseigaku Zasshi*. 1982, vol. **37**, 601-607.

35	Tsuruta H. Percutaneous absorption of organic solvents III. On the penetration rates of hydrophobic solvents through the excised rat skin. *Industrial Health*. 1982, vol. **20**, 335-345.

36	Sato A, Fujiwara Y and another. Solubility of benzene, toluene and *m*-xylene in blood. *Sangyo Igaku*. 1972, vol. **14**, 3-8.

37	Sato A, Fujiwara Y and another. Solubility of benzene, toluene and *m*-xylene in various body fluids and tissues of rabbits. *Japanese Journal of Industrial Health*. 1974, vol. **16**, 30-31.

38	Riihimaki V and Savolainen K. Human exposure to *m*-xylene. Kinetics and acute effects on the central nervous system. *Annals of Occupational Hygiene*. 1980, vol. **23**, 411-422.

39	Smith B R, Plummer J L and others. *p*-Xylene metabolism by rabbit lung and liver and its relationship to the selective destruction of pulmonary cytochrome P450. *The Journal of Pharmacology and Experimental Therapeutics*. 1982, vol. **223**, 736-742.

40	Sato A and Nakajima T. Pharmacokinetics of organic solvent vapours in relation to their toxicity. *Scandinavian Journal of Work Environment and Health*. 1987, vol. **13**, 81-93.

41	Harper C. *p*-Xylene metabolism by rat pulmonary and hepatic microsomes. *Federation Proceedings*. 1975, vol. **34**, 785.

42	Toftgard R, Haaparanta T and another. Rat lung and liver cytochrome P-450 isozymes involved in the hydroxylation of *m*-xylene. *Toxicology*. 1986, vol. **39**, 225-231.

43	Pathiratne A, Puyear R L and another. A comparative study of the effects of benzene, toluene and xylenes on their *in vitro* metabolism and drug-metabolising enzymes in rat liver. *Toxicology and Applied Pharmacology*. 1986, vol. **82**, 272-280.

44	Ikeda M. Mutual suppression of oxidation involved in the metabolism of thinner constituents. In *Voluntary inhalation of industrial solvents* DHEW, 1978, Issue ADM-79-779, 322-332.

45	Nakaiima T and Sato A. Metabolic antagonism between benzene, toluene and *m*-xylene *in vitro* . *Sangyo Igaku* . 1979, vol. **21**, 546-547.

46	Sato A, Nakajima T and another. Effects of chronic ethanol consumption on hepatic metabolism of aromatic and chlorinated hydrocarbons in rats. *British Journal of Industrial Medicine*. 1980, vol. **37**, 382-386.

47	Romer K G, Federsel R J and another. Rise of inhaled toluene, ethyl benzene, *m*-xylene or mesitylene in rat blood after treatment with ethanol. *Environmental Contamination and Toxicology*. 1986, vol. **37**, 874-876.

48   Sugihara R. High-performance liquid chromatographic studies of toluene and xylene poisoning. Part III: effect of phenobarbital on metabolism of *m*- and *p*-xylene in rats. *Acta Medica Okayama*. 1979, vol. **91**, 1441-1446.

49   David A, Flek J and others. Influence of phenobarbital on xylene metabolism in man and rats. *International Archives of Occupational and Environmental Health*. 1979, vol. **44**, 117-125.

50   Carlone M F and Fouts J R. *In vitro* metabolism of *p*-xylene by rat lung and liver. *Xenobiotica*. 1974, vol. **4**, 705-715.

51   Harper C, Drew R T and another. Benzene and *p*-xylene: a comparison of inhalation toxicities and *in vitro* hydroxylations. In *Biological reactive intermediates, formation, toxicity and inactivation. Proceedings of an international conference*. edited by D J Jollow et al. London, Plenum Press, 1977, 302-311.

52   Fujii T. Metabolism of *m*-xylene in rats after administration of chlorinated hydrocarbons. *Japanese Journal of Industrial Health*. 1977, vol. **19**, 499-503.

53   Freundt K J and Schneider J C. Drastic increase in the *m*-xylene or toluene concentrations in blood of rats after combined inhalation with acetone. *Naunyn Schmiedebergs Archives of Pharmacology*. 1986, vol. **332**, suppl. R26, abstract 104.

54   Riihimaki V, Pfaffli P and others. Kinetics of *m*-xylene in man. General features of absorption, distribution, biotransformation and excretion in repetitive inhalation exposure. *Scandinavian Journal of Work Environment and Health*. 1979, vol. **5**, 217-231.

55   Sedivec V and Flek J. The absorption, metabolism and excretion of xylenes in man. *International Archives of Occupational and Environmental Health*. 1976, vol. **37**, 205-217.

56   Riihimaki V, Pfaffli P and others. Kinetics of *m*-xylene in man. Influence of intermittent physical exercise and changing environmental concentrations on kinetics. *Scandinavian Journal of Work Environment and Health*. 1979, vol. **5**, 232-248.

57   Astrand I, Engstrom J and another. Exposure to xylene and ethylbenzene I. Uptake, distribution and elimination in man. *Scandinavian Journal of Work Environment and Health*. 1978, vol. **4**, 185-194.

58   Imbriani M, Ghittori S and others. Urinary elimination of xylene in experimental and occupational exposure. *La Medicina del Lavoro*. 1987, vol. **78**, 239-249.

59   Engstrom J and Bjurstrom R. Exposure to xylene and ethylbenzene II. Concentration in subcutaneous adipose tissue. *Scandinavian Journal of Work Environment and Health*. 1978, vol. **4**, 195-203.

60   Riihimaki V, Savolainen K and others. Metabolic interaction between *m*-xylene and ethanol. *Archives of Toxicology*. 1982, vol. **49**, 253-263.

61   Sato A and Nakajima T. Partition coefficients of some aromatic hydrocarbons and ketones in water, blood and oil. *British Journal of Industrial Medicine*. 1979, vol. **36**, 231-234.

62   Wallen M, Holm S and another. Co-exposure to toluene and *p*-xylene in man: uptake and elimination. *British Journal of Industrial Medicine*. 1985, vol. **42**, 111-116.

63   Dutkiewicz T and Tyras H. Skin absorption of toluene, styrene and xylene by man. *British Journal of Industrial Medicine*. 1968, vol. **25**, 243.

64   Stolbova A I and Smirnova T A. Study of the capacity of xylene isomers to be absorbed through unbroken skin. *Trudy Kazanskogo Meditsinskogo Instituta*. 1969, vol. **29**, 192-195.

65   Engstrom K, Xusman K and another. Percutaneous absorption of *m*-xylene in man. *International Archives of Occupational and Environmental Health*. 1977, vol. **39**, 181-189.

66   Lauwerys R R, Dath T and others. The influence of two barrier creams on the percutaneous absorption of *m*-xylene in man. *Journal of Occupational Medicine*. 1978, vol. **20**, 17-20.

67   Riihimaki V and Pfaffli P. Percutaneous absorption of solvent vapours in man. *Scandinavian Journal of Work Environment and Health*. 1978, vol. **4**, 73-85.

68   Takatori T, Terazawa K and others. An autopsy case of alkylbenzene poisoning and its clinical significance. *Nihon Hoigaku Zasshi*. 1982, vol. **36**, 654-661.

69   Engstrom J and Riihimaki V. Distribution of *m*-xylene to subcutaneous adipose tissue in short-term experimental human exposure. *Scandinavian Journal of Work Environment and Health*. 1979, vol. **5**, 126-134.

70   Dowty B J, Laseter J L and another. The transplacental migration and accumulation in blood of volatile organic constituents. *Pediatric Research*. 1976, vol. **10**, 696-701.

71   Riihimaki V. Conjugation and urinary excretion of toluene and *m*-xylene metabolites in a man. *Scandinavian Journal of Work Environment and Health.* 1979, vol. **5**,135-142.

72   Campbell L, Wilson H K and others. Interactions of *m*-xylene and aspirin metabolism in man. *British Journal of Industrial Medicine.* 1988, vol. **45**, 127-132.

73   Engstrom K, Riihimaki V and another. Urinary disposition of ethylbenzene and *m*-xylene in man following separate and combined exposure. *International Archives of Occupational and Environmental Health.* 1984, vol. **54**, 355-363.

74   Engstrom K, Husman K and others. Evaluation of occupational exposure to xylene by blood, exhaled air and urine analysis. *Scandinavian Journal of Work Environment and Health.* 1978, vol. **4**, 114-121.

75   Ogata M, Yamasaki Y and others. Quantitation of urinary *o*-xylene metabolites in rats and human beings by high performance liquid chromatography. *Industrial Health.* 1979, vol. **17**, 123-125.

76   Riihimaki V. Percutaneous absorption of *m*-xylene from a mixture of *m*-xylene and isobutyl alcohol in man. *Scandinavian Journal of Work Environment and Health.* 1979, vol. **5**, 143-150.

77   Bonnet P, Morele Y and others. Determination of the median lethal concentration of the main aromatic hydrocarbons in the rat. *Archives des Maladies Professionnelles de Medicine du Travail et de Securite Sociale.* 1982, vol. **43**, 261-265.

78   Bonnet P, Raoult G and another. Lethal concentration 50 of main aromatic hydrocarbons. *Archives des Maladies Professionnelles de Medicine du Travail et de Securite Sociale.* 1979, vol. **40**, 805-810.

79   Moser V C, Coggeshall E M and another. Effects of xylene isomers on operant responding and motor performance in mice. *Toxicology and Applied Pharmacology.* 1985, vol. **80**, 293-298.

80   Molnar J, Paksy K A and another. Changes in the rats motor behaviour during 4 hr inhalation exposure to prenarcotic concentrations of benzene and its derivatives. *Acta Physiologica Hungarica.* 1986, vol. **67**, 349-354.

81   Lazarew N W. On the toxicity of various hydrocarbon vapours. *Archiv fur Experimentelle Pathologie and Pharmakologie.* 1929, vol. **143**, 223-233.

82   De Ceaurriz J, Bonnet P and others. Chemicals as central nervous systems depressants - possibilities of an animal model. Cahiers de notes documentaires - Securite et Hygiene du Travail 3rd quarter 1981, No. 104, Note No. 1329-104-81, 351-355.

83   De Ceaurriz J C, Micillino J C and others. Prediction of the irritant effects of chemicals on the human respiratory tract Advantages of an animal model. Cahiers de notes documentaires Securite et hygiene du travail 1st quarter.   1981, No. 102, Note No. 1302-102-81, 55-61.

84   De Ceaurriz J C, Micillino J C and others. Sensory irritation caused by various industrial airborne chemicals. *Toxicology Letters.* 1981, vol. **9**, 137-143.

85   Cameron G R, Paterson J L H and others. The toxicity of some methyl derivatives of benzene with special reference to pseudocumene and heavy coal tar naphtha. *Journal of Pathology and Bacteriology.* 1938, vol. **46**, 95-107.

86   Molnar J, Paksy K A and others. Motor activity in rats during inhalatory exposure. *Kiserletes Orvostudomany.* 1982, vol. **34**, 292-295.

87   Drew R T and Fouts J R. The effects of inducers on acute *p*-xylene toxicology. *Toxicology and Applied Pharmacology.* 1974, vol. **29**, 111-112.

88   Furnas D W and Hine C H. Neurotoxicity of some selected hydrocarbons. *Archives of Industrial Health and Occupational Medicine.* 1958, vol. **18**, 9-15.

89   Patel J M, Harper C and others. Changes in serum enzymes after inhalation exposure of *p*-xylene. *Bulletin of Environmental Contamination and Toxicology.* 1979, vol. **21**, 17-24.

90   Patel J M, Harper C and another. Inactivation of pulmonary cytochrome P-450 by *p*-xylene intoxication. *Pharmacologist.* 1976, vol. **18**, 210.

91   Patel J M Harper C and another. The biotransformation of *p*-xylene to a toxic aldehyde. *Drug Metabolism and Disposition.* 1978, vol. **6**, 368-374.

92   Hine C H and Zuidema H H. The toxicological properties of hydrocarbon solvents. *Industrial Medicine.* 1970, vol. **39**, 215-220.

93   Lundberg I, Hakansson M and others. Relative hepatotoxic effects of five industrial solvents after inhalation exposure of rats. *Arbete och Halsa.* 1982, vol. **22**, 39-40. (English Summary).

155

94   Schumacher H and Grandjean E. Comparative investigations of the narcotic effectiveness and acute toxicity of nine solvents. *Archiv fur Gewerbepathologie and Gewerbehygiene.* 1960, vol. **18**, 109-119.

95   Ghosh T K, Copeland R L and others. Effect of xylene inhalation on fixed ratio responding in rats. *Pharmacology Biochemistry and Behaviour.* 1987, vol. **27**, 653-657.

96   Ghosh T K and Pradhan S N. Comparison of effects of xylene and toluene inhalation on fixed-ratio liquid-reinforced behaviour in rats. *Research Communications in Psychology, Psychiatry and Behaviour.* 1987, vol. **12**, 205-214.

97   Ghosh T K, Copeland R L and another. Behavioural effects of environmental chemicals in rats exposed in an inhalation behavioural chamber. *Federation Proceedings.* 1986, vol. **45**, 639.

98   Pryor G T, Rebert C S. and another. Hearing loss in rats caused by inhalation of mixed xylenes and styrene. *Journal of Appliced Toxicology.* 1987, vol. **7**, 55-61.

99   Lundberg I, Edkahl M and others. Relative hepatotoxicity of some industrial solvents after intraperitoneal injection or inhalation exposure in rats. *Environmental Research.* 1986, vol. **40**, 411-420.

100   Ungvary G, Tatrai E and others. Acute toxicity of toluene, *o*-, *m*- and *p*-xylene, and of their mixtures in rats. *Munkavedelm.* 1979, vol. **25**, 37-38.

101   Smyth H F, Carpenter C S and others. Range - Finding Toxicity Data: List VI. *Industrial Hygiene Journal.* 1962, vol. **23**, 95-107.

102   National Toxicology Program. Toxicology and Carcinogenesis Studies of Xylenes (mixed) in F 344/N Rats and B6C3Fl Mice (gavage studies). DHHS-NIH Publication No. 87-2583, 1986.

103   Wolf M A, Rowe V X and others. Toxicological studies of certain alkylated benzenes and benzene. *Archives of Industrial Health.* 1956, vol. **14**, 387-398.

104   Muralidhara and Krishnakumari M K. Mammalian toxicity of aromex and xylene used in pesticidal formulations. *Indian Journal of Biology.* 1980, vol. **18**, 1148-1151.

105   Harton E E and Rawl R R. Toxicological and skin corrosion testing of selected hazardous materials. Final report submitted to US Department of Transportation. 1976, Report No. DOT/MTB/OHM0-76/2.

106   Paksy K A, Molnar J and others. Comparative study on the acute effects of benzene, toluene and *m*-xylene in the rat. 317-324. *Acta Physiologica Academiae Scientarium Hungaricae,* 1982, vol. **59**,317-324.

107   Lundberg I, Hakansson M and another. Relative hepatotoxic effect of 14 industrial solvents after intraperitoneal injection in rats. *Arbete och Halsa.* 1983, vol. **22**, 17-18 (English summary).

108   Lundberg I, Ekdahl M and others. Relative hepatoxicity of some industrial solvents after intraperitoneal injection and inhalation exposure in rats. *Arbete och Halsa.* 1985, vol. **38**, 1-19.

109   Mohtashamipur E, Norporth K and others. Effects of ethylbenzene, toluene and xylene on the induction of micronuclei in bone marrow polychromatic erythrocytes of mice. *Archives of Toxicology.* 1985, vol. **58**, 106-109.

110   Tham R, Bunnfors I and others. Vestibulo-ocular disturbances in rats exposed to organic solvents. *Acta pharmacologica et toxicologica.* 1984, vol. **54**, 58-63.

111   Odkvist L M, Larsby B and others. Vestibular and oculomotor disturbances caused by industrial solvents. *The Journal of Otolaryngology.* 1980, vol. **9**, 53-59.

112   Aschan G, Bunnfors I and others. Xylene exposure Electronystagmographic and gas chromatographic studies in rabbits. *Acta Laryngology.* 1977, vol. **84**, 370-376.

113   Odkvist L M, Larsby B and others. Influence of industrial solvents on the balance system - an experimental animal model. *Int. Symp. Control. Air Pollut. Work, Environ (Proc).* 1978, vol. **2**, 76-87.

114   Odkvist L M, Larsby B and others. Positional nystagmus elicited by industrial solvents. In 'Vestibular mechanisms in health and disease' edited by J H Hood, London, Academic Press, 1978, 188-194.

115   Aschan G, Bertler A and others. The effect of organic solvents upon the central vestibulo-oculomotor system. In *Current experimental studies on organic solvents* edited by B Holmberg and I Astrand. National Board of Occupational Safety and Health, Solna, Sweden. Investigation Report 1981: 12.

116   Odkvist L M, Larsby B and others. On the mechanism of vestibular disturbances caused by industrial solvents. *Adv Oto-Rhino-Largyng.* 1979, vol. **25**, 167-172.

117   Larsby B, Odkvist L M and others. Disturbances of the vestibular system by toxic agents. *Acta Physiologica Scandinavia*. 1976, **suppl. 440**, 8.

118   Divencenzo G D and Krasavage W J. Serum ornithine carbamyl transferase as a liver response test for exposure to organic solvents. *America Industrial Hygiene Association Journal*. 1974, vol. **35**, 21-29.

119   Pyykko R, Paavilainen S and others. The increasing and decreasing effects of aromatic hydrocarbon solvents on pulmonary and hepatic cytochrome P-450 in the rat. *Pharmacology and Toxicology*. 1987, vol. **60**, 288-293.

120   Pyykko R . Inhibition of microsomal mono-oxygenases *in vitro* by aromatic hydrocarbons. *Archives of Toxicology*. 1986, **suppl. 9**, 371-373.

121   Smith B R, Plummer J L and others. *p*-Xylene induced destruction of rabbit pulmonary cytochrome P-450 and the role of metabolism by lung and liver. *Federation Proceedings*. 1981, vol. **40**, 630.

122   Holmberg B, Jakobson I and another. The effect of organic solvents on erythrocytes during hypotonic haemolysis. *Environmental Research*. 1974, vol. **7**, 193-205.

123   Gerarde H W and Linden N J. Toxicological studies on hydrocarbons. *Archives of Industrial Health*. 1959, vol. **19**, 403-418.

124   Rigdon R H. Capillary permeability in areas of inflammation produced by xylene. *Archives of Surgery*. 1940, vol. **41**, 101-109.

125   Rigdon R H. Effect of antihistamine on the localisation of trypan blue in xylene treated areas of skin. *Proceedings of the Society for Experimental Biology and Medicine*. 1949, vol. **71**, 637-639.

126   Steele R H, Wilhelm D L. The inflammatory reaction in chemical injury. *Journal of Experimental Pathology*. 1966, vol. **47**, 612-623.

127   Jacobs G, Martens M and another. Proposal of limit concentrations for skin irritation within the context of a new EEC directive on the classification and labelling of preparations. *Regulatory Toxicology and Pharmacology*. 1987, vol. **7**, 370-378.

128   Annex VI, part 11D of Council Directive 79/831/EEC concerning the guide to classification and labelling of dangerous substances and preparations: criteria for the choice of phrases indicating special risks (R-phrases) and safety advice (S-phrases), (83/467/EEC). Official Journal. No L257. 16 September 1983, p1.

129   Grant W M. Toxicology of the Eye, Second Edition. Springfield, Illinois. Charles C Thomas. 1974, 1089-1090. ISBN 0 39 802299 2

130   Kennah H E and others. An objective procedure for quantitating eye irritation based upon changes of corneal thickness. *Fundamental and Applied Toxicology*. 1989, vol. **12**, 258-268.

131   Schmid E. On the corneal disease of furniture polishers. *Klinische Monatsblaetter fur Augenheilkunde*. 1957, vol. **130**, 110-115.

132   Matthaus W. Corneal lesions in workers involved in surface varnishing in the furniture industry. *Klinische Monatsblaetter fur Augenheilkunde*. 1964, vol. **144**, 713-717.

133   Tatrai E and Ungvary G. Changes induced by *o*-xylene inhalation in the rat liver. *Acta Medica Academiae Scientarium Hungaricae*. 1980, vol. **37**, 211-216.

134   Jenkins L J, Jones R A and another. Long-term inhalation screening studies of benzene, toluene, *o*-xylene, and cumene on experimental animals. *Toxicology and Applied Pharmacology*. 1970, vol. **16**, 818-823.

135   Andersson K, Fuxe K and others. Production of discrete changes in dopamine and noradrenaline levels and turnover in various parts of the rat brain following exposure to xylene, *ortho*-, *meta*-, *para*-xylene, and ethylbenzene. *Toxicology and Applied Pharmacology*. 1981, vol. **60**, 535-548.

136   Cseh J, Mnayai S and others. Effect on rat liver of simultaneous ethanol and *o*-xylene poisoning. *Acta Physiologica Academiae Scientarium Hungaricae*. 1980, vol. **56**, 105-106.

137   Toftgard R and Nilsen O G. Induction of cytochrome P-450 in rat liver after inhalation of aromatic organic solvents. Industry, Environment, Xenobiotics. Proceedings of International Conference. Springer-Verlag, Berlin. 1981, 307-317.

138   Toftgard R and Nilsen O G. Effects of xylene and xylene isomers on cytochrome P-450 and *in vitro* enzymatic activities in rat liver, kidney and lung. *Toxicology*. 19B2, vol. **23**, 197-212.

139   Rank J. Xylene induced feeding and drinking behavior and central adrenergic receptor binding. *Neurobehavioral Toxicology and Teratology*. 1985, vol. **7**, 421-426.

140   Russo J M and Junnila M. Behavioural effects of xylene. Unpublished data.

141 Elovaara E. Dose-related effects of *m*-xylene inhalation on the xenobiotic metabolism in the rat. *Xenobiotica*. 1982, vol. **12**, 345-352.

142 Estler W. Tests on the acute narcotic effect of aliphatic and aromatic hydrocarbons - Report 2 - The effect of repeated inhalation of various concentrations of gasoline, benzene, toluene and xylene on white mice. *Archiv fur Hygiene*. 1935, vol. **114**, 261-271.

143 Batchelor J J. The relative toxicity of benzene and its higher homologues. *American Journal of Hygiene*. 1927, vol. **7**, 276-298.

144 Winslow C E A. Summary of the National Safety Council Study of benzol poisoning. *Journal of Industrial Hygiene*. 1927, vol. **9**, 61-74.

145 Honma T, Sudo A and others. Significant changes in the amounts of neurotransmitter and related substances in rat brain induced by sub-acute exposure to low levels of toluene and xylene. *Industrial Health*. 1983, vol. **21**, 143-151.

146 Toftgard R, Nilsen O G and others. Induction of cytochrome P450 in the rat liver after exposure to xylenes, dose-response relationship and dependence on endocrine factors. *Toxicology*. 1983, vol. **27**, 119-137.

147 Toftgard R, Nilsen O G and another. Changes in rat liver microsomal cytochrome P450 and enzymatic activities after the inhalation of *n*-hexane, xylene, methyl ethyl ketone and methylchloroform for four weeks. *Scandinavian Journal of Work and Environmental Health*. 1981, vol. **7**, 31-37.

148 Nilsen O G and Toftgard R. The influence of organic solvents on cytochrome P450-mediated metabolism of biphenyl and benzo(a)pyrene. Microsomes, drug oxidations and chemical carcinogenesis. *Proceedings of International Symposium. Academic Press*. 1980, vol. **2**, 1235-1238.

149 Heinonen T, Elovaara E and others. Effect of various solvents on the xenobiotic biotransformation in the liver and the kidneys of the rat: a comparative study. Extrahepatic Drug Metabolism and Chemical Carcinogenesis. *Proceedings of International Meeting. Elsevier*. 1983, 29-31.

150 Szeberenyi S, Ungvary G and another. On the liver effect of benzene and its methyl derivatives. Research Institute for Labour Safety, National Institute of Occupational Health, Budapest, Hungary. 1980, 181-192.

151 Pyykko R. Effects of methylbenzenes on microsomal enzymes in rat liver, kidney and lung. *Biochemica et Biophysica Acta*. 1980, vol. **633**, 1-9.

152 Ungvary G, Szeberenyi S and another. The effect of benzene and its methyl derivatives on the MFO system. Industry, Environment, Xenobiotics. Proceedings of International Conference. 1981, 285-292.

153 Bowers D E and Samuel Cannon M. Ultrastructural changes in livers of young and ageing rats exposed to methylated benzenes. *American Journal of Veterinary Research*. 1982, vol. **43**, 679-683.

154 Halder C A, Holdsworth C E and others. Hydrocarbon nephropathy in male rats: Identification of the nephrotoxic components of unleaded gasoline . *Toxicology and Industrial Health*. 1985, vol. **1**, 67-87 .

155 Desi I, Kovacs F and others. Maze learning in rats exposed to xylene intoxication. *Psychopharmacologia* (Berl). 1967, vol. **11**, 224-230 .

156 Yamada C. Experimental studies on the pathomorphological changes in hydrocarbon poisoning-benzene, toluene, *p*-xylene, and *n*-heptane. *Journal of Tokyo Medical College* . 1980, vol. **38**, 591-606.

157 Monsanto Company. Final report on *Salmonella* mutagenicity assay of *o*-xylene (product). Test No. LF-78-142. 1978.

158 Monsanto Company. Final report on *Salmonella* mutagenicity assay of *o*-xylene (reagent). Test No. LF-78-162. 1978.

159 Monsanto Company. Mutagenicity plate assay: *o*-xylene. Medical Project No. LF-77-84. 1977.

160 Bos R P, Brouns R M E and others. Non-mutagenicity of toluene, *o*-, *m*- and *p*-xylene, *o*-methylbenzylalcohol, and *o*-methylbenzylsulphate in the Ames assay. *Mutation Research*. 1981, vol. **88**, 273-279.

161 Connor T H, Theiss J C and others. Genotoxicity of organic chemicals frequently found in the air of mobile homes. *Toxicology Letters*. 1985, vol. **25**, 33-40.

162 Haworth S, Lawlor T and others. *Salmonella* mutagenicity test results for 250 chemicals. *Environmental Mutagenesis*. 1983, Supplement 1, 3-142.

163 Washington W J, Murphy R C and others: Induction of morphologically abnormal sperm in rats exposed to *o*-xylene. *Archives of Andrology*. 1983, vol. **11**, 233-237.

164 Florin I, Rutberg L and others. Screening of tobacco smoke constituents for mutagenicity using the Ames test. *Toxicology*. 1980, vol. **18**, 219-232.

165 Shimizu H, Suzuki Y and others. The results of microbial mutation test for forty-three industrial chemicals. *Japanese Journal of Industrial Health.* 1985, vol. **27**, 400-419.

166 American Petroleum Institute. Estimation of the mutagenicity of hydrocarbon fractions utilising the bacterial assay procedure with mammalian tissue metabolic activation. Project No. PS-4 (959). 1978.

167 American Petroleum Institute. Mutagenicity evaluation of xylene. Project No. PS-4. 1978.

168 Zeiger E, Anderson B and others. *Salmonella* mutagenicity tests: III. Results from the testing of 255 chemicals. *Environmental Mutagenesis.* 1987, vol. **9**, Supplement 9, 1-109.

169 Fel'dt E.G. Evaluation of the mutagenic hazards of benzene and some of its derivatives. *Gigiena i Sanitariya.* 1985, vol. **7**, 21-23.

170 Donner M, Mäki-Paakkanen J and others. Genetic toxicology of xylenes. *Mutation Research.* 1980, vol. **74**, 171-172.

171 Harper B L and Legator M S. Pyridine prevents the clastogenicity of benzene but not of benzo(a)pyrene or cyclophosphamide. *Mutation Research.* 1987, vol. **179**, 23-31.

172 American Petroleum Institute. Mutagenicity study of thirteen petroleum fractions. Report No. 4. Project No. U-150-14 (EA-1). 1973.

173 McCarroll N E, Keech B H and another. A microsuspension adaptation of the *Bacillus subtilis* "rec" assay. *Environmental Mutagenesis.* 1981, vol. **3**, 607-616.

174 McCarroll N E, Piper C E and another. An *E.coli* microsuspension assay for the detection of DNA damage induced by direct-acting agents and promutagens. *Environmental Mutagenesis.* 1981, vol. **3**, 429-444.

175 Maltoni C, Conti B and others. Benzene as an experimental carcinogen: up-to-date evidence. *Acta Oncologica.* 1983, vol. **4**, 141-164.

176 Maltoni C, Conti B and others. Experimental studies on benzene carcinogenicity at the Bologna Institute of Oncology: Current results and ongoing research. *American Journal of Industrial Medicine.* 1985, vol. **7**, 415-446.

177 Berenblum I. The cocarcinogenic action of croton resin. *Cancer Research.* 1941, vol. **1**, 44-48.

178 Pound A W and Withers H R. The influence of some irritant chemicals and scarification on tumour initiation by urethane in mice. *British Journal of Cancer.* 1963, vol. **17**, 460-470.

179 Pound A W. Induced cell proliferation and the initiation of skin tumour formation in mice by ultraviolet light. *Pathology.* 1970, vol. **2**, 269-275.

180 Weiss H S, Jacoby W T. Solvent effects on tumour promotion. *Federation Proceedings.* 1985, vol. **44**, 1653.

181 Ungvary G. Embryotoxic and teratogenic effects of benzene and its alkyl derivatives. *Munkavedelem Munka es Uzemegesegugy.* 1986, vol. **32**, 146-166.

182 Hudak A, Tatrai E and others. Embryotoxic effects of o-, m-, p-xylenes. *Acta Morphologica Academiae Scientiarum Xungaricae.* 1980, vol. **28**, 211.

183 Hudak A, Tatrai E and others. Study of the embryotoxic effect of *ortho*-xylene. *Morphologiai es Igazsagugyi Orvosi Szemle.* 1980, vol. **20**, 204-209.

184 Ungvary G and Tatrai E. On the embryotoxic effects of benzene and its alkyl derivatives in mice, rats and rabbits. *Archives of Toxicology.* 1985, **suppl. 8**, 425-430.

185 Nawrot P S and Staples R E. Embryofetal toxicity and teratogenicity of isomers of xylene in the mouse. *American Society of Toxicology.* 1980, 19th Annual Meeting, A22.

186 Seidenberg J M, Anderson D G and another. Validation of an *in vivo* developmental toxicity screen in the mouse. *Teratogenesis, Carcinogenesis and Mutagenesis.* 1986, vol. **6**, 361-374.

187 Tatrai E, Hudak A and others. Study of the embryotoxic effect of *meta*-xylene. *Egeszsegtudomany.* 1979, vol. **23**, 147-151.

188 Ungvary G, Tatrai E and others. Study of the embryotoxic effect of *para*-xylene. *Egeszsegtudomany.* 1979, vol. **23**, 152-158.

189 Krotov Y A and Chebotar N A. Study of embryotoxic snd teratogenic effect of certain industrial substances formed during production of dimethyl terephthalate. *Gigiena Truda i Professional' Nye Zabolevaniya.* 1972, vol. **14**, 40-43.

190 Rosen M B, Crofton K M and another. Postnatal evaluation of prenatal exposure to *p*-xylene in the rat. *Toxicology Letters.* 1986, vol. **34**, 223-229.

191 American Petroleum Institute. Parental and fetal reproduction inhalation toxicity study in rats with mixed xylenes. API report 31-31481. 1983.

192 Hudak A and Ungvary G. Embryotoxic effects of benzene and its methyl derivatives: toluene, xylene. *Toxicology.* 1978, vol. **11**, 55-63.

193 Balogh T, Tatrai E and others. Study of the embryotoxic effect of xylene mixtures. *Egeszsegtudomany.* 1982, vol. **26**, 42-48.

194 Ungvary G. The possible contribution of industrial chemicals, organic solvents to the incidence of congenital defects caused by teratogenic drugs and consumer goods. An experimental study. *Progress in Clinical and Biomedical Research.* 1985, vol. **163B**, 295-300.

195 American Petroleum Institute. Teratology study in rats: xylene. API report 26-60013. 1978.

196 Mirkova E, Zaikov C H R and others. Prenatal toxicity of xylene. *Journal of Hygiene, Epidemiology, Microbiology and Immunology.* 1983, vol. **27**, 337-343.

197 Shigeta S, Aikawa H and others. Fetotoxicity of inhaled xylene in mice. *Teratology.* 1983, vol. **28**, 22A.

198 Marks T A, Ledoux T A and another. Teratogenicity of a commercial xylene mixture in the mouse. *Journal of Toxicology and Environmental Health.* 1982, vol. **9**, 97-105.

199 Overman D O. Testing for percutaneous embryotoxicity of laboratory reagents in the hamster. *Teratology.* 1981, vol. **23**, 56A.

200 Morley R, Eccleston D W and others. Xylene poisoning: A report on one fatal case and two cases of recovery after prolonged unconsciousness. *British Medical Journal,* 1970, vol. **3**, 442-443.

201 Recchia G, Perbellini L and others. Coma probably due to accidental ingestion of xylene; treatment by haemoperfusion with activated charcoal. *Medicina del Lavoro.* 1985, vol. **76**, 67-73.

202 Al Ragheb S A, Salhab A S and another. Suicide by xylene ingestion. A case report and review of literature. *The American Journal of Forensic Medicine and Pathology.* 1986, vol. **7**, 327-329.

203 Ghislandi E and Fabiani A. Hepatic lesion due to accidental ingestion of diluent for nitrocellulose paints. *Medicina del Lavoro.* 1957, vol. **48**, 577-579.

204 Bakinson M A and Jones R D. Gassings due to methylene chloride, xylene, toluene and styrene reported to Her Majesty's Factory Inspectorate 1961-1980. *British Journal of Industrial Medicine.* 1985, vol. **42**, 184-190.

205 Sikora H and Gala J. Damage to the cardiac muscle in the course of acute xylene intoxication. *Medycyna Pracy.* 1967, vol, **18**, 75-77.

206 Tomaszewski R, Gandurski P and another. Nodal rhythm in xylene intoxication. *Wiadamosci Lekarskie.* 1978, vol. **31**, 193-194.

207 Klaucke D N, Johansen M and another. An outbreak of xylene intoxication in a hospital. *American Journal of Industrial Medicine.* 1982, vol. **3**, 173-178.

208 Arthur L J and Curnock D A. Xylene - induced epilepsy following innocent glue sniffing. *British Medical Journal.* 1982, vol. **284**, 1787.

209 Goldie I. Can xylene (xylol) provoke convulsive seizures? *Industrial Medicine and Surgery.* 1960, vol. **29**, 33-35.

210 Savolainen K and Linnavuo M. Effects on *m*-xylene on human equilibrium measured with a quantitative method. *Acta pharmacologica et toxicologica.* 1979, vol. **44**, 315-318.

211 Savolainen K. Combined effects of xylene and alcohol on the central nervous system. *Acta pharmacologica et toxicologica.* 1980, vol. **46**, 366-372.

212 Savolainen K, Riihimaki V and others. Effects of xylene and alcohol on vestibular and visual functions in man. *Scandinavian Journal of Work Environment and Health.* 1980, vol. **6**, 94-108.

213 Seppalainen A M, Savolainen R and another. Effects of xylene and alcohol on hyuman visual evoked potentials. In *Mechanisms of Toxic Hazard Evaluation.* Eds Holmstedt T R, Lauwerys M and others. Elsevier/North Holland Biochemical Press 1980, 83-86.

214 Seppalainen A M, Savolainen K and another. Effects of xylene and alcohol on human visual evoked potentials. *Toxicology Letters.* 1980, special issue No. 1, 73.

215 Seppalainen A M, Savolainen K and another. Changes induced by xylene and alcohol in human evoked potentials. *Electroencephalography and Clinical Neurophysiology.* 1981, vol. **51**, 148-155.

216   Seppalainen A M, Salmi T and others. Visual evoked potentials in short-term exposure of human subjects to *m*-xylene and 1,1,1-trichloroethane. In *Application of Behavioral Pharmacology in Toxicology.* Eds Zbinden, G. et al. Raven Press. New York. 1983, 349-352.

217   Savolainen K and Riihimaki V. Xylene and alcohol involvement of the human equilibrium system. *Acta pharmacologica et toxicologica.* 1981, vol. **49**, 447-451.

218   Savolainen R, Riihimaki V and others. Short-term exposure of human subjects to *m*-xylene and 1,1,1-trichloroethane. *International Archives of Occupational and Environmental Health.* 1981, vol. **49**, 89-98.

219   Savolainen K, Riihimaki V and others. Short-term exposure of human subjects to *m*-xylene and 1,1,1-trichloroethane. *Archives of Toxicology*, 1982, **suppl. 5**, 96-99.

220   Savolainen K, Riihimaki V and another. Biphasic effects of inhaled solvents on human equilibrium. *Acta pharmacologica et toxicologica.* 1982, vol. **51**, 237-242.

221   Savolainen K, Kekoni J and others. Immediate effects of *m*-xylene on the human central nervous system. *Archives of Toxicology.* 1984, **suppl. 7**. 412-417.

222   Savolainen R, Riihimaki V and others. Conversely exposure-related effects between atmospheric *m*-xylene concentrations and human body sense of balance. *Acta pharmacologica et toxicologica.* 1985, vol. **57**, 67-71.

223   Savolainen R, Riihimaki V and others. Changes in the sense of balance correlate with concentrations of *m*-xylene in venous blood. *British Journal of Industrial Medicine.* 1985, vol. **42**, 765-769.

224   Gamberale F, Annwall G and another. Exposure to xylene and ethylbenzene. III. Effects on central nervous functions. *Scandinavian Journal of Work Environment and Health.* 1978, vol. **4**, 204-211.

225   Anshelm-Olson B, Gamberale F and another. Co-exposure to toluene and *p*-xylene in man. Central nervous functions. *British Journal of Industrial Medicine.* 1985, vol. **42**, 117-122.

226   Hastings L, Cooper G P and another. Human sensory response to selected petroleum hydrocarbons. *Adv. Mod. Environ. Toxicol.* 1984, vol. **6**, 255-270.

227   Riihimaki V, Laine A and others. Acute solvent-ethanol interactions with special reference to xylene. *Scandinavian Journal of Work Environment and Health.* 1982, vol. **8**, 77-79.

228   Joyner R E and Pegues W L. A health hazard associated with epoxy resin-concrete dust. *Journal of Occupational Medicine.* 1961, vol. **3**, 211-214.

229   Lundberg I. Medical examination of paint industry workers with long-term exposure to a mixture of organic solvents. *Arbete och Halsa*, 1981, vol. **2**, 1-54.

230   Nelson K W, Ege J F and others. Sensory response to certain industrial solvent vapours. *Journal of Industrial Hygiene and Toxicology.* 1943, vol. **25**, 282-285.

231   Kligman A M. The identification of contact allergens by human assay. III. The maximisation test. A procedure for screening and rating contact sensitisers. *Journal of Investitgative Dermatology.* 1966, vol. **47**, 393-409.

232   Glass W I. A case of suspected xylol poisoning. *New Zealand Medical Journal.* 1961, vol. **60**, 113.

233   Hipolito R N. Xylene poisoning in laboratory workers: Case reports and discussion. *Laboratory Medicine.* 1980, vol. **11**, 593-595.

234   Kilburn R H, Warshaw R and others. Toxic effects of formaldehyde and solvents in histology technicians. A preliminary report. *Journal of Histotechnology.* 1983, vol. **6**, 73-76.

235   Kilburn R H, Seidman B C and others. Neurobehavioral and respiratory symptoms of formaldehyde and xylene exposure in histology technicians. *Archives of Environmental Health.* 1985, vol. **40**, 229-233. '

236   Roberts F P, Lucas E G and others. Near-pure xylene causing reversible neuropsychiatric disturbance. *Lancet.* 1988, vol. **2**, 273.

237   Proust B, Hannequin D and others. Solvent psychosyndrome: results of psychometric tests in 10 laboratory technicians exposed to solvents. *Archives Maladies Professionnelles.* 1986, vol. **47**, 305-310.

238   Savolainen K, Riihimaki V and another. Effects of short-term xylene exposure on psychophysiological functions in man. *International Archives of Occupational and Environmental Health.* 1979, vol. **44**, 201-211.

239   Savolainen K, Riihimaki V and others. Effects of short-term *m*-xylene exposure and physical exercise on the central nervous system. *International Archives of Occupational and Environmental Health.* 1980, vol. **45**, 105-121.

240 Savolainen K and Riihimaki V. An early sign of xylene effect on human equilibrium. *Acta pharmacologica et toxicologica*. 1981, vol. **48**, 279-283.

241 Elofsson S A, Gamberale F and others. Exposure to organic solvents. A cross-sectional epidemiologic investigation on occupationally exposed car and industrial spray painters with special reference to the nervous system. *Scandinavian Journal of Work Environment and Health*. 1980, vol. **6**, 239-273.

242 Husman K. Symptoms of car painters with long-term exposure to a mixture of organic solvents. *Scandinavian Journal of Work Environment and Health*. 1980, vol. **6**, 19-32.

243 Seppalainen A M, Husman K and another. Neurophysiological effects of long-term exposure to a mixture of organic solvents. *Scandinavian Journal of Work Environment and Health*. 1978, vol. **4**, 304-314.

244 Husman K and Karli P. Clinical neurological findings among car painters exposed to a mixture of organic solvents. *Scandinavian Journal of Work Environment and Health*. 1980, vol. **6**, 33-39.

245 Valciukas J A, Lilis R and others. Neurobehavioural changes among shipyard painters exposed to solvents. *Archives of Environmental Health*. 1985, vol. **40**, 47-52.

246 Lindstrom K. Psychological performances of workers exposed to various solvents. *Work Environment and Health*. 1973, vol. **10**, 151-155.

247 Lindstrom K, Antti-Poika M and others. Psychological prognosis of diagnosed organic solvent , intoxication. *Neurobehavioral Toxicology and Teratology*. 1982, vol. **4**, 581-588.

248 Maizlish N A, Fine L J and others. A neurological evaluation of workers exposed to mixtures of organic solvents. *British Journal of Industrial Medicine*. 1987, vol. **44**, 14-25.

249 Arlien-Søborg P, Zilstorff K and others. Vestibular dysfunction in occupational chronic solvent intoxication. *Clinical Otolaryngology*. 1981, vol. **6**, 285-290.

250 Van Vliet C, Swaen G M H and others. The organic solvent syndrome. A comparison of cases with neuropsychiatric disorders among painters and construction workers. *International Archives of Occupational and Environmental Health*. 1987, vol. **59**, 493-501.

251 Dossing M, Arlien-Søborg P and others. Liver damage following long-term occupational exposure to organic solvents. *Ugeskrift fur Laeger*. 1981, vol. **143**, 2297-2302.

252 Dossing M, Arlien-Søborg P and others. Liver damage associated with occupational exposure to organic solvents in house painters. *European Journal of Clinical Investigation*. 1983, vol. **13**, 151-157.

253 Edling C. Interaction between drugs and solvents as a cause of fatty change in the liver. *British Journal of Industrial Medicine*. 1982, vol. **39**, 198-199.

254 Sotaniemi E A, Sutinen S and others. Liver injury in subjects occupationally exposed to chemicals in low doses. *Acta Medica Scandinavia*. 1982, vol. **212**, 207-215.

255 Winnicka A, Chmielewski J and another. Xylene content and activity of certain enzymes in the blood as a result of exposure under industrial conditions. *Polski Tygodnik Lekarski*. 1977, vol. **32**, 1149-1151.

256 Fischbein A, Ross R R and another. Industrial solvents and the liver. *Lancet*, 1983, vol. **1**, 129.

257 Lundberg I and Hakansson M. Normal serum activities of liver enzymes in Swedish paint industry workers with heavy exposure to organic solvents. *British Journal of Industrial Medicine*. 1985, vol. **42**, 596-600.

258 Craveri A, Tornaghi G and others. Serum bile salts in liver screening in subjects exposed to aromatic hydrocarbons. *Giornale Clinica Medica*. 1982, vol. **63**, 322-329.

259 Kurpa R and Husman K. Car painters' exposure to a mixture of organic solvents. Serum activities of liver enzymes. *Scandinavian Journal of Work Environment and Health*. 1982, vol **8**, 137-140.

260 Zinser D, Bittinghofer P M and others. Stress and strain in workers exposed to xylene. *Arbeitsmed. Sozialmed. Praventivmed*. 1985, vol. **20**, 177-180.

261 Beirne G J and Brennan J T. Glomerulonephritis associated with hydrocarbon solvents. *Archives of Environmental Health*. 1972, vol. **25**, 365-369.

262 Zimmerman S W, Groehler K and another. Hydrocarbon exposure and chronic glomerulonephritis. *Lancet*. 1975, vol. **2**, 199-201.

263 Lagrue G. Hydrocarbon exposure and chronic glomerulonephritis. *Lancet*. 1976. vol. **1**, 1191.

264 Bell G M, Gordon A C H and others. Proliferative glomerulonephritis and exposure to organic solvents. *Nephron*. 1985, vol. **40**, 161-165.

265 Franchini I, Cavatorta A and others. Early indicators of renal damage in workers exposed to organic solvents. *International Archives of Occupational and Environmental Health*. 1983, vol. **52**, 1-9.

266 Askergren A, Allgen L G and others. Studies on kidney function in subjects exposed to organic solvents. I. Excretion of albumin and ß-2 microglobulin in the urine. *Acta Medica Scandinavia*. 1981, vol. **209**, 479-483.

267 Askergren A, Allgen L G and another. Studies on kidney function in subjects exposed to organic solvents. II. The effect of desmopressin in a concentration test and the effect of exposure to organic solvents on renal concentrating ability. *Acta Medica Scandinavia*. 1981, vol. **209**, 485-488.

268 Askergren A, Brandt R and others. Studies on kidney function in subjects exposed to organic solvents. IV. Effect on ^{51}Cr-EDTA clearance. *Acta Medica Scandinavia*. 1981, vol. **210**, 373-376.

269 Askergren A. Studies on kidney function in subjects exposed to organic solvents. III. Excretion of cells in the urine. *Acta Medica Scandinavia*. 1981, vol. **210**, 103-106.

270 Forde J P. Xylene affected platelet count. *Occupational Health*. November 1973, vol. **25**, 429-433.

271 Angerer J and Wulf H. Occupational chronic exposure to organic solvents. XI. Alkylbenzene exposure to varnish workers: effects on hematopoetic system. *International Archives of Occupational and Environmental Health*. 1985, vol. **56**, 307-321.

272 Boiko V I and Makar'eva L M. Blood picture as an indicator of exposure of employees engaged in xylene production to low intensity factors. *Gigiena i Sanitariya*. 1980, **19**, 57-59.

273 Sukhanova V A, Makar'eva L M and another. Investigation of functional properties of leukocytes of workers engaged in manufacture of xylene. *Gigiena i Sanitariya*. 1969, vol. **34**, 130-132.

274 Moszczynski P and Lisiewicz J. Hematological indices of peripkeral blood in workers occupationally exposed to benzene, toluene and xylene. *Zbl. Bakt. Hyg., I. Abt. Orig.* 1983, vol. **178**, 329-339.

275 Pap M and Varga C S. Sister-chromatid exchanges in peripheral lymphocytes of workers occupationally exposed to xylenes. *Mutation Research*. 1987, vol. **187**, 223-225.

276 Runes-Cravioto F, Zapata-Gayon C and others. Chromosome aberrations and sister chromatid exchange in workers in chemical laboratories and a rotoprinting factory and in children of women laboratory workers. *Lancet*. 1977, vol. **2**, 322-325.

277 Haglund V, Lundberg I and another. Chromosome aberrations and sister chromatid exchanges in Swedish paint industry workers. *Scandinavian Journal of Work Environment and Health*. 1980, vol. **6**, 291-298.

278 Axelsson G, Lutz C and another. Exposure to solvents and outcome of pregnancy in university laboratory employees. *British Journal of Industrial Medicine*. 1984, vol. **41**, 305-312.

279 De Ceaurriz J C, Desiles J P and others. Concentration dependent behavioural changes in mice following short-term inhalation exposure to various industrial solvents. *Toxicology and Applied Pharmacology*. 1983, vol. **67**, 383-389.

280 Kojima R. Effect of inosine, NAD and glycine or glucuronic acid lactone on acute toluene or xylene intoxications. *Igaku To Seibutsugaku*. 1971, vol. **83**, 269-274.

281 Gentry D G, Wood R W. Effects of inhaled toluene and *m*-xylene on conditioned behaviour. *Toxicologist*. 1982, vol. **2**, 164.

282 Kobayashi H, Wobara T and others. Effect of several organic solvents inhalation on systemic blood pressure. *Yamaguchi Igaku*. 1983, vol. **32**, 211-216.

283 Dyer R S, Bercegeay M S and others. Acute exposures to *p*-xylene and toluene alter visual information processing. *Neurotoxicology and Teratology*. 1988, vol. **10**, 147-153.

284 Bushnell P J. Behavioural effects of acute *p*-xylene inhalation in rats: autoshaping, motor activity and reversal learning. *Neurotoxicology and Teratology*. 1989, vol. **10**, 569-577.

285 Bushnell P J and Peele D B. Conditioned flavour aversion induced by inhaled *p*-xylene in rats. *Neurotoxicology and Teratology*. 1988, vol. **10**, 273-277.

286 Wimolwattanapun S, Ghosh T K and others. Effect of inhalation of xylene on intracranial self-stimulation behaviour in the rat. *Neuropharmacology*. 1987, vol. **26**, 1629-1632.

287 Morvai V, Hudak A and others. ECG changes in benzene, toluene and xylene poisoned rats. *Acta Medica Academiae Scientiarum Hungaricae*. 1976, vol. **33**, 275-286.

288   Engelhardt W E and Estler W. Investigations into the acute narcotic effect of aliphatic and aromatic hydrocarbons. The effect of a single inhalation of different concentrations of gasoline, benzene, toluene and xylene on rabbits and cats. *Archiv fur Hygiene.* 1935, vol. **114**, 249-260.

289   Chenoweth M B. Ventricular fibrillation induced by hydrocarbons and epinephrine. *Journal of Industrial Hygiene and Toxicology.* 1946, vol. **28**, 151-158.

290   Hobara T, Kobayashi H and others. Effects of organic solvents on superoxide dismutase activities in erythrocytes and organs of dog. *Yamaguchi Igaku.* 1981, vol. **30**, 439-443.

291   Braier L. A comparative study of isocyclic hydrocarbons in animals and in man. *Haematologica.* 1973, vol. **58**, 491-500.

292   Braier L and Francone M. Haemolytic phenomena due to benzene andits homologues. *Archives des Maladies Professionnelles.* 1950, vol. **11** , 367-369.

293   Wood R W, Coleman J B and another. Anticonvulsant and antipunishment effects of toluene. *Journal of Pharmacology and Experimental Therapeutics.* 1984, vol. **230**, 407-412.

294   Patel J M and Harper C. The effect of rat liver alcohol and aldehyde dehydrogerase activities on the pulmonary toxicity of *p*-xylene. *Federation Proceedings.* 1977, vol. **36**, 990, Abstract No. 3797.

295   Roberts A E, Bogdanffy M S and others. Lung metabolism of benzo(a)pyrene in rats treated with *p*-xylene and/or ethanol. *Journal of Toxicology and Environmental Health.* 1986, vol. **18**, 257-266.

296   Roberts A E, Bogdanffy M S and others. Alteration of benzo(a)pyrene metabolism in rat lung by the organic solvent, *p*-xylene. *Toxicologist.* 1985, vol. **5**, 168, Abstract No. 672.

297   Mikiskova H. Determination of the electrical excitability of the motor cerebral cortex and its use in pharmacology and toxicology. *Archiv Fur Gewerbepathologie und Gewerbehygiene.* 1960, vol. **18**, 300-309.

298   Gerarde H W. In *Toxicology and Biochemistry of Aromatic Hydrocarbons.* Amsterdam, Elsevier, 1960. Elsiver monographs on toxic agents, No 8.

299   Gut I, Kopecky J and others. Metabolic and toxic interactions of benzene and acrylonitrile with organic solvents. Proceedings of an International Conference on Industrial and Environmental Xenobiotics. 1981, 255-262.

300   Ungvary G and Donath T. Effect of benzene and its methyl derivatives (toluene, *p*-xylene) on postganglionic noradrenergic nerves. *Zeitschrift fur Mikroskopisch Anatomische Forschung, Leipzig.* 1984, vol. **98**, 755-763.

301   Holmberg B and Malmfors T. The effect of industrial solvents on adrenergic transmitter mechanisms. Wenner-Gren Centre. International Symposium Series. *Proceedings of International Symposium.* 1974, vol. **22**, 191-200.

302   Edelfors S and Ravn-Jonsen A. Calcium uptake in rat brain synaptosomes after short-term exposure to organic solvents. *Acta pharmacologica et toxicologica.* 1985, vol. **56**, 431-434.

303   Castranova V, Bowman L and another. Toxic effects of organic solvents on rat alveolar macrophages. *American Review of Respiratory Diseases.* 1980, vol. **121**, 227.

304   Li G L and Yin S N. Benzene-specific increase in leukocyte alkaline phosphatase activity in rats exposed to vapours of various organic solvents. *Journal of Toxicology and Environmental Health.* 1986, vol. **19**, 581-589.

305   Smyth H F and Smyth H F. Inhalation experiments with certain lacquer solvents. *The Journal of Industrial Hygiene.* 1928, vol. **10**, 261-271.

306   Kashin L M, Kulinskaya I L and another. Changes in the animal organism with chronic exposure to low concentrations of xylene. *Vrachebnoe delo.* 1968, No. **8**, 109-112.

307   Ormos G, Cseh R J and another. Excretion of progesterone given i.v. in a large dose from the circulation of female rats after exposure to organic solvents, partial hepatectomy, and binding of the bile duct. *Kiserletes Ovostudomany.* 1984, vol. **36**, 547-552.

308   Gusev I S. The toxicology of low concentrations of aromatic hydrocarbons. AICE survey of USSR of air pollution literature. *American Institute of Crop Ecology, Silver Spring.* 1972, vol. **15**, 19-34.

309   Gusev I S. Comparative assessment of the effect of small concentrations of benzene, toluene and xylene. *Gigiena i Sanitariya.* 1967, vol. **32**, 3-6.

310   Yakushevich Y E. Experimental data on the hygienic evaluation of the continuous and intermittent action of benzene, toluene and xylene. *Gigiena i Sanitariya.* 1973, vol. **38**, 6-10.

311   Battig K, Grandjean E. Industrial solvents and avoidance conditioning in rats. *Archives of Environmental Health.* 1964, vol. **9**, 745-749.

312   Kyrklund T, Kjellstrand P and another. Brain lipid changes in rats exposed to xylene and toluene. *Toxicology*. 1987, vol. **45**, 123-133.

313   Savolainen H and Seppalainen A M. Biochemical and physiological effects of organic solvents on rat axon membranes isolated by a new technique. *Neurotoxicology*. 1979, vol. **1**, 467-477.

314   Toftgard R. Effects of xylene exposure on the metabolism of antipyrine *in vitro* and *in vivo* in the rat. *Toxicology* 1983, vol. **28**, 117-131.

315   Szuldrzynska J. Motor activity of rats chronically poisoned with toluene and xylene vapours. *Bromatologia i Chemia Toksykologiczna*. 1980, vol. **13**, 365-370.

316   Mikhailova A and Khalkova Z. Biochemical studies of the lungs with experimental exposure to xylene and noise. *Probl. Khig*. 1985, vol. **10**, 88-93.

317   Ivanovich E, Antov G and others. Combined effect of some physical and chemical factors. *Journal of Hygiene, Epidemiology, Microbiology and Immunology*. 1985, vol. **29**, 105-110.

318   Kjellstrand P, Bjerkemo M and others. Effects of solvent exposure on testosterone levels and butyrylcholinesterase activity in mice. *Acta pharmacologica et toxicologica*. 1985, vol. **57**, 242-249.

319   Romanelli A, Falzoi M and others. Effects of some monocyclic aromatic solvents and their metabolites on brain dopamine in rabbits. *Journal of Applied Toxicology*. 1986, vol. **6**, 431-435.

320   Mutti A, Falzoi M and others. Brain dopamine as a target for solvent toxicity: Effects of some monocyclic aromatic hydrocarbons. *Toxicology*. 1988, vol. **49**, 77-82.

321   Navrotskii V K and Kashin L M. Comparative evaluation of the action of small concentrations of benzene, toluene and xylene on animals in a chronic experiment. Collected papers on the subject: Scientific bases of occupational health and eradication of infectious diseases, hygienic significance of low-intensity environmental factors. Kharkov. 1970, 17-24.

322   Faustov A S, Rramsakov V V. Immunobiological reactivity of the organism with chronic ethyl benzene and xylene intoxication. *Trudy Voronezhskogo Gosudarstvennogo Meditsinskogo Instituta*. 1968, vol. **73**, 41-46.

323   Rosengren L E, Rjellstrand P and others. Irreversible effects of xylene on the brain after long-term exposure: A quantitative study of DNA and the glial cell marker proteins S-100 and GFA. *Neurotoxicology*. 1986, vol. **7**, 121-136.

324   Condie L W, Hill J R and another. Oral toxicology studies with xylene isomers and mixed xylenes. *Drug and Chemical Toxicology 1988*, vol. **11**, 329-354.

325   Mirkova E, Hinkova L and others. Xylene neurotoxicity in pregnant rats and fetuses. *Activas Nervosa Superior (Praha)*. 1979, vol. **21**, 265-268.

326   Fabacher D L, Hodgson E. Hepatic mixed-function oxidase activity in mice treated with methylated benzenes and methylated naphthalenes. *Journal of Toxicology and Environmental Health*. 1977, vol; **2**, 1143-1146.

327   Bernard A M and others. Evaluation of the subacute nephrotoxicity of cyclohexane and other industrial solvents in the female Sprague-Dawley rat. *Toxicology Letters*. 1989, vol. **45**, 271-280.

328   Gershbein L L. Liver regeneration as influenced by the structure of aromatic and heterocyclic compounds. *Research Communications in Chemical Pathology and Pharmacology*. 1975, vol. **11**, 445-466.

329   Bakhtizina G Z. Experimental study of the effect of xylene on the thyroid gland and adrenal cortex of rats in postnatal ontogenesis. Endokrin Sistema Organizma i Toksich. Faktory Vnesh. Sredy. Materialy I-i Vses. Konf., Ufa. 1979, 5-10.

330   Speck B and Moeschlin S. The effects of toluene, xylene, chloramphenicol and thiouracil on the bone marrow. Experimental autoradiographical studies with ^{3}H-thymidine. *Schweizerische Medizinische Wochenschrift*. 1968, vol. **98**, 1684-1686.

331   Wecher R A and Scher S. Bioassay procedures for identifying genotoxic agents using light emitting bacteria as indicator organisms. *Serono Symposium Publications*. Raven Press. 1982, vol. **1**, 109-113.

332   Gerner-Schmidt P and Friedrich U. The mutagenic effect of benzene, toluene and xylene studied by the SCE technique. *Mutation Research*. 1978, vol. **53**, 313-316.

333   Zhong B, Tang Q and another. A comparative study of the cytogenetic effects of benzene, toluene and xylene. *Hereditas*. 1980, vol. **2**, 29-31.

334   Ungvary G, Varga B and others. Study on the role of maternal sex steroid production and metabolism in the embryotoxicity of *para*-xylene. *Toxicology*. 1981, vol. **19**, 263-268.

335   Tatrai E, Ungvary G and others. Embryotoxic effect of *para*-xylene. *Acta Physiologica Academiae Scientiarum Hungaricae*. 1980, vol. **56**, 90-91.

336   Ungvary G, Ormos G and others. Importance of the liver and sexual steroids in embryotoxicity caused by solvents. *Kiserletes Orvostudomany*. 1986, vol. **38**, 191-196.

337   Choroszewska A. Effect of xylene on implantation, course of pregnancy and offspring in rats. *Medycyna - Dydaktyka - Wychowanie*. 1977, vol. **9**, 218-219.

338   Teslina O V. Study of permeability of the placenta to I[131] on exposure to the action of xylene. Experimental study. *Akusherstro i ginekologiya*. 1974, No. **7**, 63-64.

339   Levchuk V S. Influence of xylene on the oestrus cycle in white mice. Kemerovo. 1964, *Clinical features of occupational diseases of chemical aetiology*, 147-155 Trans HSE No 12559 B.

340   Haley T J. A review of the literature on ethylbenzene. *Dangerous Properties of Industrial Materials Report*. Jul/Aug 1981, vol. 1, (6), 2-4.

341   Snyder R. (Editor). Ethel Browning's Toxicity and Metabolism of Industrial Solvents, Second Edition. Volume 1: Hydrocarbons. Elsevier, 1987. ISBN 0 44 490391 7.

342   European Chemical Industry Ecology and Toxicology Centre (ECETOC) 1986, Report No. 7 Ethylbenzene : CAS 100-41-4. Joint Assessment of Commodity Chemicals, Brussels.

343   Cragg S T, Clarke E A and others. Subchronic inhalation toxicity of ethylbenzene in mice, rats and rabbits. *Fundamental and Applied Toxicology*. 1989, vol. **13**, 399-408.

344   Barlow S M and Sullivan F M. Reproductive hazards of industrial chemicals. London Academic Press. 1982. ISBN 0 12 078960 4.